A PAGEANT
OF THE THEATRE

Books by Edmund Fuller

John Milton

A Star Pointed North (novel)

Brothers Divided (novel)

George Bernard Shaw: *Critic of Western Morale*

Vermont: *A History of the Green Mountain State*

Tinkers And Genius: *The Story of the Yankee Inventors*

Man In Modern Fiction

Books With Men Behind Them

The Corridor (novel)

A Pageant Of The Theatre

A PAGEANT
OF THE THEATRE

BY EDMUND FULLER

NEW REVISED EDITION

THOMAS Y. CROWELL COMPANY · NEW YORK

ACKNOWLEDGMENT is made with thanks to the following for permission to quote from copyrighted material. W. W. Norton & Co., Inc. for an excerpt from *The Greek Way*, by Edith Hamilton. Charles Scribner's Sons for excerpts from *Four Plays by Lope de Vega*, translated by John Garrett Underhill. E. P. Dutton & Co., Inc., and J. M. Dent & Sons Ltd., London, for excerpts from *Peer Gynt*, by Henrik Ibsen, translated by R. Farquharson Sharp, in the Everyman Library. The Public Trustee and The Society of Authors, London, for excerpts from *Heartbreak House*, by George Bernard Shaw.

Preface

IT IS IMPORTANT to understand what a book is trying to do and what it does not claim for itself. This book's title was chosen most carefully—A *Pageant of the Theatre*. It hopes to show its readers a display, an exhibit, of aspects of the history and variety of one of man's most ancient, persistent, and exciting arts. It hopes to be entertaining and informative as a good pageant or show should be.

Though the history of the theatre is its material, we have not called the book a history. To do so would imply solemn obligations beyond our pleasant purpose. There are several comprehensive histories of the theatre and many studies of national theatres and of technical, professional aspects of the art. Also there are abundant surveys of the drama as literature, both national and world-encompassing. All of such are designed to serve the student making a formal study of the subject.

A *Pageant of the Theatre* is for general readers, for those who enjoy the theatre but have not thought about studying it formally. Perhaps this will tempt a few to do so. It is a companion to pleasant theatregoing and playreading, designed to enhance those pleasures by giving some account of how the theatre was created, the many forms it has taken, the numerous peoples and cultures that have contributed to it, and to give brief introductions to some of its principal writers, actors, and associated artists.

We have tried to be accurate in what is related here, but have not tried to exhaust the subject—the bibliography will offer some starting points for those who wish to read more.

The theatre of here and now is all around you. You can buy tickets and see the show. You can read about personalities in the theatre, its techniques, and its inevitable controversies in newspapers, magazines, and current books. Lecturers throughout the country report what's afoot on Broadway each season. Also you will see some of both the old and the new in movies and television, those modern extensions of the stage. On long-playing records, you can hear whole plays and operas done by fine casts.

Because of this profusion we bring our story only to the threshold of the present. Beyond that, the detail is too vast and what seems notable this year may be remembered by no one five years from now. The main story this book tells has been proved by time. Its events and people are remembered now and will be for years to come.

If you enjoy the theatre, try our pageant. You may be surprised to discover how much lies behind your present evening's pleasure at a play.

Edmund Fuller

Kent, Connecticut

Contents

Illustrations

A PAGEANT
OF THE THEATRE

Chapter 1

How Drama Was Born

Greek tragic mask of the Hellenistic period. *Athens National Museum*

A ROARING FIRE blazes in the night. In the vast blackness primitive men and women huddle in a ring within the circle of light and warmth. They are grateful for this fire, one of the most precious of man's possessions; it will serve their kind in times to come in ways unimaginable to them now.

Let's pretend that we have leapt back into remote time and are part of this company of cave men. The season is changing; green things have begun to appear again. This very night has seen the first thunderstorm of a new spring. Nature is full of fearsome, awe-inspiring happenings.

What is the fiery, forked dragon tongue that leaps across the sky? What is the dreadful beast that roars with each flash, yet is never seen? What if he should spring upon us now, as he sometimes does when the fire leaps downward and a tree is blasted? What is this mysterious, benevolent, kindred flame that crackles before us, giving warmth, frightening off prowling beasts? Some of us are charged with guarding it, to nurture it watchfully lest it

1

flicker away unfed in the embers sometime and leave us cold, unlighted, undefended, for we have not yet become its masters and cannot call it into being at our will.

Whence comes this fresh greenness? Where are the sleet and snow that so lately harassed us? What is the sighing creature of the winds, tearing and cruel for so long, now gentle and mild? These are the mysteries of our lives which alternately threaten or promise, save or destroy, starve us or give us food.

One among us says, "There is a mighty Being who rules these things. Now He is kind to us. Let us please Him, lest He smite us again with the tongue from the skies, or the cold, or the drought." Who is this Being? One of us springs into the inner band of the firelight. "He is like this!" He dances crudely, imitating by all the emotions he knows the might and power of the unknown god. Others follow his example and the ancient ritual dances representing the gods and their powers have begun.

As early men grappled with such mysteries, attempting to understand the nature of their lives and their world, they found their own features inadequate to represent the hidden powers. They fashioned terrifying, grotesque masks, images of their makers' imaginings of gods and demons.

When bad luck strikes they will put on their hideous masks. Perhaps the demon persecuting them will be terrified by this seeming presence of another and will flee, leaving them in peace. It was countless ages before men gave up such notions; indeed, among primitive peoples they still exist. Even our Halloween false faces are reminders in play that they were once used to ward off the evil spirits said to be abroad on All Hallows' Eve.

In our imagined prehistoric scene we were witnesses to a great event: the birth of drama. The world's whole storehouse of drama springs from this ancient source of men seeking in their superstitious fear to understand something of the awful mysteries of their lives. The history of drama is the history of man. Some of us may first meet it and chiefly think of it as entertainment, but that was its last development and least important aspect. Drama played, and still plays, a part in religion, education, and politics. It is an art which unites in its service all of man's other arts.

Today every great city has theatres where live actors perform in the presence of their audience. All but the smallest towns have movie theatres, millions of homes have television sets, and by these modern media plays good and bad are brought before numberless people continents and oceans apart.

Going to see the living theatre is a simple matter. You purchase your ticket, appear at the proper time, and the play is performed by a company of actors and an assisting technical crew. You take it for granted but much has gone into its preparation; someone has written the play; someone has assembled the actors, the director, the stagehands, and the materials—that is called producing it—and here it is for your enjoyment.

The infant primitive theatre knew no such organization. There were no trained professionals specializing in the many skills required for a modern theatre performance. There were no stages or auditoriums where performers and spectators could come together, for men were not yet living even in well-built houses but in caves, huts of earth and stones, rude tents of hides.

There was little time for contemplation or amusement—indeed, such concepts were unknown. It was a desperate life of constant conflict with the elements and with animals. A man's life was occupied with hunting, fishing, finding a mate, feeding, sheltering and defending his family. Thomas Hobbes, a seventeenth-century English social philosopher, summed up the condition of the cave man: "No arts; no letters; no society; and which is worst of all, continual fear and danger of violent death; and the life of man, solitary, poor, nasty, brutish, and short."

Yet these primitive people planted the seedling of the world's drama. How could this art take form? What principle guided its development?

The great principle, which remains a powerful element in every field of art, is *rhythm*. It is easy to see how compelling this principle was to early men. They saw that everything around them was rhythmic: the motions of sun, moon, and stars, the changing of seasons, the movements of waters and winds, the pace at which they walked or ran, the motions of the great cats, the undulations of snakes, and even inexplicable impulses springing up in their own bodies which they expressed by beating upon hollow logs or by shaking rattles. All of nature was rhythm; man, seeking to understand and to master through imitation, followed rhythm and developed the first form of drama: *dance*. Amid all the other forms of drama that branched from it, the dance remains important in man's life. We watch with pleasure the disciplined art of ballet companies, and we step onto the dance floor ourselves in modes as varied as the waltz, the square dance, or the latest jazz style of the year.

At the cave man's fires gods and demons are not the sole subjects of his pantomimes. Someone wishes to boast of the hunt. Language is crude, men do not yet speak much beyond short syllables and grunts. Someone cries, "I met a beast and slew him." He imitates the actions of the hunt, the slinking pursuit, the cornering, the flung spear, the flailing of the stone axe, the kill. We, his fellows, understand his triumph and approve.

These men have uncovered a great mystery. What is this magic beside the campfire? How is it that my neighbor here, a man long known, is both before us now and yet is also back in the hunt of hours, even days, ago; the hunt which I remember myself, for I was there? More puzzling, he is my neighbor but he has suddenly become the fierce victim of the chase whom I remember well, having flung my own spear at him. What is this mystery? How can a man be himself and yet a god, demon, or beast? What makes this change which is not really a change yet which all of us believe?

Today we are long accustomed to men pretending to be other than themselves, but to the primitive mind it was a thing of magic. Familiar as we are with the art of acting, it is still this same magic, this glamorous mystery of changing identities, which is the lure of the stage.

That which the primitive men began was partly art, partly religion. The actors were witch doctors, later priests. Drums and the first strings and wind instruments ruled its rhythms. The dramatic actions became ceremonies, rituals, formal and traditional. Each season, each occasion, spring and winter, birth, death, or marriage, had its appropriate dramatic expression.

History was born of this as men re-enacted the legends and traditions of their ancestors. This was the only way, for ages before writing was invented, that man communicated his heritage of knowledge and lore from generation to generation. Bards sang or recited long stories in forms that were prized for their repetition exactly as men remembered hearing them before.

Wherever man dwelt, there the dance-drama grew by slow evolution, becoming more complex in its symbols and forms with the growing intellectual power of man, his ability to have *ideas*. The original religious importance of the dance-drama lay in the belief that the performer became the vessel for the spirit of the god, beast, or man impersonated. Most important of all, man had begun to create a realm of the imagination into which he could pour his ideas and emotions, a world separate from the "real" one of nature around him, yet with a reality of a different kind of its own. That is the world of art. Its development was a sign of the growing creativity of the species, one of the attributes that sets man apart from the other beasts.

Theatre of the fourth century B.C. at Epidaurus. *The Bettmann Archive*

Chapter 2

The Theatre of Greece

WE ARE IN Greece, a little more than four hundred years before the birth of Christ. We find ourselves part of the crowd in an outdoor amphitheatre as large as some famous ones which harbor the American weekly autumn ritual of the football game. For hours, the citizens of Athens have been gathering to witness an exciting event, many coming early in search of a good seat. We are to see the first performance of the newest comedy by the witty, popular, prize-winning Aristophanes.

The play is called *The Clouds* and rumor has it that it contains an attack upon the well-known teacher-philosopher Socrates who is currently in some disfavor with the government. Can it be that Aristophanes, an irreverent satirist often frowned upon by the authorities, is now taking the side of the government against the greatest teacher in Athens? Will there be any protest from the admirers of Socrates? Some in the audience think hopefully that perhaps there will be another near riot as when certain of Eurip-

6

ides' plays were performed and shocked the public with their views about the gods and the state. Come what may there is plenty of excitement stirring.

A mood of high-spirited fun lies upon these people all about us. The occasion is no ordinary performance of a comedy. It is the comedy contest in the Great Dionysia of 423 B.C., the semiannual festival of Dionysus, patron god of the Greek theatre. People are eating and drinking amid the hubbub. We smell garlic blended with the fragrance of strong wines and olive oil.

A hush falls over the crowd. The play is beginning. It is about an old man, Strepsiades, who is overwhelmed with debt because of the extravagance and betting on horses of his son, Phidippides (whose name means horse-lover). He goes to the Thoughtery, the house of Socrates, head of the school of philosophers, desiring to be taught the art of false reasoning so that he may evade the payment of his debts by winning lawsuits. Strepsiades is finally turned away by Socrates, who finds him too old and stupid to learn. In his place, the wastrel son Phidippides is sent. As soon as his education is complete, Phidippides sets upon his father and beats him, justifying this outrageous conduct by the false reasoning he has learned from Socrates.

The crowd suddenly bursts into laughter. On the stage Strepsiades is approaching the Thoughtery. Above his head hangs none other than the mock Socrates, who has just been lowered from above by a crane and is comfortably swinging "between heaven and earth" in a basket, there to expound his teachings.

STREPSIADES   [*Not seeing* SOCRATES *at first*]
Socrates! My little Socrates!

SOCRATES   [*Calling from above*]
Mortal, what do you want with me?

STREPSIADES   [*Looking up in astonishment*]
What on earth are you doing up there? Tell me, I beseech you.

Before we can hear the explanation from the basketed sage the play is interrupted by a great burst of laughter and appreciative applause. Look! Not far away, just a little below us, someone has risen to his feet! The crowd is in an uproar! It is the real Socrates! He is standing on his seat, a little man, his bald crown circled by puffs of curly hair, his homeliness accented by a bulbous nose. He has stood in order that all may see him and appreciate the cleverness of the actor's caricature. It is a rare gesture of sportsmanship. At last the tumult subsides and the play continues.

Socrates' good nature was the more remarkable since this mockery of his teachings was utterly unjust. Perhaps this is why the play, in spite of much lusty, rowdy humor, was not successful. This time the usually triumphant Aristophanes received only the third prize. The setback, for which he never quite forgave the Athenians, was deserved, for in attacking the best mind of Athens from the viewpoint of the ignorant and those suspicious of learning, the comic playwright was not worthy of himself.

The theatre was an important part of Greek national life. The main occasions for dramatic performances were the semiannual festivals of Dionysus, in winter and spring. At these times three days were devoted to dramatic contests.

We have just seen a brief moment in the performance of a comedy. The first and greatest event of the dramatic festivals, however, was the tragedy contest. Each dramatist desiring to compete for the prize was required to write three or four tragedies developing a single story. That is why the earlier Greek dramas were planned as trilogies or tetralogies, sets of three or four. The tragedies were followed, by custom, with a short satyr play, or low comedy, to carry the audience back into the mood of celebration after the purging of the emotions through tragedy. Each contestant had a separate day set aside for the performance of his works.

The preliminaries to the plays were elaborate, vivid pageantry. Thousands of spectators watched these colorful displays. The theatres were related to the temples. The ceremonies began with a

Modern performance of an ancient Greek play at Epidaurus. *National Tourist Organization of Greece*

Euripides' *Ion* at Epidaurus Festival. *National Tourist Organization of Greece*

solemn religious procession. Priests of Dionysus led the march, followed by the actors, the chorus, the dramatists and their sponsors (wealthy citizens who financed the work of the dramatists). The procession visited the sacred grove of Dionysus. The statue of the god was removed from the grove by the priests and borne at the head of the procession to the theatre where it stood upon an altar throughout the performances. A libation, or offering, of oil was poured upon the altar before the beginning of each play. At the close of the festival the statue was ceremoniously replaced on its pedestal in the grove. Thus, twice a year, Dionysus attended the theatre of which he was patron deity.

The Greeks arrived at this theatrical splendor by the road of religious worship. As the myths told it, about three thousand years ago, down from the hillsides of Thrace in northeastern Greece came a young man called Dionysus. He was handsome, vigorous, filled with the joy of life, preaching by word and example a free devotion to revelry, wine, and pleasure. Scholarly men would call him a "hedonist," which means one who makes pleasure the chief aim of life. This indulgent, often dangerous and destructive teaching nevertheless contained elements of beauty, celebration of the loveliness of nature, the exuberance of living. It led to excess, but wise men, taking the wheat from the chaff, owed something to the belief and fervor of Dionysus and his worshippers.

Dionysus, whom we also know by his other name of Bacchus, is the symbol of a spirit which no doubt created him rather than being his creation. In the Greek myth he is the son of Zeus, the supreme god, and Semele, a mortal woman. Thus he is a half-god and rightly the head of his own religious order.

Dionysus is the father of the Greek theatre which grew out of the rites of Dionysian worship. On many special occasions, such as the annual pressing of the wine, the early Greeks would gather for revelry and celebration in honor of this deity, patron of the wine and, like its effects, sometimes joyous and sometimes terrible.

There would be dancing and singing and some persons masked themselves as *satyrs*, wild mythological creatures half man and half goat who were the attendants and servants of Dionysus. From these creatures the earliest crude comedies, which were little more than roughhouse, took the name *satyr plays*.

At first everybody present took part. They thought that during the festivals the spirit of the god entered into everyone, giving each man and woman an element of godhood in his own right. This was exciting and lots of fun, but a simple idea often becomes more complicated as time passes. It came about that there were some who stood out above the others in celebration; they danced with greater agility or sang with greater fervor. Others would gather about to watch and thus a *performance*, with spectators and performers apart, came into existence. A general celebration still took place but the special performers had come to stay and their importance grew from year to year. Professionalism was being born.

A new problem arose: a large audience had to be able to see, which is not possible when just standing around. The people sought out semicircular hillsides sloping gently toward a flat place. In these hollows the flat areas were stamped down, as we might roll a tennis court, into what was called a *dancing circle*. Dancing circles, nestling in the hollows of the hills, were the first stages; the curving hillsides, the first *theatrons*, or "seeing places." Such theatres of the open air were in use throughout Greece by about the year 600 B.C. Later, from the Latin, we also began to call our theatres *auditoriums*, or "hearing places," where the audience, the "hearers," sat.

These earliest Greek dramas were altogether group affairs. They were performed by a chorus which sometimes sang, sometimes chanted the story, accompanied by dances. Around 535 B.C. a man named Thespis, of whom we know only that he was a prominent leader of the chorus, stepped out from the group and recited certain portions of the drama alone. He was the earliest actor. For the first time an individual played a separate part in dialogue with the chorus. To traditionalists this may have seemed scandalous, as all new departures do, yet to this day, because of Thespis' originality, actors are frequently called *Thespians* after him.

The way was open now to a much more elaborate kind of drama. A more vivid style than choral narrative was revealed and it was not long before the first of the great Greek dramatists, Aeschylus, took advantage of the idea to introduce not only one but two individual speakers. Later Sophocles ventured to the use of three and the barriers were down. The Greek dramas had become plays, essentially as we know them today, still using the chorus, but with numerous separate characters.

There is an enormous contrast between the theatre of Dionysus in Athens, where we recreated a scene a short while ago, and the plain dancing circles of the Greek theatre in its infancy. The development of the drama after the introduction of actors required more elaborate staging than the simple natural amphitheatres could offer. The theatre changed to keep pace with the growing needs of the drama.

Instead of the grassy banks, there were marble seats placed in the amphitheatres, many tiers in height, sloping toward a now paved dancing circle with an altar in its center. This form is embodied in the magnificent theatre at Epidaurus, which still stands in impressive beauty and where plays are performed every year.

The dancing circle was called the *orchestra*. This latter word has altered its meaning in two ways for us. Groups of musicians playing in theatres inherited the name "orchestra" from the section of the theatre they occupied. Americans have extended the meaning of the word loosely to include the whole first level of seats (the English call this section "stalls").

The actors had to have formal places for their entrances and exits. Dressing rooms were needed and a place of concealment for actors not on the stage. A low building was developed, at first

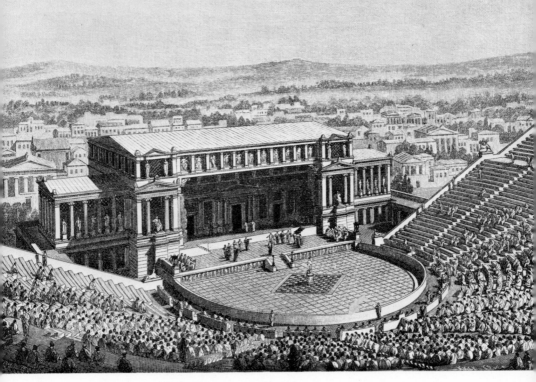

Reconstruction of Theatre of Dionysus at Athens. *The Bettmann Archive*

little more than a hut, located in full view of the audience directly behind the orchestra. This was called the *skene* (skay-nay) and from this we derive the theatre term *scene*.

The *skene* became a standard background. As the stories of the plays became more complicated and the actors increased in number it was felt that some place of prominence should be provided so that the actors might be seen and heard to the best advantage. The flat roof of the original, low *skene* became the new playing area, or stage, above the level of the orchestra. At the back of the stage another structure was built up that evolved as an increasingly elaborate formal background for the players, including doors for entrances and exits, which also could be opened to display a scene within.

When this happened the enlarged *skene* cut a slice from the old dancing circle which became a semicircle, still used by the chorus for some time to come, but no longer used by the main actors. In time the orchestra was forsaken altogether, actors and chorus sharing the stage. This change can be seen in the ruins of the theatre of Dionysus at Athens.

We don't really know how much painted scenery the Greeks used. Probably the formal background of the *skene* usually took the place of scenery. If you have seen pageants, plays, or operas in the open air you may realize how unimportant realistic scenery is. The Greeks are said to have used devices called *periaktoi*, three-sided columns with a different scene painted on each side. By turning these at the sides of the stage they may have indicated the nature of the scene, leaving the rest to the imagination. There isn't much difference between this and the practice in Shakespeare's time of placing on stage a simple sign saying, "This is the Forest of Arden."

Greek costumes were richly beautiful. They also used stage machinery and masks. Some claim the Greeks used revolving turntables, like many modern theatres, to bring new tableaux (motionless posed groups of actors) into view. They sometimes used wheeled platforms for this purpose, as in the *Agamemnon* of Aeschylus when the great central doors of the *skene*, representing palace doors, might be swung open at the end so that the body of the king, murdered within, might be brought forward into the view of the audience.

In some Greek plays gods arrived from the heavens or departed to them. For these effects, or such comic tricks as suspending Socrates in a basket, they used cranes. *Deus ex machina*, or "god from the machine," was the term for these crane-lowered deities whose function was often to impose divine order on the tangled affairs of the play. The phrase has passed into our language as a metaphor for any last-minute, external solution to a problem.

Masks were standard equipment for the Greek actor and to this day the grimacing tragic and comic masks are universal symbols of dramatic art, common in the decoration of theatres and on play-

Performer in Epidaurus Festival of classical Greek drama. *National Tourist Organization of Greece*

Tragic mask of the Hellenistic period in Greece. *Athens National Museum*

bills and posters. We have spoken of the superstitious, ritualistic use of masks by witch doctors. The Greeks used them for a combination of practical and artistic reasons. Many spectators in the great amphitheatres were too far away to see natural facial expressions. The exaggerated conventional designs of the masks were visible to all. Yet still more important, the Greeks liked the effect of this extreme representation of an emotion which, to them, expressed the eternal quality of all tragedy or all comedy.

Greek drama was richly poetic. They loved a rich, beautiful

voice and power of declamation more than any other quality in an actor. The masks were carved of wood and some have suggested that they possessed acoustical properties to magnify the voice like megaphones. It is quite possible that they were resonant and increased the richness and carrying power of the voice. But this was not essential. The Greeks built their theatres with an extraordinary sense of natural acoustical properties. If you visit the enormous theatre at Epidaurus you can verify for yourself the fact that a quiet spoken word down in the orchestra can be heard clearly in the highest seats.

Greek theatre was conventional. This means it did not try to imitate life literally but to suggest the most important qualities of life. Often in modern times stage and film have been given over to close imitations of nature. Yet even the most realistic dramatic performance is filled with conventions which we do not think about consciously.

A convention in the artistic sense means an approved and commonly understood technique. Beating one's breast or tearing one's hair are conventional gestures of despair. People do not sing their way through life but that is a convention we accept in opera or musical comedy. Close-ups, dissolves, and zoom-shots are conventions of movies and television. Animated cartoons are completely conventional with their highly standardized action patterns which show a character mashed or blown up or meeting some other frightful fate at one moment and vigorously in the chase again at the next.

Formalism—a style in which the form in which things are represented is essential to the whole effect—has been a major aspect of theatrical art from the Greeks onward. They used the chorus to discuss and interpret the events of their plays. They talked about off-stage happenings more than they showed events themselves, yet such was their mastery of word, recitation, and gesture that they lost no dramatic power. The chorus not only chanted or sang, but also danced or marched about the stage in formal patterns.

Form is the essence of all art. It follows that to respond to art you must understand the form, either by absorbing it as you grow up in a culture where it is all about you, or by deliberate study of the form and conventions of the art of any time or place.

Tradition says that in Greece, somewhere between eight and ten centuries before Christ, there was a blind poet named Homer. He is supposed to have been one of the ancient bards who wandered from city to city reciting the mythic stories in epic verse. To him are attributed two of the poetic masterpieces of antiquity, shapers of style ever after them, alive and vital in literature today: the *Iliad* and the *Odyssey*. Much of the substance of these epics was passed down in the memorized oral tradition by many generations of bards, but the works we call Homer's represent their most ancient written versions.

For a while in the nineteenth century it was the fashion of some scholars to suggest that Homer was not a real person but a traditional name attached to work that was really an accumulated product of many unknown persons or sources. Speculation also has suggested that the two great epics are a hundred years or so apart in date and even that the author of the *Odyssey* was a woman. Yet some modern scholars have turned back to the belief in a single authorship of their written form because of the unity and harmony of the works which outweigh the inconsistencies. An old rhyme captures the irony of the way in which the world often treats its great artists:

> *Seven cities claimed Homer dead,*
> *Through which the living Homer begged his bread.*

Whoever, whatever, Homer may have been, the *Iliad* and the *Odyssey* contain much of the vast lore of Greek mythology, reflecting the Greece of prehistory when men and gods mingled, when dreadful monsters inhabited land and sea, and when Greeks fought a ten-year war with Troy to recover the runaway wife of a

Greek king. So much of Greek history and religion is in this framework of myth that it is impossible to unravel. A great modern historian, Arnold Toynbee, has said of the *Iliad* that "anyone who starts reading it as history will find that it is full of fiction but, equally, anyone who starts reading it as fiction will find that it is full of history."

From the same heritage of myth come the great Greek tragedies, four centuries or more after Homer. Greeks did not go to the theatre to be surprised by a new tale. The dramatists used traditional stories and characters with which their audiences were thoroughly familiar. The playwright dramatized the old story to bring his own fresh insights to it and to compel us to see its meaning through his eyes. To experience the powerful, enduring impact of Greek drama you must come to it with some reasonable background of reading in Greek mythology, which you also need for a full response to any literature right down to our own time.

It is the peculiar power of drama that a play can be utterly gripping to its audience even when everyone knows perfectly well how it is going to end. Indeed, it often draws its greatest force from the fact that we *do* know what is coming. The suspense of anticipation is greater than that of surprise, for the real nature of suspense is anguish, concern for the characters because of our sympathy for and identification with them. What fascinates us is how they respond to what happens.

The three greatest dramatists of Greece were Aeschylus, Sophocles, and Euripides. Their lives overlapped, though each carried the form of his art a distinctive step forward, and as poets they share equal honor. They were individuals whose slightly differing views of the world can be seen in their plays.

Aeschylus lived from 525 to 456 B.C. He fought bravely in the wars in which Greece held off the assaults of the huge Persian empire and, although he became famous as a playwright, on his tombstone he was identified as a soldier-hero of the battle at Marathon.

This man was the father of tragic drama, the introducer of the second actor who made possible the interaction of characters that we understand as dramatic action, the inventor of many of the Greek stage machines and techniques. Looking upon life he saw men as in the grip of the gods; he saw that what happened to them was often unjust and terrible; he said that men must face their destinies strongly and struggle against what was evil; behind the many gods of mythology he sensed the presence of the one God; he did not accept what satisfied most men around him: "I hold my own mind and think apart from other men."

He had fought in war to defend Greek freedom but like his two peers in drama he knew the corruption and horror of war and exposed it as he saw his beloved nation beginning to work her own ultimate downfall by wars against others such as the Persians had waged against Greece.

The Greeks loved satire and mockery and were witty, often cruel masters of both. Some derided the austere Aeschylus and when he was dead said he had been killed by an eagle who mistook his bald head for a rock and dropped a tortoise on it to break the shell. Yet the people of Athens, abruptly aware that a mighty voice was still, revoked a strict rule prohibiting the revival of plays that had once been performed at the religious festivals so that Aeschylus' works could be performed from season to season.

His *Agamemnon*, one of the "slices from Homer's banquet" as he modestly called some of his plays, is part of the epic of the Trojan War and its aftermath. It is one of the precious surviving seven of the ninety plays he is said to have written. With it begins his trilogy, the *Oresteia*, the only one of the complete, connected Greek trilogies that we possess.

Agamemnon, king of Argos, was commander-in-chief of the Greek armies at Troy. He was the brother of Menelaus, king of Sparta, whose wife Helen had run off with Paris, one of the sons of Priam, king of Troy. The war was fought to recover her and lay waste the offending city. The sailing of the Greek armies from the harbor of Aulis was delayed by unfavorable winds. Agamemnon sacrificed his daughter, Iphigenia, to propitiate the gods and get fair winds.

The play opens more than ten years later. A long-awaited signal fire reveals that the war is ended by a Greek victory; Agamemnon is returning. For years, Clytemnestra, his wife, has nursed hatred of him for killing their daughter, and she has plotted against him with a lover, Aegisthus. When the king arrives she welcomes him before the palace but then, leading him in to his bath, casts a net over him and murders him with an axe.

That grim deed is one more link in a chain of crimes and vengeances that in primitive codes can have no end. In the second play, the *Choephoroe* (Ko-eff'-ory) ("Libation Bearers"), Orestes, son of Agamemnon, in league with his sister Electra, commanded by the god Apollo, slays his mother Clytemnestra and her lover Aegisthus to avenge his father.

The third play is the *Eumenides*—the title, "The Kindly Ones," is a Greek euphemism, or prettifying phrase, for the Furies, supernatural pursuers of persons guilty of unpunished crimes. Orestes is haunted by the Furies who demand his death. Here Aeschylus speaks his own mind against primitive feud tradition. He brings Orestes to trial in Athens. The judges divide equally for and against him. Then the goddess Athena (*dea ex machina*) intervenes and casts the acquitting vote. She appeases the Furies—in effect retiring them honorably, their era ended—and decrees that chains of crime and vengeance must be broken. The chorus chants:

> *The thirsty dust shall nevermore*
> *Suck up the darkly streaming gore*
> *Of civic broils, shed out in wrath*
> *And vengeance, crying death for death!*

The second of the great dramatists was Sophocles, who lived from about 496 to 406 B.C. Acceptance, endurance are the notes of Sophocles, mingled with great tenderness for suffering. He stood somewhat apart and gazed upon the life of man as a hard course. But if men must accept what the gods will, if they must endure what cannot be helped, they need not do so passively. Passivity is not dramatic. Sophocles shows us that they can choose good rather than evil even if evil triumphs and destroys them; they can cry out against injustice even as they endure it, protesting the way things are; in death, they can choose to die well. Sophocles is pessimistic and conservative; he does not believe literally in the multitude of mythic gods but the moral-ethical law of the God behind the gods is the standard by which he measures human conduct. He is said to have remarked that he portrayed people as they ought to be, whereas Euripides portrayed them as they are. There is value in each way. Sophocles brought conservative judgment to bear upon his own nation which was beginning its ruin by betraying its principles.

We have only seven of the one hundred and twenty plays attributed to him. He introduced the third actor and other technical developments. He was the most flawless craftsman of the three tragic dramatists and the most consistently popular with Athenian audiences.

He knew that events are ironic, turning in ways dreadfully different from what they had led us to expect. The deepest expression of this occurs in his greatest play, the most technically perfect and stunning of all Greek tragedies, *Oedipus Tyrannus* (in Latin, *Oedipus Rex*, in English, *Oedipus the King*).

Here is the background of that play: A male child was born to Laius, king of Thebes, and his wife, Jocasta. It was prophesied that this child would kill his father and marry his mother. To avoid that curse, the child was exposed to die on a mountainside with a spike driven through his feet. A shepherd rescued the infant and took him to Corinth where the boy was adopted by the king and queen of that city and raised to believe himself their own son. He was called Oedipus ("swollen-foot") because of his injured feet.

When he was a young man, Oedipus was told by the oracle of Apollo that it would be his fate to slay his father and marry his mother. To avoid this awful disaster he left Corinth, vowing never to return while his supposed parents lived. At a crossing of three roads he met King Laius of Thebes who arrogantly ordered him to stand aside. A quarrel followed and the high-tempered youth slew the older man, quite ignorant of who he was.

Proceeding to Thebes, Oedipus delivered that city from a monster called the Sphinx which had been terrorizing the people. Hailed as the city's hero, he married its widowed queen, Jocasta. They had two sons, Eteocles and Polyneices, and two daughters, Ismene and Antigone.

All this information is woven into the drama in its appropriate time, but as the play opens we know nothing of it. Oedipus has ruled Thebes well for years and is loved and admired. Yet now a pestilence afflicts the city. Oedipus' brother-in-law, Creon, brings word from the oracle of Apollo that the city is polluted by the un-known slayer of Laius and that the pestilence will end when he is expelled. Oedipus announces that he will find the slayer at all costs.

A blind prophet, Teiresias, is questioned and asserts that Oedipus is the murderer of Laius. The king is enraged but is forced to realize that it is indeed so. Still he does not realize what the rela-tionship had been. He presses his investigation. Jocasta is first to realize the full truth; she urges Oedipus to stop his quest but he will not; she withdraws into the palace and takes her life. A mes-senger comes with what is intended to be good news for Oedipus: the old king and queen of Corinth have died, it is now supposedly safe for him to return there, free of any curse. At the same time he discovers that they were not his real parents. He knows, now, who he is and that circumstances have fulfilled the terrible prophecy that all had long ago attempted to avoid. He rushes into the pal-ace, finds the dead queen, and in anguish and guilt scratches out his eyes with the pins of her brooches. Coming out before the hushed, appalled, and sorrowing people, he abandons the throne to his sons, Eteocles and Polyneices, and asks to be led from the city.

Though Sophocles wrote two more plays related to the tragic royal house of Thebes, *Antigone* and *Oedipus at Colonus*, they were not written in sequence but stand independently. One of his innovations was to depart from the practice of writing plays as formal trilogies or tetralogies.

Antigone is another of his most widely performed plays. The sons of Oedipus, Eteocles and Polyneices, were pledged to rule the city in alternate years, but Eteocles, who started first, refused to step down at the end of his first year. The betrayed Polyneices brought the armies of seven allied kings and laid siege to Thebes to claim his rights. The invaders were repulsed but the brothers slew each other in personal combat. Their uncle Creon became king. This story is told in Aeschylus' *Seven Against Thebes*, for in their different ways the three tragic dramatists worked with many of the same materials.

At the opening of Sophocles' play Creon has decreed that because Polyneices had brought an army against his own city his body shall lie out on the battlefield without burial. It is a dishonor to deny burial to the dead, for it bars them from repose in the other world, and it is also an affront to the gods to whom the dead belong, a fact that Creon ignored. Although death is the penalty for disobedience to the order, one of the sisters of Polyneices, Antigone, determines to bury her brother's body. She asks for Ismene's help in this pious, sisterly duty but the other sister is timid and lacks the courage for such defiance. Antigone speaks in characteristic Sophoclean utterance:

> . . . be what thou wilt; but I will bury him: well for me to die in doing that. I shall rest, a loved one with him whom I have loved, sinless for my crime; for I owe a longer allegiance to the dead than to the living: in that world I shall abide for ever.

She fulfills her pledge but is caught. The angry Creon has her walled up in a cave to die. Creon is then persuaded that he has been too harsh. Relenting, he orders Antigone to be released but she has slain herself to avoid a lingering death. His own son, who had been betrothed to Antigone and pleaded for her, has also slain himself, as has Creon's wife, in grief at her son's death.

The youngest of the three tragic dramatists was Euripides, born about 480 B.C., although he may have died in 406 B.C., the same year as Sophocles, who outlived him by a little. He was a much more savage critic of Athenian society and policies than either Aeschylus or Sophocles, although both of them had brought the city-state under moral judgment. Euripides was the true rebel and radical. He threw over the mythic gods altogether. The Greek scholar Edith Hamilton contrasts the line of Sophocles: "Nothing is wrong which gods command" with Euripides': "If gods do evil, then they are not gods."

To him the war of Greeks against Sparta in his own time was an evil like the war of legendary Greeks against Troy. Out of this conviction sprang *The Trojan Women*. Its protest against wars of conquest has never been surpassed and speaks with undiminished eloquence today.

Its dramatic power derives from its moral passion for there is little action. The setting is the plain before the smoking ruins of the sacked and burned city of Troy. Hecuba, the widowed queen of the fallen city, lies on the ground. Two gods, Poseidon (or Neptune), god of the sea, who has always supported the cause of Troy, and Athena, who has been the supporter of the Greeks, hold a conversation. Here Euripides unmasks the victors. The Greeks, in their mad vengeance upon the city, had even profaned the temple of their own goddess and protectress. Now she has washed her hands of them, she tells Poseidon, and gives him her full consent to harass and destroy them as he will by the fury of the seas on their way home.

The rest of the play is one long outcry of grief by the women of the fallen city and the tragically noble Hecuba. The victorious Greeks heap useless cruelty and humiliations upon the vanquished survivors and expose themselves as merciless in the pride of triumph. The gods have given the clue that a divine retribution awaits them as bad as the vengeance they have poured upon the defeated.

This scorching play was cast into the teeth of the Athenian populace a scant few weeks after the Greeks had annihilated the small neighboring island of Melos, putting its men to the sword and taking its women into bondage, for merely refusing to ally themselves with the Greeks in the war against Sparta. The episode and the negotiations that preceded it are told in Thucydides' *The Peloponnesian War*.

It was a bold stroke, characteristic of Euripides, but dangerous. This was open challenge to the policy of Athens. Even though he had many admirers and won the dramatic prize often, there were sometimes riots when his plays were performed. Around 408 B.C. he was too controversial a figure to remain in Athens. He accepted what was surely not a voluntary exile and lived and wrote for the short remainder of his life in Macedonia where, according to legend, he was accidentally torn to pieces by the hunting dogs of his host, King Archelaus.

We have more of his work than any of the other tragedians, though it is only nineteen plays and fragments from a probable output of eighty or ninety. In exile he who had often won the prize in the contests dedicated to Dionysus wrote the powerful play *The Bacchae* (Bacchantes, or devotees of Bacchus), which exposed the appalling frenzy and madness that were possible in Dionysian worship.

We know Greek comedy through only two playwrights whose works have survived. They represent distinctly different expressions of the comic spirit. The "Old Comedy" is that of Aristophanes; the "New Comedy," of Menander.

Aristophanes, who lived about 448 to 380 B.C., was the master of the Old Comedy which, in spite of its name and antiquity, is right up to the present moment in spirit. Wholly unsentimental, it is satirical, bristling with the barbed wit that criticizes, mocks, exposes, or deflates its target. Aristophanes had a scatter-shot style that spared neither persons nor institutions.

He was opposed to the war with Sparta and mocked the government's war policies, the generals, the diplomats, the orators. It was not only officials who felt the sting of his wit but also well-known personalities of the city, philosophers such as Socrates (who also opposed the war and the government), and the three writers of tragedies, each of whom he admired in some ways but whose styles and ideas nevertheless drew his laughter wherever he thought he saw flaws or pomposity. The people at large, too, felt his lash as he jibed at the follies of Athens' total democracy. People often follow their petty emotions instead of their considered judgment. The Athenians had a practice called "ostracism" by which a prominent man might be sentenced to a ten-year exile for any reason that impelled the voters. It takes its name from the *ostrakons*, shards of pottery, by which the votes were cast. Once the Athenians ostracized one of their finest leaders, Aristides. There is a story that Aristides, unrecognized, asked a citizen whom he had seen cast an *ostrakon*, why he was voting for exile. The man replied that he had nothing against Aristides, but, "I'm tired of hearing him always called 'the just.'"

The pace of the comedies was headlong; the tone, raucous. The spirit resembles that of irreverent satirical reviews and nightclub entertainments that have been popular in recent years in England and the United States. Yet in spite of the considerable freedom of language and subject in this latter half of the twentieth century, we have not approached the unrestricted expression of Aristophanes. His earthy, coarse language and action would still lie beyond what is permitted in public performance. This aspect of Greek comedy is put in perspective by Edith Hamilton, both a distinguished scholar and a woman of the utmost refinement and taste, in her fine book, *The Greek Way*.

The comic theatre was a means of working off the exuberant energy of abounding vitality. There were no limitations to the subjects it could treat or the way of treating them. The result is that the distinctive quality of the Old Comedy cannot be illustrated by quotation. The most characteristic passages are unprintable. Something completely indecent is caricatured, wildly exaggerated, repeated in a dozen different ways, all fantastically absurd and all incredibly vulgar. The truth is that the jokes are often very funny. To read Aristophanes through at a sitting is to have Victorian guide posts laid low.

He is so frank, so fearless, so completely without shame, one ends by feeling that indecency is just a part of life and a part with specially humorous possibilities. There is nothing of Peeping Tom anywhere, no sly whispering from behind a hand. The plainest and clearest words speak everything out unabashed. Life looks a coarse and vulgar thing, lived at the level of nature's primitive needs, but it never looks a foul and rotten thing. Degeneracy plays no part. It is the way of a virile world, of robust men who can roar with laughter at any kind of slapstick, decent or indecent, but chiefly the last.

Lysistrata, one of Aristophanes' antiwar plays, is performed often in modern times in slightly restrained form. It offers the simplest antiwar stratagem of all time when the women of Athens agree together to deny themselves to their husbands until the war is stopped.

The chorus of frogs in his play, *The Frogs*, with its repeated chant of

Brekekekex co-ax, co-ax

sounds like an ancient ancestor of the football cheer.

We have eleven out of an uncertain total number of plays by Aristophanes. Among the last, lost ones was a play that is said to have changed its style in the direction of what is called the New Comedy.

The added element that distinguishes the New Comedy is

sentiment: a love story. It is a softer, gentler mode of humor, more of a story and less of a display of wit or clash of ideas. Menander is the only Greek author in this vein whose work we possess—even so, a mere three imperfectly preserved plays and fragments from perhaps as many as a hundred.

His stories deal with confused questions of the parentage of children, mistaken identities, surprising revelations and happy endings. This formula was adopted by the Roman comic writers and continues through the Italian comedies to emerge in our language in Shakespeare's *The Comedy of Errors* which, although much more elaborate in plot and counterplot, has the spirit of the Greek playwright.

Menander lived about 342 to 292 B.C. Tradition says that he was drowned at Piraeus, the harbor of Athens.

Aeschylus. *Rome Museum*   Sophocles. *Lateran Museum, Rome*

 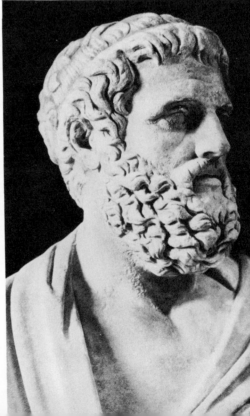

The Greek theatre produced not only the first tragedies and comedies but gave rise to the earliest criticism of drama. The philosopher Aristotle, who lived from 384 to 322 B.C., was a pupil of the illustrious philosopher Plato and later served as tutor to the youth remembered as Alexander the Great.

Aristotle was one of the first "universal minds"—men whose curiosity and intellectual power seem to reach into every realm of knowledge and study. Aristotle wrote on the natural sciences, logic, metaphysics, ethics, politics, history, rhetoric, and poetry. Under the latter subject drama is studied, in an essay called *Poetics*.

In it he sets forth general observations on dramatic technique based on what was done by Aeschylus, Sophocles, and Euripides. All drama is the imitation of action, he says. Comedy differs from

Euripides. *Naples Museum*

Menander. *National Tourist Organization of Greece*

tragedy in that "the one seeks to imitate worse, but the other better men than are." Yet, he adds, comedy does not seek to represent all the vices of men "but the ridiculous only." The chief end of tragedy, he said, was to purge the emotions through pity and terror.

Two words are especially important in the study of Greek drama: "*hubris*" and "Fate." *Hubris* means overweening, arrogant pride, that defiant pride which the Jewish and Christian tradition also regard as the deadliest sin, by which the angels fell. In Greek tragedy again and again we see the fall of a great man brought about by *hubris*, which is the true sense of the ancient proverb: Pride goeth before a fall. It is foremost of the tragic flaws that are common to even the noblest of human natures.

"Fate" in the Greek sense is a complex idea. It is the way things are going to be and not even the gods can alter it. In the *Iliad*, Zeus wishes to protect the life of Hector, the Trojan hero, in his fight with the Greek Achilles, but when the supreme god tosses their names into the scales of Fate it is Hector who must lose.

Yet Fate does not cancel responsibility. As in the case of Oedipus, Apollo foresees, with a god's vision, what all the people involved are going to do—but at the same time it is by their own choices that each event in the tragedy takes place. To foresee it is not to cause it. We are drawn close to the conclusion that to a great extent character is Fate—what we are deeply influences what happens to us and determines the way we accept what we cannot control.

History supported those Greek playwrights and philosophers who opposed the war with Sparta although the government ignored them and the people would not heed. That war dragged golden Greece into weakness and ultimate destruction. That majestic civilization first staggered under the weight of its own armor and finally fell under the dominance of a new world power: Rome.

The Roman Coliseum. *Italian State Tourist Office*

Chapter 3

Roman Spectacle

IF YOU TOOK an ancient Roman to a modern football game or a heavyweight championship fight he might have a good time in a tepid way and thank you politely for it, but secretly he would have thought it tame and felt that you might have asked for your money back.

The two features most highly prized by the average Roman audience were tremendous spectacle and violence. Uniquely Roman entertainment seldom amounted to much else. The spirit of the Rose Bowl Tournament on New Year's Day is quite like that of a Roman game day, insofar as it consists of processions and general festivities winding up with the gathering of thousands of citizens in the amphitheatre for the main event. But unlike the

33

bumpy passage of a football a hundred yards or so back and forth, before the bloodthirsty masses in a Roman arena more than a few persons would lose their lives in contests of man against man, or man against beast.

There were many different kinds of spectacles. Rome, in its centuries of splendor and might, built many more stadiums and arenas for such events than for plays. These had names still glamorous to us today: *circuses* and *hippodromes*. Circus takes its name from the enclosed circle for games or races. Hippodrome is from the Greek *hippos*, horse, and *dromos*, course.

Even so, smaller Roman theatres for plays can be seen all around the Mediterranean shores and in France and Britain. Just outside Rome, in the huge tumbledown estate of Hadrian's villa, the emperor had one theatre in the characteristic Greek architectural style for tragedy, and some distance away another in the slightly modified Roman style for comedy, both of which may be seen today.

Since spectacle was the predominant mode of Roman entertainment, we shall look at its many forms in spite of the fact that they are not pure theatre. The greatest of the structures for spectacle was the Circus Maximus. It was in the shape of a long oval, slightly flattened at one end. Here were located stalls for the horses and chariots at the start of the race. The circus was nearly a mile around and at the height of its use could accommodate more than two hundred thousand persons.

The Circus Maximus was in use over a vast span of Roman history, from the early days of the Republic or even the later kings to the years of slow collapse of the state under the last emperors— from long before Christ until several centuries into the Christian era.

For years only the lower tiers of seats were of stone, the upper sections being made of wood, like bleachers in a ballpark. The wooden seats were destroyed by fire many times and rebuilt. Once, in an accident that sounds familiar because it happens today, too, many people were killed when a section of the wooden stands collapsed during games. At the height of the empire the structure was altogether of stone.

Julius Caesar constructed a ten-foot-wide, water-filled moat to separate the arena from the first tier of seats. At animal games the spectators needed protection from any beast that might run amuck and attempt to plunge into the seats. Anyone who has sat in the front row at a bullfight and seen a furious bull hurl himself over the barrier immediately below him will recognize the problem. Later, Nero had the moat filled up, possibly because it cramped the style of the chariot races.

Down the middle of the long amphitheatre ran a low, narrow wall, called the *spina*, or spine, as the divider of the oval race course. Roman chariot races were run in seven laps. On the *spina*, in addition to sculptures and other decorations, seven large oval objects were conspicuously set up like eggs in a rack. One of these was taken down at the finish of each lap so that, in the tension and excitement, charioteers and spectators alike could tell at a glance how much of the race remained. These races were among the greatest popular traditions of Rome and are part of the image we all hold of that period. You will have a good sense both of the contest and of such structures as the Circus Maximus if you have seen the film *Ben Hur* or any one of numerous other spectacular motion pictures involving Roman times.

Though no seats or architectural features now remain, one may visit the Circus Maximus in the heart of Rome today, near the Forum, between the Palatine and Aventine hills. You may walk around that clearly defined course where for so many centuries chariots careened and men and beasts struggled.

At various periods Rome also contained the Circus Flaminius, Circus Neronis, and Circus of Maxentius, the latter of which is still a quite well-preserved ruin.

The great arena which most captures the imagination and is one of the symbols of the city is the Coliseum (sometimes spelt

Colosseum), which we know by that name not because it is so huge, as one might think, but because beside it once stood a colossal statue of the emperor Nero. The original amphitheatre on that site was destroyed in the burning of Rome in Nero's time. The present structure, begun by the emperor Vespasian in A.D. 75, was known to Romans as the Flavian Amphitheatre.

It is the most spectacular single structure among the ruins of ancient Rome, where it stands, a gaunt skeleton, tradition-saturated, unmistakable when the eye first beholds it. Like so many ruined buildings it was long pillaged for its fine dressed stone, like a handy quarry, and incorporated into palaces and great houses. Otherwise it would be in a better state of preservation, for man is much more destructive in the short haul than time, which works with slow patience. It is the home of thousands of cats that lie in the sun, quarrel with each other, and spit or snarl alarmingly at tourists roaming the dark corridors of the upper galleries. They seem like miniature haunting spirits of the great cats that tore men to pieces there for the entertainment of the crowd. From its highest tiers we can gaze down at the Arch of Constantine, the Arch of Titus, and beyond it the Forum, and feel antiquity all about us. The English poet, Lord Byron, expressed in a few lines an old belief of the city:

> *While stands the Coliseum, Rome shall stand;*
> *When falls the Coliseum, Rome shall fall;*
> *And when Rome falls—the World.*

In the days of its use the Coliseum had many remarkable features. The arena could be flooded for the staging of mimic sea battles, of which more later. Underground were labyrinthine cellars, exposed now in the ruins, where gladiators made ready, prisoners were held, and many kinds of beasts were caged, all awaiting their fatal moment before the Roman crowds. Byron again summed it up:

> *Butcher'd to make a Roman holiday.*

More than eighty thousand persons could be seated there. Like a huge circus ring, it had a canvas top, a great awning stretched across to protect the crowd from the cruel summer sun.

Combats between gladiators were enormously popular. Military in nature, they were said to have sprung from a military motive. They were begun about 100 B.C., under the Republic, by the consul Gaius Marius. He was about to lead Rome into extensive wars and some thought he planned the games to accustom the Roman people to the idea of bloodshed—a theory which sounds just a bit too neat.

At first prisoners of war were made to do the fighting. As public taste for the spectacle grew, certain citizens took part, as amateurs, to display their prowess at arms. In time a professional gladiatorial rank grew and became a guild, also serving as an auxiliary militia.

Familiarity makes many things acceptable. Roman tolerance of bloody sports ripened into appetite. You might see men against men, or against beasts, or animal against animal. You could have hurried one day to buy your ticket to see an elephant fight a rhinoceros.

For a prisoner of war or a slave, the deadly game might be a chance to win freedom if he could enlist the favor of the crowd by valor. Even a defeated fighter could hope to have his life spared if he was not disliked by the emperor or the president of the games. When a gladiator had beaten his man, he hesitated before the death blow, and turned to the audience. If the people clamored for the kill and turned thumbs down in the gesture of rejection, the defeated man was slain. If the loser had been brave the verdict might be thumbs-up and he was spared. The emperor always had the final decision and could overrule the crowd.

Plain sword duels were the simplest of fare. Romans demanded novelty in the matching of opponents and weapons. It was popular to pit an armored man with shield and short sword against a nearly naked man with a trident (three-pronged spear) and a net, in the meshes of which he would seek to entangle the swordsman.

The net was a deadlier weapon than you might suppose and the formidable armored man was often the loser.

The moral standards of Roman life sank steadily lower under the succession of Caesars. Even in the age of Augustus, under whose reign Christ was born, the historian Titus Livius, also called Livy, lamented in the beginning of his *History of Rome* that "our vices have attained to such a height of enormity, that we can no longer endure either the burden of them, or the sharpness of the necessary remedies." A great deal worse was to come. Sportsmanship and the fighting chance in the games gave way to wholesale bloodshed. The people who paraded captive kings and warriors through the city in their victories, pitted many of these prisoners unarmed against beasts in the arenas to watch them be torn to pieces. The same treatment was accorded many early Christians struggling to defend their religion in hostile Rome. Whether the Coliseum was actually a site of these Christian martyrdoms is uncertain although a great cross at the edge of the arena commemorates the tradition.

We mentioned a moment ago that the Coliseum could be flooded for mimic sea battles. They were called *Naumachia* and were popular. Opposing fleets of small vessels manned by slaves were set against one another. At the opening of the spectacle the fleets were sailed or rowed in procession around the artificial lake. Then they formed in fighting ranks and battled in deadly earnest until one fleet or the other was destroyed. Many lives were lost in these fights and ships were burned or sunk. The water turned red. When this miniature naval engagement was over, the basin was drained so that the wreckage and bodies might be removed.

Such contests were held in other arenas, too. The emperor Claudius, fifth in the succession of Caesars, once staged a battle on a large lake near Rome. When the slaves did not fight ferociously enough he ran stumbling along the shore shouting threats and orders at them. If slaves were not given the promise of freedom for good fighting they often faced the grimmer promise of death to follow if they did not wholeheartedly court death in battle.

The expense of all these lavish displays was usually borne by the emperor, or occasionally by some wealthy family, or by some general who had private ambitions. The sponsor, when other than the emperor himself, was given the title of President of the Games. The cost was sometimes enough to bankrupt even a wealthy citizen. More than once a malicious emperor ruined a man by compelling him to give a festival of games which he could not afford, yet which, since it was a command performance and a supposed honor, he dared not skimp for fear of his life.

All this is a dark but unfortunately characteristic side of Roman taste in entertainment. Even more vile and cruel displays were sponsored by such mad, degenerate emperors as Caligula, Nero, and Caracalla. The hulking ruins of the baths of Caracalla, by the way, are now each summer in Rome the impressive setting of outdoor opera performances. A visitor wandering through the crumbling baths in other seasons may happen upon stacks of scenery panels stuck away where there is a sheltering roof remaining.

To be just to the Romans, they were not wholly a bloodthirsty people without virtues. They did not have the deep-rooted, natural instinct for culture and graceful living possessed by the Greeks. Yet they were an intelligent, vigorous, and often progressive people. Their genius was for military strategy, for organization and government, for construction, conquests, and orderly law. Rome developed legal codes and systems to which the whole free Western world is indebted. Until general social rot set in, Romans practiced the complicated arts of civil administration superbly. They imposed order on the known world and after their great conquests preserved a relatively stable peace, the famous Pax Romana, for centuries, until the slow erosion of standards of conduct, the vanishing of the old civic virtues, caused the empire to fall into ruins.

Because practical and especially military matters occupied their thoughts so much, Romans were content to let their culture be largely an imitation of Greece. Most of what they did in all the arts fell below Greek achievements. Yet Roman order and organization, even Roman imitation, did us the service of preserving the remnants, traditions, and records of Greek culture.

Literary forms other than drama reached high levels in Rome. In poetry these ranged from the short satirical poems of Catullus to the odes, epistles, and satires of Horace, and Virgil's *Aeneid*, the Roman equivalent of the epics of Homer. The orations of Cicero match those of the Greek Demosthenes. Roman history is distinguished, not only in Julius Caesar's accounts of his own wars in Gaul, but in the books of the historians Tacitus, Livy, Pliny, and others.

Tragedy never flourished in Rome. Seneca, a member of the Senate, was the best-known tragic dramatist of the first century of the Christian era. Born in Spain around 4 B.C., he was brought to Rome as a child. He lived in the most dangerous of times for a man to move in high circles—through the reigns of the mad emperor Caligula, by whom his life was threatened, the emperor Claudius who banished him for a time under false charges, and the emperor Nero. When the youthful Nero came to power Seneca, who had been his tutor, enjoyed a period of considerable influence in the affairs of Rome and though he could scarcely help being blackened by some of the events of that dreadful time, he is credited with helping to restrain Nero, for a while, from the worst of excesses. The emperor was jealous of all around him and Seneca renounced public life and wealth, trying to withdraw from the world to follow his interests as writer, philosopher, and dramatist. But Nero would not forget him and in A.D. 65 sent soldiers to Seneca with the command that he take his own life. Like others before him, the philosopher accepted this calmly and obeyed.

Seneca's tragedies, such as his *Oedipus* and *Medea*, are adaptations from the works of the Greek dramatists. Probably they were intended more for formal readings than for stage performance. They have less life and passion than their models yet, passed down through the heritage of Latin literature, they had great influence—

not for the good—upon the drama of Europe centuries later, as we shall see.

Roman drama, in addition to owing all its inspiration to the Greeks, suffered from the Roman taste for bigness. To the average Roman citizen quantity was more impressive than quality. Parades and triumphal marches crept into stage plays where they did not belong. In Roman writings we find complaints from men of taste and judgment against the interruption of the story of the play for lavish, meaningless processions produced for the personal glorification of the wealthy sponsor of the performance.

In comedy the Romans were far more creative and inventive than in tragedy. Even though the influence of the Greek Menander was strong, the Romans made large contributions of their own to comic tradition. More important, it was their comedies which survived to help shape the plays of later centuries, rather than the scanty fragments left from Menander.

Roman comedy also sprang in part from improvised folk plays in the provinces outside the city. Etruria was especially rich in comic imagination. These plays were not in pure Latin but in local dialects. The Etruscans called actors *istri*; from the Latin version of the word, *istriones*, we get the English word *histrionic*, referring to acting. Some of the performers were also called *mimi*—we would say mimes, mimics, or imitators. Those who danced or acted out stories solely by movement were called *pantomimi*, from which we get *pantomime*.

Rome was constantly visited by troupes of provincial players, traveling like small circus companies. Some from the northern provinces, from Gaul, as France and part of Germany then was called, wore barbaric costumes, juggled, did acrobatics, and exhibited trained animals. On a crowded market day such a troupe of players might come tumbling through the streets, singing, improvising, in rough-and-ready street entertainment. When formal Roman theatre died out it was the popular traditions that lingered to revive, centuries later, in the *commedia dell' arte*.

The greatest writer of comedies, which also entitles him to be considered the chief Roman dramatist, was Titus Maccius Plautus, born in 254 B.C. As a young man he came to Rome from the province of Umbria. As an actor he became well acquainted with the tastes of Roman audiences, which were not lofty. For a time he left the stage and went into business, failed, worked as a miller, and did odd jobs. Unsuccessful at anything else, in middle age he began to write plays.

All the plays of Plautus are based on the Greek New Comedy so it is to him that we owe much of our knowledge of the original. Yet he was much more than a mere translator or imitator. What he took from the work of other men he went on to make into something of his own and something distinctly Roman. With his action-crammed stories and rowdy comedy he became the most popular dramatist of his day and made money. His fame and wealth won him the honor of Roman citizenship, which entitled him to the use of three names. Plautus, which he had been called until then, was a nickname meaning "flatfoot." His true name was Titus. When the citizenship was bestowed upon him, he took the middle name of Maccius, meaning "clown." Thus we could call him, in English, Titus Clown Flatfoot.

Roman audiences did not expect to be surprised at how a story turned out. At the beginning of each of Plautus' plays a Prologue came forward and made a mock-serious speech, outlining the entire plot of the play to follow. The action was carried only to the point immediately before the end, as a rule, and the final outcome was explained by the Epilogue who then asked the audience for applause in a manner which has perhaps been carried to its height before modern television studio audiences. Perhaps it seemed as offensive to some, then, as it does now.

In the *Asinaria,* or *Comedy of Asses,* the Prologue begins: "Kindly give us your entire attention now, spectators: I heartily hope it will result in benefit to me, also to you, and to this company and its manager, and to those that hire them. (*Turning to a*

Herald.) Herald, provide all this crowd with ears at once . . . and put it in the bill!"

At the close of the play *Amphitryon* the leading character turns to the audience and says, "Now, spectators, for the sake of Jove almighty, give us some loud applause."

Amphitryon is about the amorous interest of Jupiter in the wife of Amphitryon, a general of Thebes. This tale from the myths is so popular that it has been adapted for the stage again and again down to our own times. The French playwright Jean Giraudoux wrote a version which he called *Amphitryon 38*, claiming that it was the thirty-eighth adaptation of the story since its origin. Adapted for the American stage by S. N. Behrman, *Amphitryon 38* was one of the hits of the Broadway season of 1937, starring a famous husband-and-wife acting team, Alfred Lunt and Lynn Fontanne.

In one of the scenes of Plautus' version, Sosia, a cowardly servant of Amphitryon, is approaching his master's house at night. The god Mercury is lying in ambush, awaiting him, in the form of Sosia himself, whom he is impersonating to aid Jupiter's designs on the general's wife. Sosia, dimly seeing someone lurking ahead of him, becomes alarmed.

SOSIA

Oh Lord, my teeth do itch! He's going to give me a welcome on my arrival, he surely is . . . a fisty welcome! He's a kind-hearted soul, I do believe. Seeing how master's kept me awake all night he's going to up with his fists now and put me to sleep. Oh, I'm dead entirely! For God's sake look at the size of him, and strong, heavens!

MERCURY

I tell ye, any man that comes this way shall eat fists.

SOSIA

No you don't! I don't care about eating at this time o' night. It wasn't long ago that I dined. So if you've got any sense you just bestow that dinner on the hungry.

MERCURY

My fists are rampant.

SOSIA

If you intend to put 'em through their paces on me, for heaven's
sake break 'em in first on the wall.

It is an added shock to Sosia to find that the menacing stranger
is his double.

Jerome Kern's lovely and popular song "Smoke Gets in Your
Eyes" has its idea anticipated in another of Plautus' plays when
two lovers have been reunited. "This lady you're hugging isn't
smoke, is she?" "Smoke? Why so?" "Well, your eyes are water-
ing; that's why I asked."

One of the best of Plautus' plays is the *Aulularia*, or *The Pot
of Gold*. This is the story of a comic miser, Euclio, who finds a
pot of gold and lives in a state of exaggerated terror lest it be discovered by someone and stolen from him. Through a series of
ridiculous complications a pair of lovers, to whose match he has
been an unwitting obstacle, are enabled to marry when they bring
about the return of the pot of gold after it has been stolen from
Euclio by the servant of the young lover.

Many of Plautus' finest comedy lines and strokes of characterization occur in this play. Megadorus, a wealthy old man, is urged
by his sister to take a wife. Appalled at the suggestion he says:
"You're knocking my brains out with such a proposition, my dear
girl; you're talking cobblestones . . . . I'll marry anyone you please,
on this condition, though: her wedding tomorrow, and her wake
[funeral] the day after."

Euclio says to a servant: "Now I trust you won't mind answer-
ing the questions I'm going to ask," and gets the reply: "No, no
. . . that is, if you don't ask any I don't want to answer."

Two servants discuss the miser: "Why, when he goes to bed,
he strings a bag over his jaws." "What for?" "So as not to chance
losing any breath when he's asleep." And again: "Do you think

the old buck could be induced to make us a present of a couple of hundred dollars to buy ourselves off with?" "Lord! He wouldn't make you a loan of his hunger, no sir, not if you begged him for it. Why, the other day when a barber cut his nails for him, he collected all the clippings and took 'em home."

Euclio's housekeeper says to the cook, who has come to prepare the marriage feast: "We haven't got any firewood in the house." "Any rafters in it?" "Mercy, yes." "There's firewood in it, then: never mind going for any!'

In all, Plautus wrote some hundred and thirty comedies of which only twenty-one have survived. One of them, *Menaechmi*, was the immediate source of Shakespeare's *Comedy of Errors*, about separated twins who are reunited in confusing circumstances. As we've observed, the tradition of this story reaches back to Menander. Plautus was content with one set of twins; Shakespeare added a whole new dimension of farcical confusion by giving these brothers twin servants as well. There is such appeal to the old tale that modern Broadway has seen a successful musical comedy based on Shakespeare's version and called *The Boys from Syracuse*.

Publius Terentius Afer, commonly called Terence, was the next best Roman author of comedies. He was born in slavery in Carthage around 190 B.C. At an early age he was brought to Rome by his master who soon recognized his great talents and set him free. He loved the Greek literary style and imitated it closely, often with beauty and distinction. Yet his comedies were not sufficiently noisy and lusty for Roman audiences who relished the roughhouse of Plautus. Terence was not a popular success and fell back on a consolation to which many writers after him have resorted: pride in writing for a limited but discriminating audience. After a brief, frustrating career in the theatre he set out for Greece which he loved so much. Some writers say he died of a broken heart at losing his translations of the plays of his idol, Menander.

Mosaic of tragic and comic masks from Pompeii. *The Bettmann Archive*

In fact he was lost at sea at around the age of thirty. In spite of his popular failure he influenced later writers because of his polished style.

Roman comedy is the source of some of the oldest jokes and well-worn comic routines that are still with us with superficial changes of costume, language, and topical reference. Sometimes the changes are not even very great. In 1962 a musical comedy opened on Broadway called A *Funny Thing Happened on the Way to the Forum*. Its story was woven together ingeniously from choice threads from a number of Roman comedies, good songs and dances were thrown in, along with pretty girls and a cast of veteran comedians headed by Zero Mostel. The show was an immediate hit with critics and public alike and ran for more than two years. It was a triumph for the principle that there's no joke like an old joke if it was good to begin with.

The first Roman stage was simply a wooden platform set up in the Circus Maximus for Etruscan players, the troupes of *mimi* who came in from the country. The plays of Plautus and Terence were first produced on such stages. The actors used masks and costumes. The chorus was not used, for it had disappeared even from the late era of Greek comedy. With the city's growing splendor theatres became part of the public architecture that was its glory. Elaborate Roman theatres resembled those of Greece but with differences. The seating section (the Greek *theatron*) was connected to the stage (the Greek *skene*), making the theatre one structure instead of two. The Romans may have invented the stage curtain, though not as we know it today. Roman writers sometimes speak of the curtain being *down* while the play was going on. From this, and from slots which can be seen in the ruins of some Roman theatres, it seems that the Roman curtain was pulled *up* from a roller to shut the stage from view, and lowered to expose it.

Romans held the first elaborate theatrical performances at night. Since the theatres were open to the sun, as in Greece, there seems to have been little reason for this other than the characteristic Roman love of novelty. The performances were lit by flares.

Actors in Rome did not enjoy high social standing. Most of them were slaves. Sometimes one who distinguished himself might be made a freeman. This good fortune could attend the success of a playwright, too, as in the case of Terence who earned freedom by his ability. Roscius, the most famous actor, was made a Roman knight in the time of the Republic. Roman actors invented one evil which has plagued the stage ever since: the paid claque, a group of persons hired by an actor, or opera singer, to applaud his appearances enthusiastically and persistently and force him to come before the audience for repeated bows, or "curtain calls" as the modern theatre calls them.

The insane tyrant Caligula, fourth in succession of the Caesars, was slain at a theatrical performance. Robert Graves has written

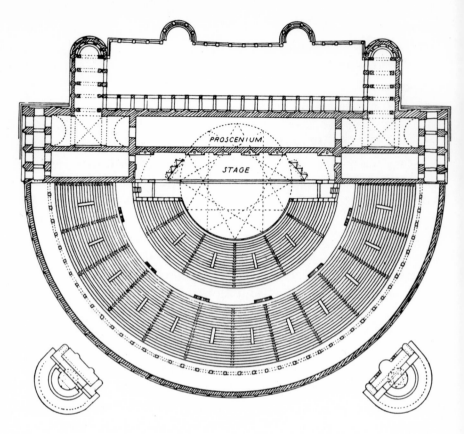

Floor plan of Roman theatre. *Streit, "Das Theater"*

two fine novels about Rome, *I, Claudius* and *Claudius the God*.
In his version of the event, Caligula was attending a tragedy being
played by the Greek, Mnester, an actor of great fame. Mnester
played the role of a murdered tyrant. In standard stage practice,
when he was supposedly stabbed, he spouted red fluid all over his
robes from a concealed bladder. The play having ended, Caligula
was set upon in a corridor and killed. Panic spread. Caligula's
dreaded German bodyguards were about to massacre the audience
when, according to Graves, Mnester saved the situation by making a speech in which he declared that Caligula had been saved
miraculously and was now addressing the people in the Forum.

Before the guards discovered that the story was false the audience escaped.

The most dramatic plays, full of make-believe bloodshed and fighting, could not compete with the genuine bloodshed and fighting to be seen in the arenas. Romans wanted the real thing more than stage substitutes. As the satirical poet Juvenal said, Roman rulers were able to keep the mass of people happy under all abuses with *panem et circenses*, bread and circuses.

As the old empire declined and the old beliefs crumbled, Christianity filled the vacuum, first as a faith, and then, following the conversion of the emperor Constantine, as a political power. There were historical ironies in this event, for religious worship and life inevitably become compromised when they are involved with worldly rule and authority.

Roman governments under Christianity set about to stamp out all that remained of the old pagan customs and thought. The theatre was attacked with a zeal unmatched until centuries later Puritans briefly suppressed the theatre in England.

Even the pagan Republic had experienced its own form of puritanism. The first Cato, called the Censor, sternly condemned popular pastimes of the people, believing that Roman manhood and military strength would be undermined by indulgence. He imposed a long, effective ban on theatrical performances. When the great general Pompey, onetime co-ruler with Julius Caesar, wanted a private theatre he got around the law by an ingenious deception. Above the many tiers of seats in his beautiful theatre he built a small shrine to Venus, with an altar and a statue of the goddess. He evaded the law by announcing that he had built a temple and that the tiers of seats were steps leading up to the shrine. Such tricks were not necessary for long. Cato's fears were justified to the extent that under the emperors Roman morality decayed altogether—which was not the fault of the theatre.

The early Roman Christians denounced the theatre as the shrine

of heathen gods, and pointed for example to Pompey's once pretended temple of Venus. They added that Greek theatre had been
part of the worship of Dionysus whom they called, in partial
truth, a god of drunkenness and debauchery.

The most effective foe of the theatre was Tertullian in the second century of the Christian era. In his *De Spectaculis* ("Of Spectacles") he stormed about the wickedness of the theatre and the
frightful consequences likely to afflict those who attended it.

> Why may not such men be in danger of devils entering into
> them? for the case hath happened, the Lord is witness, of that
> woman who went to the theatre, and returned thence with a devil.
> Wherefore when the unclean spirit, in the exorcism, was hard
> pressed because he had dared to attack a believer, he boldly said,
> "and most righteously I did it, for I found her in mine own place."
> It is well known, also, that there was shown to another in her
> sleep, on the night of the day in which she had heard a tragedian,
> a linen cloth, upbraiding her with that tragedian by name, and
> that this woman, at the end of five days, was no longer in the
> world. . . .

Such are the ways when a new order is sweeping away an old
and men are aroused to excesses of zeal. Tertullian's campaign was
successful. The decaying theatre of Rome, like its other institutions, collapsed without much struggle—but rather to sleep than
to die. The empire was in fragments under barbarian attacks. The
so-called Dark Ages, not entirely justly named by any means, were
beginning. It was almost five hundred years before the theatre was
born again in Europe; the irony is that it sprang into new life
within the Christian churches.

A kabuki performer. *Consulate General of Japan, New York*

Chapter 4

The Theatre in Asia:
China—Japan—India

IF YOU LIKE a profusion of brilliant colors, costly costumes, exotic music and dances you would have found much to enjoy in the classical theatre of the Orient. If you prefer plays of swift action and complicated plots, staged with realistic settings then the traditional theatre of the East is not for you. In the past there could not have been a better example of the differences between East and West than their tastes in entertainment. Now, to some extent, modern communications, the shrinking of distances through jet travel, and the greater sophistication produced by these, have introduced East and West to each other's arts and developed mutual influences.

There are many different theatrical styles in the Orient, including those of the smaller countries such as Thailand, Malaysia, Burma, Cambodia, and others, many of whose names, national

51

identities, and boundaries are shifting bewilderingly today. China, Japan, and India, the three largest nations of the East, whose cultural patterns have been the most influential, are all we can examine. Because their theatrical traditions are so unlike ours we must once more regard ourselves as tourists in times past and places distant and see what we find.

THE COLLEGE OF THE PEAR GARDEN

Let us suppose ourselves in China, sometime in the early years of the eighth century. At that time the theatre of Europe was in the long eclipse of the Dark Ages.

We will go to see a play with our Chinese hosts. Performances were generally given on a portable stage. In mild weather we may find our entertainment in the open air; otherwise it may be in some borrowed public building. Some companies of actors traveled and performed on river boats, like the Mississippi showboat companies of a century ago.

Our hosts seem quite easygoing about time. They are unconcerned about arriving at the beginning, for this entertainment does not have a clearly defined beginning such as we would expect. It is like a long loaf of bread and you can slice a piece out of it anywhere. The show starts in the afternoon and rambles on until midnight or later. In spite of this non-stop performance it isn't one story but a seemingly endless succession of short plays. One set of actors comes on stage as soon as the previous group has finished and we can scarcely tell these transitions from entrances and exits within the action. Even if we understand the language we will be confused for the conventions of this theatre are utterly unlike ours.

The audience is not paying close attention. Many people are talking with their neighbors. Almost everyone is eating or drinking. As soon as we have found our seats we can buy refreshments if we wish. Attendants are passing among the spectators with trays of boiled rice, fruits, candies, boiled eggs, and other tidbits. In Western theatres refreshments are sold between the acts. Indeed, in England you can have an elaborate tea brought right to your seat. Here in China, as if at a baseball game or circus back home, the selling, eating, and drinking proceeds in competition with the players, and nobody minds.

We must not conclude that the entertainment is boring or that the audience is being rude. This kind of theatre does not require the steady attention we give to a Western play. You can look and listen when you feel like it, then turn away to talk and eat. It is all the same. The performance will be going on when you look back. When you have had enough of any of its various pleasures you will get up and leave. The performance will go right on. New-comers will take your seats.

As an extra service, much appreciated by most of the audience but not altogether welcome to us, an attendant comes around from time to time offering to wipe our faces with a damp towel shared by all. We decline this offer, although if the show is indoors we too may have foreheads beaded with perspiration, for the crowded room can get uncomfortably warm. We long for the air conditioning of modern theatres.

Now let's see what's going on upon the stage. What a weird assortment of characters! It looks like a scene of the Mardi Gras or a Chinese New Year's Day parade. Costumes and make-up are not at all realistic so we cannot recognize the individuality of any of the actors. The rest of the audience knows them well because they are familiar with the convention.

A few inquiries help us out. Although we can't make head or tail of the story at least we learn something about the assorted people on the stage. Their faces are heavily coated with make-up. They do not wear masks, as the Greeks and Romans did, but they might just as well do so. The person in the red veil is a bride. A very white face, chalk white, is the mark of a wicked person, so we can spot the villain. One character has long strips of paper hanging from his right ear. Now that we have the key to the whole thing we know that this is someone who has died and returned to make a spectral visit like the ghost of Hamlet's father. Though we would not see the murdered king of Denmark in our own theatres with strips of paper hanging from his ear, we would see him in a ghastly light, with pale face and hollow voice, perhaps accompanied by eerie music—we have our own conventions for such things.

Sometimes dead persons appear in black veils, which would be familiar enough to us. Divine personages, like the gods who appeared on the Greek stage, would have gilded faces. Sick persons would appear in heavy yellow veils. A robber would have a streaked face.

The most important figure on the stage is a man clad completely in black who is constantly puttering about assisting the actors in one way or another. He is the Property Man, indispensable to any Chinese play. The black costume signifies invisibility and indeed, although we Westerners are distracted by his activities, the rest of the audience seems not to notice him at all. They have accepted his invisibility. This same convention is used in elaborate Oriental puppet plays, in which life-sized puppets are manipulated by black-clad handlers.

We watch the Property Man place a chair in the center of the stage. It has become a mountain to be climbed by the hero. When the hero has stepped down again the chair is removed. Another time he shuffles forward with a ladder and holds it while a character climbs it, ascending to heaven. He may step forward to light somebody's pipe, or hold an actor's coat so that it will not be soiled when he falls upon the stage in pretended death. There is nothing that this ever-present Property Man does not do; no mystery of stage illusion that he does not produce with the same simple, childlike obviousness. This is a theatre that depends more than most upon the imaginations of its spectators.

The Chinese theatre also has a chorus of a sort. The chorus is a single actor who seems to wander about at random, stepping forward from time to time with a few explanatory words or comments.

It is surprising that for all the richness of their ancient culture the Chinese did not have a very literary drama. The finest writers of China, her poets, novelists, and philosophers, scorned the theatre as a popular medium too commonplace to be worthy of their efforts. Playwriting was left to humbler writers, hacks who were looked down upon by literary men. Fine literature was regarded as the special province of the noble mandarin class.

The plays are not really as difficult to understand as may have been suggested. The confusion arises from the many unfamiliar conventions by which they are performed. Generally they are simple melodramas, with the exaggerated, disproportionate emotions characteristic of this kind of play.

In the Chinese plays a virtuous student foils the wicked villain and saves his mother from poverty, then marries an equally virtuous girl. A hero fights off invaders singlehandedly, saves his native land, then ascends to his reward in heaven. The plays are classified in two major groups: civil and military, according to whether they deal with patriotism and heroic exploits in battle, or with the homely heroisms of ordinary life. The actors take great liberties with the sketchy texts and change their lines at will, as inspiration moves them.

The actor's task in this theatre is difficult. He requires long and rigorous training to master countless detailed conventions of gesture, voice, and dance. He must know a thousand fine points of technique so that, in this strangely artificial and mechanical style of acting, he can portray to the knowing eye subtleties as great as the fine points of realistic acting. The theatre historian Sheldon Cheney observed that the Chinese actor might have to fight a duel with an imaginary opponent, using imaginary weapons, fall dead, then rise and walk off the stage in such a manner that the audience would know his body is being carried away by four bearers.

The Chinese love the art of acting; to them, it is the greatest attraction of their stage. They know precisely what is to be expected of the actor in a particular characterization. If the position of the little finger of the right hand is not exactly correct in the conventional posture representing a definite emotion they are dissatisfied with the performance. There is a great deal of ballet in this acting style, as is true of all the Oriental theatres.

Music is also an important element, a continuous, baffling music. To the Western ear it is more puzzling than a strange tongue. We cannot translate this music. It arises wholly out of the Eastern temperament and seems meaningless to a Westerner unless he has made a profound study of it. It seems unmusical, discordant, monotonous, almost maddening. We wonder how the audience can endure its persistent droning, yet they relish it as part of the whole.

Our most accessible pleasure is in the splendor of the costumes. They are lavish in material and astonishing in workmanship. Nor are they mere imitations of grandeur, but made of genuinely fine materials. Even the rags of the actor who plays a beggar are silken.

The stage itself is a simple platform, with a formal painted background for the entrances and exits of the actors. No scenery is used and there is no curtain. One of the effects a curtain produces is that of beginning and end, and we have seen already that the Chinese do not think in these terms. Their drama is nonclimactic. It does not follow a progressive, steady development toward a climax so stirring that its audience will be deeply moved and feel a sense of finality as the last curtain falls.

Conventions are just commonly understood ways of doing things. In spite of prevailing conventions there is never any law against doing something differently. Often Western playwrights break away from our own conventions, sometimes borrowing from the Chinese. Our Town, by Thornton Wilder, which won the Pulitzer Prize in 1938 and is performed frequently all over the world, uses modified Chinese techniques. No scenery is used in staging the play. The Chinese Property Man and chorus are combined in the person of the Stage Manager who arranges simple objects around the stage to serve as properties, such as placing a board across the back of two chairs to make a soda fountain. He also comments at length on the characters and events of the play. Yet for all these unusual and effective devices, the play is by no means Chinese in style of performance and emotional spirit. Its characterizations and acting are realistic and it progresses, however ramblingly, to a peak of emotion. In the Chinese theatre the lack of climax accounts for the casual coming and going of the audience. No one would think of leaving in the middle of *Our Town*, or of coming late.

The classical Chinese theatre with its rigid conventions unchanged for centuries survived into modern times. A Chinese performer, Mei Lan-fang, was regarded as one of the leading actors of the world. He toured the United States in 1930, reviving ancient Chinese plays. He played women's roles as well as men's, for tradition long banned women from the Chinese stage, as was true of the Elizabethan theatre in England.

Chinese theatrical performances such as we have imagined ourselves to be witnessing may occasionally be seen in the Chinatowns of New York or San Francisco. They may have something of the flavor of the museum or tourist attraction about them, but no doubt elderly Chinese might attend them with nostalgia for a vanishing tradition.

The origin of Chinese theatre is wrapped in charming legend. We cannot tell how many centuries ago forms of the dance began to play their inevitable part in the religious rites of the Chinese. The theatre is said to have been introduced by the emperor Ming Huang around A.D. 700. Ming Huang was believed to have visited the moon. There he was entertained by plays and players, a sight then unknown upon earth. After his return he built a stage and established a theatre in his pear garden. Ever afterwards, Chinese actors have been called members of the College of the Pear Garden.

FLOWER PATH AND PINE TREE STAGE

Now let us cross the Yellow Sea and do some theatre-going in neighboring Japan. The first thing we'll discover is that there are two types of theatre, quite separate and distinct, for us to choose between. These are the kabuki, the popular theatre of the common people, and the *noh*, the aristocratic theatre of the upper classes.

First we'll go to a kabuki performance. This is somewhat later in time than our Chinese visit. Kabuki was at the height of its popularity and vigor in the early eighteenth century. Here the plays do not go on as interminably as in the Chinese theatre. We have managed to arrive a little early. As there is no curtain in this theatre either, we can observe the design of the popular Japanese stage. Once again it is a platform stage, a simple place for acting. But there is a special feature which we have not encountered before. From the front of the stage a long, narrow runway extends back through the audience to the rear of the hall. We take seats near this and many of the actors will make their entrances and exits almost above our heads. Some of the action of the play may even flow onto this narrow strip.

The Japanese call it the Flower Path. In modern times it has turned up in the Western theatre occasionally in musical comedies, reviews, and burlesque shows, to enable chorus girls, and sometimes comedians, to carry their cavortings out into the midst of the audience.

The kabuki stage also employed trap doors and even turntables, making possible a variety of theatrical tricks and illusions. Like every other theatre we have seen develop, the kabuki had religious origins and because of this, over the stage is a roof in temple style. In later years they did not always trouble to construct the roof but satisfied themselves with painting it on the background, perhaps with other suggestions of scenery.

As the play begins and we attempt to follow the story through its pantomime, we will discover that in spite of its elaborate rituals and formalisms there is somewhat more of a story, as we understand it, than we found in the Chinese theatre. We are seeing one of the more famous and popular plays of kabuki tradition, *The Forty-Seven Ronins*. It is classed as an epic music drama, or *joruri*.

In this tale of revenge a Japanese nobleman tries to kill a high official who has insulted him. The attempt is balked and the nobleman is arrested and sentenced to commit hara-kiri, the ceremonial suicide long practiced in Japan. Forty-seven of his servants, employees, and counselors become outlaws, or *Ronins*, and pledge themselves to avenge him. The official knows of their oath and has himself heavily guarded at all times. For a year the *Ronins* go about separately, some in disguise, others appearing to be drunkards or cowards, patiently waiting to catch their quarry off guard. Inevitably he relaxes his watchfulness as time passes. The *Ronins* attack his house and capture him after a fierce battle. They offer the official the opportunity to perform honorable hara-kiri. He is too cowardly, so they slay him and offer his head as a sacrifice to their dead master. But the codes of their society are strict; having violated the peace, they, too, must die, even though all Japan honors them for their faithfulness. Accordingly, all forty-seven *Ronins* perform hara-kiri, in what may be the greatest number of last-act deaths in theatrical history, and are buried with honors near their master's grave.

This famous play is based upon an historical occurrence of the year 1703. It is typically Japanese in spirit and elaborately spun out in presentation. It reflects a rigid code of honor under a feud system of eye-for-eye, tooth-for-tooth, before which even the ratio of forty-seven lives for one was of no importance. "Oh, admirable and faithful man!" is the praise given the leader of the *Ronins*, who abandons his wife and children for the sake of the honor of himself and his dead master.

Many versions of this tale were played on the popular Japanese stage. Probably one of them was by Chikamatsu Monzayemon, an eighteenth-century playwright whom some have called the Japanese Shakespeare, which we may take to be a slightly exaggerated comparison. Chikamatsu, a member of the samurai, or noble warrior class, himself became a *Ronin*.

As in China, the Property Man is much in evidence, doing his helpful chores, but where the Chinese actor would have ridden an imaginary horse, the Japanese actor rides a mount composed of two men in the front and back of a horse costume which, if we are to consider it a move toward realism, is a slight one indeed.

Japanese acting is highly formalized, again in part a sort of slow ballet, and the art is composed of many conventional gestures and still poses. When the actor desires to emphasize a special point he strikes a rigid, fixed pose, with eyes wide open and staring. This is called a *Mie*. To leave no chance that the audience might overlook this important stance the assistant stage manager claps wooden blocks together loudly.

Music accompanies the play continuously in keeping with its dance aspects. Kabuki is supposed to have had its origin in the religious dances of a priestess named *O-Kuni* about 1600 The first kabuki theatre was opened in Yedo, now called Tokyo, in 1624 which, in terms of the Western theatre, is just a few years

Scene from a kabuki play. *Consulate General of Japan, New York*

after Shakespeare's death and the close of the great era of Elizabethan drama.

Kabuki plays were often performed in the popular puppet theatres. As we mentioned before, these puppets were not little hand dolls or marionettes on sticks or strings, but were life-size figures in beautiful costumes. Several puppeteers might work a single figure, one supporting it, one steering it about the stage, with separate ones moving arms, legs, and head. Like the Property Man, the puppeteers were clothed wholly in black, for invisibility, even wearing black hoods and gloves.

Traditional kabuki performances have been played by Japanese companies visiting this country in recent years, being seen both in theatres and on television. The large Japanese puppets have been seen here, too. One of the features of kabuki most impressive to American audiences is the lion dance in which the performer, wearing a long, trailing wig, longer than his own body, representing the mane, swirls it about in wild gyrations by neck movements alone, a remarkable feat, for the mane is extremely heavy and could sprain or even break the neck of an unskilled person attempting it.

When we attend the aristocratic *noh* theatre we find a different atmosphere. The audience is select and exclusive. Though we sometimes hear the term *"noh* play" in English this is actually repetitious, for *noh* means "drama."

Noh is the oldest form of Japanese theatre, having its beginnings in the fourteenth century, earlier than kabuki. A *noh* is short, being no longer than an average one-act play. Usually three or more were performed in one program, carefully chosen for their related effects as the Japanese arrange flowers. Sometimes comic interludes were played between *nohs* to break the emotional strain of the performance, although to us, untrained in these conventions, there will seem to be very little emotion at all as we think of it.

A *noh* does not have as plain and straightforward a story as we found in kabuki. It is delicately poetic, extremely formal and cere-

monial. Probably the closest equivalent in Western theatre would
be the English court masques of Ben Jonson's time that we will
consider later. One must be a connoisseur, a student, schooled in
the tradition of *noh* and its proper style of performance, in order
really to appreciate it. This is the theatre of a people who make
an extremely complex ritual called the Tea Ceremony for sharing
a cup of tea together.

There are six main types of *noh*. The *Kami-mono*, or God Piece,
praises the gods and celebrates their deeds and glories. The *Shura-
mono*, or Battle Piece, relates tragedies of the battlefield or other
accounts of warfare. In the *Katsura-mono*, the Wig Piece or
Woman Piece, men impersonate women and there is much dancing. *Kurui-mono* is the Lunatic Piece, presenting the tragedies of
the insane. Occasionally it is combined with the *Onryo-mono*, or
Revenge Piece. The *Genzai-mono*, or Earthly Piece, is the *noh*
in which the greatest number of living people appear, in contrast
to the general domination of *noh* by ghostly characters. Finally
comes the *Kiri-no-mono*, or Last Piece, at the end of a program;
it is made up of spirit dances and appearances of supernatural
beings.

The stories are not acted out in straightforward action. They
are told by the spirits of the dead persons to whom the events had
occurred in life. The narration is accompanied by formal movements, poses, and groupings appropriate to the story within this
strict convention.

The stage is another simple platform for acting. The chief decoration is a pine tree painted on the background. It symbolizes faithful endurance. Leading in from the audience's left is a runway for
the entrances of the actors. It is decorated with three small pine
trees symbolizing heaven, earth, and humanity. This theatre was
traditionally called the Pine Tree stage. On the right side is the
"Hurry Door," used for the exit of persons who have been killed
or who have died during the play. Here again a Western playwright
has borrowed something. In Thornton Wilder's one-act play *The*

Long Christmas Dinner, in which the lives of several generations of a family flow together in the course of a single meal, one side of the stage is solely for the entrance of the living and the other side for the exit of the dead.

No representational scenery is used. The familiar Eastern Property Man is not needed for, with the rarest of exceptions, only one property is used in the *noh*: a fan which the actor handles in accordance with well-understood rules to indicate whatever article he is supposed to be holding.

The precise and formal style of acting is said by some to be based upon the stiff movements of puppets, a case of humans imitating dolls instead of the other way round. The cast contains certain definite figures. There is the "first actor" called *Shite,* and a "second actor" called *Waki.* These are not the names of characters but technical terms for the actor's function in the play, as we might speak of a "leading man" or a "supporting actor." The first and second actors of the *noh* in turn are supported by companions known as *Tsure,* or sometimes by a boy called *Ko-Kata.*

Noh players using the traditional masks and fans. *Consulate General of Japan, New York.*

The design of the stage is related closely to the actors' movements. The roof of the *noh* stage is supported by four pillars. One of these is called the "first actor's pillar" and the *Shite* stands beside it when he is not reciting. Diagonally opposite is the *Waki's* or "second actor's pillar," to which he retires to stand when he has finished his part. A third is called "the flute player's pillar," where that important musician takes his place. The fourth is called the "mark pillar," and is a fixed point used as a guide to the actor in keeping the precisely correct position as he moves about upon the stage.

Each actor enters to a special musical theme and begins his role by singing or reciting a song, accompanied by a dance. The voice is never used in its natural pitch but is forced into shrill or low tones on a monotonous note in order that it may override the persistent music of flute and drum.

When the actor has finished his part he taps with his foot before withdrawing. In keeping with this wholly formal style of acting, a simple tap on the knee indicates that the character is in a state of excitement. The audience understands this perfectly. The actors are masked and the cast includes a chorus of men who stand or squat on the stage and chant from time to time in comment on the story.

We see that the *noh* is the height of convention, formalism, stylization—almost interchangeable terms all familiar in the theatre. Detail of performance and refinement of technique are as important as the content of the drama; indeed, are inextricably involved with it. This kind of tradition generally lasts only as long as the specific society or class that developed it. The *noh* existed for six hundred years, almost unchanged in all that time, until Japan felt the influence of the West.

Once again we find legendary religious origins for this art. In time past, the sun goddess decided to go into retirement. Of course the world was plunged into darkness. The other gods and goddesses, desperate, up-ended some wooden tubs in front of the sun's retreat and danced upon them. The sun goddess, curious to see what was making all the racket, came out from hiding.

This legend of the origins of *noh*, and the evolving form, of which dance was an integral part from the beginning, were preserved and cherished for centuries by Buddhist priests. Buddhist philosophy is the root of all *nohs* and partly accounts for the strangeness of the plays to Western minds. The importance of the human being is reduced almost to nothing and human lives are viewed as of no more individual account than flowers or birds in the universal scheme of things. This leads to what strikes us as a most remote and impersonal sort of theatre.

Scene from a *Noh*, showing the stage decoration typical of this form. *Consulate General of Japan, New York*

Most *noh* playwrights were Buddhist priests. Two of them are best remembered: Kwanami Kiyotsugu, and his son, Seami Motokiyu, who lived in the fourteenth century, the greatest age of ancient Japan.

One of Kwanami Kiyotsugu's plays, *Sotoba Komachi*, has been translated into English by Arthur Waley. It is a *Katsura-mono,* or Wig Piece, but it also has some of the qualities of a Revenge Piece. It is narrated chiefly by the character of Komachi. Once the most beautiful woman in Japan, she had been courted by many men. To one lover in particular she had pledged herself in marriage upon the condition that he make a difficult journey to visit her for one hundred nights in succession. He was not allowed to see her, but was required to make a mark upon a bench as evidence of his visit. Her suitor fulfilled the conditions faithfully, under great hardship, but on his last visit he died. Since then Komachi has been possessed, or haunted, by the spirit of the dead suitor (the Japanese regarded the spirits of the dead as extremely powerful and dangerous). She has grown old and hideous, racked with remorse for her heartlessness. After her story has been told, the spirit of the suitor finally releases the aged Komachi so that she may find peace.

Komachi, speaking of her wretched wanderings, says:

> *Westward with the moon I creep*
> *From the cloud-high City of the Hundred Towers.*
> *No guard will question, none challenge*
> *Pilgrim so wretched: yet must I be walking*
> *Hid ever in the shadow of the trees.*
> *Past the Lovers' Tomb,*
> *And the Hill of Autumn*
> *To the River of Katsura, the boats, the moonlight.*

The chorus, speaking in the voice of the dead suitor whose spirit possesses Komachi, tells of his ordeal:

Swiftly, swiftly coming and going, coming and going . . .
One night, two nights, three nights,
Ten nights (and this was the harvest night) . . .
I never saw her, yet I traveled;
Faithful as the cock who marks each day the dawn,
I carved my marks on the bench.
I was to come a hundred times;
There lacked but one . . .
Oh the pain! and desperate,
Before the last night had come,
He died,—Shii no Shosho the Captain.

During this account, spoken by the chorus both for the spirit of the suitor and for her, Komachi dances and pantomimes the action of the night journey.

One of the best-known plays of Kiyotsugu's son, Seami Motokiyu, is the *noh* entitled *Hachi-no-Ki*. In this story a wandering priest, lost in a snowstorm, seeks shelter at a hovel. He is met by a woman who says that her husband is not in so that she cannot admit the stranger. Then the husband arrives, but he says that there is room in the hut for only two. The priest goes on his way. As he is disappearing in the snowstorm, the husband and wife are overcome by shame at their lack of hospitality and call him back. They entertain him, regardless of sacrifice, giving him their own food and burning their most cherished possessions, some dwarf trees, to warm him. Questioned by the priest, the husband says that his name is Tsuneyo, and that he is a nobleman who has been thrust out of his rightful place by usurpers.

It later develops that the wandering priest was really a nobleman named Tokiyori. He becomes ruler of Japan and orders all persons of noble birth to appear before him. He asks that the poorest of the lot be brought forth. This proves to be Tsuneyo, who is in rags. Tokiyori restores him to his titles and possessions.

The character of the priest-ruler is based upon an actual Tokiyori who ruled Japan from 1246 to 1256. It was said that he became a priest and traveled about the land to study the needs of his subjects.

Because of its poetic, rather than dramatic, quality the *noh* exists now chiefly as literature. Many *nohs* have been translated into English.

Modern Japanese plays and films have made the world acquainted with the traditional stories in a form distinctly Eastern yet quite accessible to the West. There has been an odd cross-fertilization. *The Magnificent Seven* was an American Western film following faithfully the outline of a *samurai* hero tale of the same name about the rescue of a town from outlaws.

Rashomon, a modern Japanese play on an old theme, is the story of a crime involving a *samurai,* his wife, and an outlaw. The events are enacted four different ways, from the point of view of each of the three principals and a spectator. *Rashomon* in turn was transplanted to an American Western setting in a film called *The Outrage.*

With both ancient and modern materials, Japan has made itself an honored place at international film festivals.

A GOD-CREATED DRAMA

Hindu mythology and religious lore give a detailed account of how the theatre of India came into being. In a time before history the world enjoyed a Golden Age. Then there was no drama, for in the Golden Age there was no pain, sorrow, grief, hardship, or violence. Everything was tranquil and perfect. The drama could not exist without any of those elements of which plots are made and which arouse the sympathies or terror of an audience.

Golden Ages, alas, do not last forever, in the mythologies of any country, for we must always get around to explaining how things came to be the way they are now. In the Indian story, as in others, a Silver Age followed, still good, but enough imperfection and error had crept into the world to provide the working materials for drama. The All-Father, Brahma, was approached by the other gods, who asked him to create a new art which should combine in itself all the other arts. He took elements of literature, recitation, pantomime, painting, and music and combined them into one. The god Shiva added the dance, which was a specialty of his own.

The gods then caused a stage to be constructed. A sage named Bharata was commissioned as director of the new art. The Silver Age also ended and passed forever into legend, but the drama created by the gods then has remained with man down to this concrete and steel age in which we live.

The historical origins of Hindu drama appear to date back before even that of Greece, but its time of greatest vigor and lasting achievement comes much later, from about the fourth to the ninth centuries of the Christian era.

Hindu drama differs greatly from the Chinese and Japanese. In general it is more literary and poetic. The Japanese *noh*, with its beautiful poetry, is one exception to this rule, of course. To the Western mind, Hindu drama seems mild and cloyingly sweet. The Hindu play is essentially idyllic, descriptive, narrative, rather than actively dramatic. It uses gentle, charming, often pastoral subject matter. The essence of good taste in Hindu drama is the rule that no play must offend by any unseemly violence of emotion, or the presentation of any vulgarly direct conflict. This is almost an effeminate drama; it lacks vigor.

In one aspect it does resemble the *noh*: in its classical form it is the theatre of a small, aristocratic class. Yet popular variations on the old forms were played by traveling troupes at festival times, generally dealing with mythical stories such as the adventures of the hero Rama and the monkey god, Hanuman.

The aristocratic drama was confined by the caste system. The divisions and subdivisions of ancient Hindu social organization begin with the Brahmins at the top and work down many levels to the Untouchables. Modern India still has not finished the long task of ridding itself of the remnants of the caste system.

The formal rules of dramatic style were more complicated in India than even in the Japanese drama, just as the social system was more complex. Hindu scholars defined twenty-eight important divisions of the drama: ten of the higher, eighteen of the lower form. It was all so involved that the art could not flourish. Only specializing scholars would be interested in pursuing the details.

The Hindus did not build theatres. Plays were court or market-place entertainments and makeshift stages were set up wherever one was to be given. The stage was formed by marking off a playing area with hanging draperies. Aside and apart from this, the general surroundings of splendid palaces or courts were allowed to serve as background, for the classical plays dealt only with subjects which were suited to such a setting. No scenery was used and few properties.

The progress of a Hindu play was extraordinarily flexible. A king might be disclosed in conversation with one of his ministers. The minister might suggest that the journey they are now making is tiring and that they should stop for a rest. The king might reply that they must press on for they will soon overtake their hunting party. A moment later, although no one has gone anywhere, the lines will reveal that both the time and the place have changed again. The Hindu audience took these progressions in stride. The absence of scenery was a help in this imaginative scene-shifting.

Again that versatile and experimental American playwright, Thornton Wilder, whom we have cited several times, has adopted this convention of changing place continuously without stage movement. His one-act play *The Happy Journey to Trenton and Camden*, a touching and entertaining piece, is played in two rows of straight chairs that represent the front and back seats of an automobile. Sitting in these and talking, a family drives from Trenton to Camden, and while remarking the sights on the way, also enact a warm family comedy rich in characterization.

The two most important playwrights of ancient Hindu drama are Kalidasa and King Shudraka. *Shakuntala,* by Kalidasa, whom the Hindus called the Bridegroom of Poetry, is the greatest Hindu classic. *The Little Clay Cart* is the best known of King Shudraka's works. Both are sentimental idylls. They have been translated into several English versions and can be found in almost any large public library.

Shakuntala is a charming but very long play. Shakuntala, a beautiful young girl, is the ward of a holy hermit. Dushyanta, the king, while on a hunting trip, discovers her in the garden of the hermitage. He woos and weds her secretly. When he is recalled to court for affairs of state he gives her a ring and promises to return soon and take her back to the capital as his queen.

While the king is away, Shakuntala accidentally and unknowingly offends a saint who places a curse upon her by which Dushyanta shall be caused utterly to forget about her. Shakuntala is unaware of this, but some of her friends, who know it, plead with the saint for mercy. He consents to modify his curse, saying that if Shakuntala shows the king the ring he had given her, he will then remember her again.

When the king does not return, as he had promised to do, Shakuntala's guardian sends her to the court. She still does not know about the curse and is grief-stricken when the king does not recognize her. She remembers the ring and decides to show it to him, but discovers that it has been lost. She is in despair and the king is perplexed, when a nymph intervenes and carries Shakuntala off to the home of the gods for protection.

The ring turns up in the hands of a fisherman who returns it to the king. It had fallen into a pool and been swallowed by a fish. Dushyanta then remembers everything and is filled with sorrow, fearing that he has lost Shakuntala forever.

The story wanders while Dushyanta, at the request of the gods, goes off to kill a race of giants. Finally, the lovers are reunited in a sacred grove and all misunderstandings are cleared up. In the meantime, Shakuntala has borne a child, a son who in infancy matches the feats of the infant Hercules for wisdom and strength. We are told that he is destined to be the equal in splendor and might of his noble father. Thus everything is brought to a happy ending.

The formal dialogue has a rather naive charm. When Dushyanta first discloses himself to Shakuntala and her young friends, the maiden asks, aside:

SHAKUNTALA

How is it that the sight of this man has made me sensible of emotions inconsistent with religious vows?

THE KING

[Gazing at the girls]
How charmingly your friendship is in keeping with the equality of your ages and appearance!

PRIYAMVADA

[Aside to another of the girls]
Who can this person be, whose lively yet dignified manner, and polite conversation, bespeak him a man of high rank?

When the king is wondering anxiously if Shakuntala loves him he watches her secretly, hoping for some sign.

THE KING

Shakuntala seems indeed to be seriously ill. (Thoughtfully) Can it be the intensity of the heat that has affected her? or does my heart suggest the true cause of her malady? (Gazing at her passionately) Why should I doubt it? The maiden's spotless bosom is o'erspread with cooling balsam; on her slender arm her only bracelet, twined with lotus-stalks, hangs loose and withered; her recumbent form betokens languor. Ne'er could noon-day sun inflict such fair disorder on a maid—No, love, and love alone, is here to blame.

Somewhat later the king, himself, falls prey to the ravages of love and resorts to poetry:

THE KING

I certainly am becoming thin from want of sleep:
As night by night in anxious thought I raise
This wasted arm to rest my sleepless head,
My jeweled bracelet, sullied by the tears
That trickle from my eyes in scalding streams,
Slips toward my elbow from my shrivelled wrist.
Oft I replace the bauble, but in vain;
So easily it spans the fleshless limb
That e'en the rough and corrugated skin,
Scarred by the bow-string, will not check its fall.

The play continues in this vein, characteristic of Hindu drama; it is too exaggerated and flowery a style for Western taste.

Hindu drama is written down in Sanskrit, the classical written language of India. In performance more common spoken dialects were used.

Little vestige of classical Hindu drama remains today. Hindu dance, however, is known and admired throughout the world, largely due to the brilliant performances of a troupe led by Uday Shankar. His brother, Ravi Shankar, has made popular the haunting, improvised musical form called the *raga*, played on a strange, difficult ancient stringed instrument, the *sitar*, capable of a great range of sound and variety of effects.

Modern India has made notable contributions to the art of the motion picture. One of the finest achievements in the cinema is the Bengali trilogy, *The World of Apu*, produced and directed by India's leading film artist, Satayajit Ray. It is a realistic and profound story of life in modern India. Ravi Shankar supplies it with a memorable musical score.

Performance of a mystery play at Coventry, England. *The Bettmann Archive*

Chapter 5

Miracles and Mysteries

THE GREAT TOWN square before the imposing bulk of the cathedral is filled with noisy, eager people. The crowd mills and shoves about, impatient for the spectacle to begin. We are at Mons, in France, in the year 1501. A mystery play is about to be performed. But don't be misled by the name. This mystery is not a murder thriller to be solved by some medieval private eye. It is not even

74

one single play. It will be a series, or cycle, of dramatized biblical stories, ranging from the creation of the world to the Crucifixion of Christ, a large order for a theatrical entertainment. It will last for days, but even so, its span is not considered extraordinarily great. Some religious play cycles of the Middle Ages progressed confidently to the Last Judgment.

When the performance begins, wondrous things unfold to the great satisfaction of the people. The creation of the world is enacted before our eyes with effects of thunder and lightning. There are seas of real water in which live fish swim. The Garden of Eden abounds with spring flowers. Trees are heavy with fruit, both real and artificial. A snake wriggles into this scene of pastoral loveliness, tempts Eve with the forbidden apple, then wriggles away, crawling into the most impressive of all the stage creations before us: Hell Mouth.

The jaws of a fearsome dragon loom up as big as a house. They open and shut constantly with a spine-shivering crunch. Red flames, fireworks, and jets of steam shoot forth from the jaws. From the smoky, steamy, sulphur-smelling interior come screams of anguish and torment. Through other openings we catch glimpses of scenes like a torture chamber. Red devils armed with pitchforks harry unfortunate spirits. Other fiends rush forth in cunning disguises to tempt the virtue of characters in the drama, or to drag some doomed soul struggling and screaming into the fearful jaws. This was one of the grandest and most popular stage effects of the Middle Ages.

At other scenes we find still more wonders. The rains fall and the great flood engulfs the world so vividly and convincingly that nearby spectators are drenched by the splashing. Noah's Ark floats before us with its zoological cargo. In the Passion scenes Judas hangs himself with appalling realism. Gossip among the crowd says that last year the actor playing Judas was dead before he could be cut down—who knows? Christ is fastened to the Cross with cunningly imitated spikes. This simulated Crucifixion was a strenuous ordeal and the actor might faint from the strain and pressure of the ingenious metal brackets that actually held him on the Cross.

A tremendous cast, anticipating the "cast of thousands" of modern movie epics, takes part in this performance. It all costs a great deal of money. Months of preparatory work have gone into it. It has not been wasted effort. The throngs of spectators love it; the Church which sponsors it, the guilds which organize it, also are pleased.

The stage manager's working script and expense accounts of this actual performance at Mons in 1501 still exist and show the astonishing care with which the elaborate stage effects were planned and carried out. The long list of properties purchased or made for the production includes such varied items as:

> 3 baskets of earth
> 18 wagonloads of grass
> birds, rabbits, lambs, fish and other animals, all alive. (For the Creation, Abraham's sacrifice, etc.)
> various trees
> apples, cherries, fig leaves, various fruits, real and imitation. (To be tied on trees for the Garden of Eden.)
> flame-throwing instruments for Hell
> false body of St. John
> imitation sword of Herodias
> pulleys with which Judas hangs himself
> the soft batons with which Jesus is beaten
> roots of trees. (To embellish Hell.)

The services of many artisans were engaged. The expense account lists:

> Item for 4 pivots of iron, each having four iron bands and 4 rings to turn handles, 16 staples to attach them to two large copper tubs for making thunder in Hell, weighing 24 pounds, at 2s. per pound: 48s.

> To Godefroy du Pont for five and one half days of his time employed by him for the fitting of serpents with pipes for throwing flames, at 8s. a day: 44s.

To Master Jehan du Fayt and his assistants numbering 17 persons for having helped in Hell for nine days during the said Mystery at 6s. a day to each, 45£. 18s.

The stage manager's script contained, in addition to the financial record, lengthy and explicit stage directions.

Note: Cain should kill Abel directly over the secret [passage] where there will be the child who plays Abel's blood who cries for vengeance.

Remind those who work the secrets of the thunder barrels to do what is assigned to them by following their instruction slips and let them not forget to stop when God says: Cease and let tranquillity reign.

The mystery play at Mons was an impressive spectacle. It was not a solitary occurrence. Throughout Europe and England, during the Middle Ages, religious pageants of this sort flourished. Even today in Germany, Spain, Italy, England, and other parts of the world such performances are duplicated, carefully preserving tradition.

This is quite a different scene from the last glimpse we had of the theatre in Europe. Then the great Roman Empire was far gone in its decline. The last remnants of pagan theatre were driven out by the fierce attack of Tertullian and other embattled early Christians. How have we reached this point where the theatre is reborn under the sponsorship of that same Church?

For some three hundred years after the triumph of Tertullian, the art of theatre was almost extinct in Europe. In these centuries there was only the haphazard entertainment of wandering minstrels, famous in song and story. Jugglers and animal trainers also roamed about, seeking food and shelter where they might find it in return for their entertainments. A strolling singer would chance upon some castle in the evening. He would sing and recite for his supper and lodging, prolonging his stay if he found a warm welcome. It was such a minstrel, Blondel, whom romantic legend credits with finding and rescuing Richard the Lion-Hearted when the king had been captured and imprisoned for ransom on his way home from one of the crusades.

For the spirit of some of the medieval minstrelsy listen to a recording of the *Carmina Burana,* by the modern composer Carl Orff, who has captured the quality of this old music.

Some of the peoples of Europe were still close enough to barbarism to observe the age-old primitive rites of spring. Pagan May dances and other festivals were annual events in many places but there was no sign of anything that could be called theatre.

During the so-called Dark Ages after the crumbling of the Roman Empire, and the later centuries called the Middle Ages, power was held chiefly by feudal lords who, with their armed men, ruled their immediate neighborhoods. They either fought with rival lords or formed loose federations with them. The earliest kings ruled through the loyalty of the feudal barons who could unseat a king or curb his power if they wished.

The common people were peasants and serfs. From them slowly emerged a class of skilled workmen, artisans in stone, wood, metals, skins, and fabrics. It was such artisans who combined their skills to build the great Gothic cathedrals. They formed guilds which became influential and wealthy. A class of tradesmen and merchants came later.

The other great class was the clergy, who had a virtual monopoly on learning for centuries. The Dark Ages had only one illumination: faith. The Church preserved the remnants of ancient pagan knowledge along with its religious heritage through the uncertainties of the age of feudalism. The Church was also a great worldly power and in Western Europe the pope was a political force as great as any king.

Something of these times can be seen, even if romanticized, in the stories of King Arthur and his Round Table, the tales of Robin Hood, and such novels as Sir Walter Scott's *Ivanhoe* and Sir Arthur Conan Doyle's *The White Company.*

An illiterate peasantry could not understand the Latin Mass;

there were no printed books for them even if they had been able to read. Manuscripts themselves were a rarity, preserved and copied in the libraries of monasteries. For the people to know the great Bible stories and the traditions of their Faith they had to hear them told in a common tongue or see them enacted. In a sense the medieval religious drama was begun by the Church as a teaching device and an encouragement to piety.

Sometime in the tenth century, at St. Gall in Switzerland, those who attended Easter Mass saw a new thing. In front of the altar was a representation of the cave tomb of Christ. Seated before it was an angel. Up the aisle, in mournful procession, came the three Marys, weeping for the crucified Jesus. The angel explained in pantomime that Christ had arisen and showed them the empty tomb. Probably at this point the choir sang hymns celebrating the Resurrection.

Such simple additions to the liturgy, or order of worship, were the beginning of the new birth of the drama. They were well liked and spread throughout Europe. Such miniature plays, which soon became more than pure pantomime, were called "tropes," literally "turns," dialogues inserted in the Mass. Soon tropes were not performed at Easter only but also at Christmas, Corpus Christi, and many other feasts or saints' days of the Church.

The stories of the plays became much more elaborate than the simple discovery of the empty tomb. Other popular subjects were Nativities, or Christmas plays, the death of John the Baptist, and the encounter between the resurrected Jesus and the travellers on the road to Emmaus. In time all the Bible stories and lives of the saints became possible material.

At first these plays, like the Mass, were in Latin but they soon changed to the dialects of the people. The playwrights were priests. Drama had arisen again, once more as a religious expression, once more in the charge of priests.

As the dramas became more ambitious the playing space ex-

panded from just before the altar to include the entire front of
the church and the aisles. Inevitably a time came when the plays
demanded more room than the interior of a church could provide.
The drama moved to the broad expanse of the front steps which
made an admirable elevation for playing, with the whole length
and breadth of the streets and the public square for the overflow.

This kind of staging offered little opportunity for changing
scenery. The medieval audience, unlike the literate and sophisticated Greeks, was not content with formal architectural backgrounds. Ingenious ways of solving the problem were worked out.
Series of "stations" or "mansions" were set up, possibly suggested by
the Stations of the Cross that every church contained, and by the
words of Jesus: "In my Father's house are many mansions." These
progressions occupied an enormous amount of playing space. The
succession of stations might require the whole width of the cathedral and the entire public square. Starting at a high point, at one
side, with an elevated scene representing Heaven, the stations
would progress with suitable settings for all the important episodes
to be included in the course of the play, winding up at the opposite
extreme from Heaven with the fiery, awesome Hell Mouth. The
actors either moved from one playing station to another as the
action required, or else different companies played different scenes.
No mode of theatre has ever occupied more territory.

Whenever possible the natural advantages of steps and building
fronts were put to use. Where this could not be done, platforms,
booths, or wagons were set up. As the actors moved the members
of the audience moved with them, except for those fortunate
enough to be able to command a general view of the whole scene
of action from a high place. In some cases simultaneous action
occurred on a number of levels which offered the spectators the
embarrassment of riches of a three-ring circus.

Human nature being what it is, in time elements crept into the
religious drama which the Church did not like but at which it had
to wink. The natural animal spirits of the people and their occa-

sional irreverence, remnants of pagan celebrations, together with breaches of discipline by some of the younger clergy, led to sacrilegious parodies of sacred ceremonies. In Europe these were commonly called the Feast of Fools, or the Feast of Asses. Sometimes there were mock performances of the Mass, with the choir braying like donkeys instead of singing proper responses. In England there was a popular festival of the Boy Bishop. A boy would be "ordained" as bishop and invested with mock dignity. Or it might happen that a grave performance of a religious play would be followed by a wild burlesque of all that had gone before, as satyr plays followed solemn tragedies in the Greek theatre. People seek relief sometimes from any intense mood.

Developments of this sort alarmed and discouraged the Church. Whereas the clergy at first had been the sole participants in the productions, the religious drama now began to slip into other hands. The saint plays became community undertakings, though still usually with the patronage and blessing of the Church. The actual responsibility for production was assumed by various guilds of craftsmen, artisans, or tradesmen. For a long time priests continued to be the playwrights until education had spread enough so that others could read and write. Many of the plays hardened into traditional forms in versions identified with specific localities.

The religious dramas are called miracle or mystery plays—terms which are practically interchangeable. They were called miracle plays because of the miraculous nature of the stories told. Those that dealt with the lives of saints were often called saint plays. When the productions passed out of the hands of the priests and were taken over by the craft and trade guilds they were called mysteries from the Latin word, *ministerium*; the old French word, *mester*; and the Old English, *misterie*, all meaning "trade." We saw that the stage directions from Mons referred to the devices by which certain stage effects are achieved as "secrets," in the sense of being related to a "mystery." Both words have changed drastically in their current usage.

The assignment of duties to the various guilds was highly appropriate and sometimes amusingly literal. Plasterers would perform the scene of the creation. Carpenters and shipwrights and drawers of water would enact the scene of the flood and the building of the ark. Goldsmiths, jewelers, and tailors would perform the adoration by the Wise Men, for they alone could produce the finery for the kings of the Orient and their retinue. Butchers and bakers would produce the Last Supper, the wedding feast at Cana, and the feeding of the five thousand. Fishermen would do the miraculous draught of fishes. The Crucifixion was performed by smiths. The baptizing of Christ was the work of the barbers. The production of the many plays forming the cycles of religious drama were genuinely community activities, wherein men contributed according to their skills.

Several of the fine mystery cycles of England have been preserved, ranging over a period from about 1328 to the time of Queen Elizabeth in the sixteenth century. The oldest of these cycles is the Chester Mysteries, twenty-five plays with a delightful and touching blend of piety and folklore. One of these is *Christ's Descent Into Hell* which deals with the events between His death and Resurrection. It was produced, appropriately, by cooks and innkeepers. Also known as *The Harrowing of Hell* (mentioned in all the great creeds of the Christian Church: "He descended into Hell"), it portrayed Christ's journey into Hell to redeem and deliver the great figures of the Old Testament who had died before His coming to redeem mankind, and also to deliver the spirits of the virtuous pagans.

In the play Christ is challenged by Satan, who is convinced that he is being wronged by Christ's intervention on the part of mankind. Satan takes the position that he is justly entitled to the souls of men as a result of his successful transaction with Adam in the Garden of Eden. Christ and Satan then proceed to argue this point and to threaten each other in the homeliest of terms.

SATAN

Adam came hungry to me, and as suzerain I made him do homage; he is mine and all his race for an apple which I gave him.

CHRIST

Satan, mine was the apple which thou gavest him; the apple and the apple-tree were both my creation. How could you, then, dispose of goods which belonged to another? Since he has, therefore, been bought with my own, he is mine by right.

SATAN

Retain heaven and earth for thyself; leave the souls in Hell to me. Let me retain what I have! what you have you may peacefully possess.

CHRIST

Be silent! For you have cast double-ace! [The lowest throw in dice.] Do you think I have died for naught? By my death mankind is redeemed. Those who have served me shall dwell with me in heaven. You shall suffer greater pains than anyone in this place.

SATAN

None can do worse to me than I have already borne. I have suffered so great evil that it is indifferent to me where my lot fall. If you rob me of mine, I will also rob you of yours. I will go from one man to another, and draw away many from you.

CHRIST

God knows, I will speak a word with you, and compel you to keep peace. I will bind you so firmly that you will rob me of few. Only the smaller devils of little power will be permitted, henceforth, to go among men, and to get possession of all those who will not resist them.

Accordingly, Christ binds Satan and releases from their torments all those whom he had thus far held in bondage. The brief passage quoted teaches one of the Church's doctrines: that no man is tempted beyond his power to resist.

One of the finest English mysteries is the Middle English, or Brome, *Abraham and Isaac*. At its climax, Abraham has led young Isaac to the mountain top where God has commanded him to sacrifice the boy on an altar. The trusting child has no suspicion of his father's purpose until Abraham draws forth a great sword.

ISAAC

Yes, father, but my heart begins to quake to see that sharp sword in your hand. Why do you bear the sword drawn so? I wonder greatly at your looks.

ABRAHAM

Oh! Father of Heaven, I am so full of woe, this child breaks my heart in two!

ISAAC

Indeed, father, you must have something in your mind that grieves you ever more and more.

ABRAHAM

Oh! God of Heaven, send me thy grace, for my heart was never half so sore.

ISAAC

I pray you, father, let me know whether I am to suffer any harm or no.

ABRAHAM

Oh! Isaac, Isaac, I must kill thee!

ISAAC

Kill me! father, alas! What have I done? If I have in aught trespassed against you, you may make me full mild with a rod; but with your sharp sword kill me not, for I am only but a child, father.

ABRAHAM

I am full sorry, my son, to shed thy blood; but truly, my child, I have no choice.

ISAAC

Now I would to God my mother were here on this hill; she would kneel for me on both her knees to save my life. And since my mother is not here, I pray you, father, change your looks, and kill me not with your sharp knife.

When Abraham explains God's command the child resigns himself. In the nick of time, however, God sends a ram into the bushes as a substitute in the sacrifice, and Isaac is spared because of his father's unquestioning obedience to God. With a perceptive touch of characterization, the child, although reassured somewhat, remains suspicious. Abraham asks him to stoop and help kindle the fire for the altar. Isaac hesitates and says, "But, father, if I stoop down low, Ye will not kill me with your sword, I trow?"

There was no greater cycle than the Towneley Mysteries, a series of thirty-two plays, ranging from the creation to the Crucifixion. It was performed at Woodkirk, in the vicinity of Wakefield (by which name it is sometimes known also), but takes its principal name from the landed Towneley family which sponsored the plays and preserved them.

This cycle contains an early classic of English drama: the *Secunda Pastorum* or *Second Shepherd's Pageant*. It shows the gradual increase of nonreligious elements in the mysteries. Most of it seems to be merely a simple folk comedy. Abruptly, almost at the end, it changes its nature and becomes a Nativity transplanted to an English beath with that same simplicity by which medieval and Renaissance painters portrayed biblical scenes in Italian settings.

A group of shepherds are tending their flocks. They complain of the bitter cold and the hardness of their lot as compared to the gentry or great folk who oppress them with taxes. In an ancient comic vein they also lament the unpleasantness of married life with wives who are scolds and less than lovely. They are joined by Mak, a man whom all suspect of sheep stealing and whom they insult openly. Mak is thick-skinned and insists upon remaining and sharing their supper. He refuses to depart even as they prepare for sleep. They compel him to lie down in their midst so that he may not slip away and steal any of their sheep.

When the others are fast asleep Mak casts a spell over them to prevent them from waking. He takes a choice lamb and runs off to his own hovel with it, giving it to his equally unscrupulous wife, Gill. He then hastens back and takes up his place with the other shepherds. When they awake the following morning, they do not know that he has not been with them throughout the night, and he takes his leave casually.

Soon they discover the theft of the lamb. In rage, feeling that some trick of Mak's must be behind it, they follow to his hovel. Mak hears them coming. Hastily he bundles his wife into bed. They swaddle the lamb in baby clothes, put a bonnet on its head, and tuck it into a cradle beside her. When the indignant shepherds arrive Mak protests injured innocence at their suspicion and says that of all times for such a charge this is the worst, for his wife has just given birth to a fine baby boy. At this point, Gill chimes in, as if in pain and outrage:

> *Ah, my middle!*
> *I pray to God so mild,*
> *If ever I you beguiled,*
> *That I eat this child*
> *That lies in this cradle.*

Which is precisely what she means to do.

The shepherds search the house, find no trace of their lamb, and leave grudgingly. Outside, they repent of the injustice they have done and decide that they should go back and give a christening present to Mak's baby. Mak doesn't want to admit them again but can hardly refuse. One shepherd says that he wishes to give sixpence as a gift and stoops to kiss the child before he can be stopped.

> *Give me leave him to kiss, and lift up the*
> *   clout [cloth]. (He glimpses the sheep.)*
> *What the devil is this? He has a long snout!*

In the immediate confusion, Gill feigns surprise and claims that the child is a changeling.

> *He was taken with [by] an elf,*
> *I saw it myself;*
> *When the clock struck twelve,*
> *Was he forshapen [transformed].*

Unconvinced, the angry shepherds drag Mak out and toss him in a blanket. Just at this point the farcical false nativity is displaced by the true Nativity. A bright star passes and an angel's voice tells them to go to Bedlem (Bethlehem) to see the Christ Child.

The shepherds go, rejoicing that they shall see what patriarchs and prophets of old had wished to see. In a stable they find Mary and the Child, and offer simple gifts: a bob of cherries, a bird, and a ball. Mary says:

> *The Father of heaven, God omnipotent,*
> *That set all on seven [made all in seven days], his*
> *   Son has he sent . . . .*
> *And now is he born.*
> *He keep you from woe!—*
> *I shall pray him so.*
> *Tell forth as ye go,*
> *And min on [remember] this morn.*

The English cycles were generally staged in one of two ways. Usually the performance was played on wagon stages, either moving in procession from one playing station to another in towns, or lined up in a row in the country.

Each wagon contained a setting and carried the actors necessary to its scene. The usual occasions of performance were Corpus Christi and Whitsun Week, which occur in spring, and therefore had a reasonable prospect for mild weather.

When the presentation was in a town the starting wagon would take up a position before the mayor's house and perform the first play. When finished, it would move on to the next appointed spot, there to repeat the performance. Meanwhile, behind it, all along the route, the other wagons with their many varied pageants followed in procession, each one playing over and over its part in the slowly unfolding cycle. It was a chain theatre. The big wagons were probably somewhat like the elaborate floats in the New Orleans Mardi Gras parade, or the Tournament of Roses in California.

Peasant theatre on the market place (from an engraving by Breughel). *The Bettmann Archive*

In the country, the wagons were lined up in stationary ranks and the audience moved from one to another to follow the cycle.

The performers did not limit themselves to the small playing space of the wagon settings but spread out freely onto the surrounding ground. A stage manager's direction of the period reads: "Herod shall rage on the pagyn [wagon] and also on the ground." From this archaic word for the wagon stage, "pagyn," comes our familiar word "pageant." Herod, of the biblical slaughter of the innocents, was the favorite villain of the mystery plays.

The acting was broad and filled with bombast to delight the hearts of the simple audiences (the "groundlings," as they are called by Shakespeare, for they stood on the ground to watch), who conceived of all stage emotion in the broadest possible terms. Shakespeare must have seen the mysteries played. The style of acting popular in them carried over into the later nonreligious theatre and distressed discriminating men. That is the allusion made by Shakespeare in Hamlet's speech to the players, counselling them against overacting.

> O, it offends me to the soul to hear a robustious periwig-pated fellow tear a passion to tatters, to very rags, to split the ears of the groundlings, who for the most part are capable of nothing but inexplicable dumb-shows and noise . . .; it out-herods Herod; pray you, avoid it.

Another form of drama, unlike the mysteries but still religious in nature, was the morality play. They were chiefly allegorical, using personification; their characters were not human individuals but qualities, traits, or ideas, embodied as personalities for the sake of drama. Traditional characters in the moralities were Virtue, Faith, Christian, God, the Devil, Vice, Avarice, and so forth. Perhaps the best known of all allegories, though in a different medium and later in date, is John Bunyan's *Pilgrim's Progress*.

One of the English moralities has achieved an immortality and is read and played today. *Everyman*, by an unknown author, probably a priest, for all its archaic phrasing and moralistic content, is astonishingly moving and human. It is simply and honestly rooted in one of the profound and universal experiences common to all men, to "every man": the confrontation with Death and the mysteries of the hereafter.

At the opening of the play, God, discouraged by Mankind's neglect of spiritual for worldly matters, determines to demand a reckoning of Everyman. He sends Death forth with a summons. Everyman is taken by surprise. He is dismayed when Death identifies himself and orders him to prepare for the long journey. He pleads for a stay, for more time, which Death refuses him. Everyman pleads that he is not ready, that he has had insufficient time, that his book of reckoning is in no condition to face judgment. When Death will give him no stay, Everyman asks for the right to beg his friends to accompany him on the long journey.

> Shall I have no company from this vale terrestrial
> Of mine acquaintance, that way me to lead?

This request Death grants, saying that he may have the companionship of anyone who will venture forth with him.

In despair Everyman looks for Good Deeds, only to find that Good Deeds cannot rise from the ground. He is weak and weighted down helplessly by Everyman's sins. Good Deeds would go with him but cannot. Then Knowledge enters, bringing Confession with him. By their advice, through penance, the heavy burden of sin is lifted from Good Deeds and he is free to arise, to accompany Everyman. They are joined by Strength, Discretion, and Five Wits, and together, after Everyman has received the last rites of the Church from a priest, they set out upon the journey.

When they come in sight of the grave even Strength, Discretion, and Five Wits desert. Knowledge says that he can go no farther than the grave's edge, although he does not fear. Only Good Deeds can and will go the whole way. Thus Everyman, realizing how misguided he has been in not loving Good Deeds most through all his life, enters the grave with this faithful companion, his book of reckoning in order, confident of being saved.

The simple humanity of *Everyman* has not lost its force in many centuries, nor will it do so in all that may come, for Everyman still awaits his final confrontation with Death. No other known morality play is of comparable quality. In the commonplace ones, Vice and the Devil often were played for popular comic relief. In the sixteenth century a device called the Interlude was introduced. As the name suggests, interludes were short comic sketches inserted between acts, or between one morality play and another. Interludes were a sign of the transition from the religious drama to a new secular theatre.

Although secular theatre was reborn after the Middle Ages, religious drama has not disappeared. At Oberammergau and Freiburg in Germany, since the seventeenth century, traditional Passion plays have been performed, roughly every ten years or so, with considerable irregularities in the cycle due to wars and other circumstances. In Spain and other Latin countries religious dramas are still performed in the ancient manner. There is a tendency for all such spectacles to become tourist attractions; if piety draws some, curiosity brings others, which was probably true in older times to some degree.

In England the York and Chester cycles have been given splendid revivals in recent years. One of England's leading composers, Benjamin Britten, has composed a simple folk opera, *Noye's Fludde*, based on the Noah play in the Chester cycle, which is delightful and is widely performed. At Lancing College, in Sussex, England, it is played in the spring once every four years. A French playwright, André Obey, wrote a *Noah*, in the spirit of the mysteries, which has been done on Broadway.

The Union Theological Seminary in New York some years ago established a department of religious drama which produces plays and encourages writers.

Scene from the Passion Play of Oberammergau, showing Christ risen from the dead and appearing before Mary Magdelene. *Ewing Galloway*

New York Pro Musica, an organization devoted to the performance of medieval and Renaissance works, has produced the plays of *Daniel* and *Herod* in recent years.

Even in a commercial theatre religious subjects inevitably are persistent for they are involved with universal ultimate problems of life and death and good and evil that are the very heart of drama.

Some famous modern plays, unmistakably religious in character though widely varied in style and content, are Shaw's *Saint Joan;* Marc Connelly's *The Green Pastures* (a miracle play in terms of southern Negro biblical folklore); Anouilh's *Becket,* T. S. Eliot's *Murder in the Cathedral,* and Robert Bolt's *A Man for All Seasons* (all modern saint plays, the first two about St. Thomas à Becket, the latter about St. Thomas More); Archibald MacLeish's *J. B.,* which is an adaptation of the book of Job; and Paddy Chayevsky's *Gideon.* An early example of the so-called "theatre of the absurd," Samuel Beckett's *Waiting for Godot* is considered by some to be a kind of religious drama whose mysterious, unseen, patiently awaited Godot is identified with God.

All this is evidence that the theatre, born and reborn in formal religious contexts, always has profoundly religious elements present in it.

Renaissance stage setting. *The Bettmann Archive*

Chapter 6

I Pagliacci—The Clowns

ON A DAY in the latter half of the sixteenth century, in the central square of the city of Florence, Italy, a great crowd gathers, laughing and talking, pushing and shouting in excitement. The players have come; the antic comedians of the Italian popular theatre, the *commedia dell' arte*. A wooden stage has been erected upon stilts

94

and sawhorses. It is hung about with curtains to hide the off-scene players and provide entrances and exits. The hangings are more likely to be of humble sackcloth than silks or satins. When the actors appear they are dressed in familiar, conventional costumes, quite apt to be shoddy. Such an unimpressive, tatterdemalion outfit makes us wonder at the eagerness of the waiting audience.

When the comedy begins we find that the appeal lies not in the trappings but in the action. Before the responsive, happy crowd gathered about this crude stage, a rough-and-tumble comedy, scandalous and impertinent, sentimental and tender, cruel and libelous by turns, plays at a tempestuous pace. The audience rocks with laughter, shouts with pleasure at new twists brought to old situations, sighs with shared emotion when the lover meets with frustration or else seems about to triumph in his courtship. There seems to be no end to the resourceful inventiveness of these players. The native Italian wit bubbles freely. When the play is ended the audience clamors loudly for more. Clearly we have met a direct descendant from the old Roman comedy.

This is the time of the Italian Renaissance, that era beginning in about the fourteenth century, in which Europe stirred with new life. Before we go further in examining the theatre we should consider what is happening, though we can do so only in the most broadly generalized and oversimplified terms, for the subject is immense.

The somewhat misleading name "Dark Ages" for the aftermath of Roman decline was due to the considerable eclipse of the light of freely exchanged knowledge, the breakdown of centralized government, the collapse of communications, and the isolation of people from one another as a result of these things. The relatively orderly world, maintained for so long by the Pax Romana, the Roman peace, had given way to anarchy and the fragmented local rule of feudalism.

In a process involving several centuries and moving with glacial slowness, order again emerged from civil disorder. Small fragments of power or rule united with others into units at least as large as cities and their immediate surrounding lands. There sprang up city-states such as Rome, Florence, and Venice, somewhat like those that had existed in Greek times. Communications were restored; travel became more safe; ideas could be exchanged over greater distances once again. Men began to look about more confidently, to venture afield from small places, to try new ways of doing practical things, to invent new things to do, to express themselves with a renewed and growing confidence in humanity. Streams of energy and ideas flowed together, became a current, and produced what has been called historically the rebirth, Renaissance, of Western culture. Ideas, inventions, forms of government, economic systems, trade routes, arts, sciences, geographical discoveries crowded upon one another.

These exciting things began and for a long time centered in Italy and it is that country with which we are concerned in this chapter. The rebirth in other countries, particularly England, is another story. The European Renaissance in general covers roughly the three hundred years from 1300 to 1600. Five factors, not all Italian, all of which occurred between 1300 and 1517, gave momentum and permanence to this development, so that Europe did not slip back into the feudal provincialism from which it was emerging.

The mariner's compass, by aiding navigation to break away from the visual landmarks of coastal cruising, helped to spur the expansion of trade and exploration, which in turn stimulated the rise of the merchant class to a position of power and wealth, and also put the Western world in touch with the Orient and the American continent.

Around 1400 gunpowder and firearms arrived to end abruptly the feudal military system. Weapons more effective than the swords and spears of knights or the bows of yeomen changed the nature of war and broadened the struggle for power among city-states or kingdoms.

In 1450 Gutenberg invented printing from movable type, one of the greatest inventions in the history of mankind. Ideas, information, religious teachings, instruction, and the literary arts could begin to spread more widely than ever before through the printed word.

The discovery of the new world of the Americas in 1492 shrank the Mediterranean basin in the eyes of men. The Pillars of Hercules, the Strait of Gibraltar, was no longer almost the end of the Western world. Power began to shift away from Mediterranean states to the Atlantic seaboard of Europe. The currents of new thought and science began to flow strongly in France and England.

In 1517 the Protestant Reformation, led by the German priest, Martin Luther, broke the unified political power of the Roman Catholic Church, necessarily changing the degree of influence the pope could wield over distant kings, if they no longer acknowledged Rome as the supreme seat of religious authority.

The Renaissance was an age astonishingly vigorous and colorful. Its vast burst of energy often produced abuses or excesses. Genius flourished in all branches of art and learning. It was an age of achievers. Michelangelo, Leonardo da Vinci, Benvenuto Cellini, Raphael; Machiavelli, Boccaccio, Petrarch, Dante, Lorenzo de' Medici (Lorenzo the Magnificent), Caterina Sforza, Savonarola, and, somewhat later, Galileo, are among the brilliant names scattered across the era, in art, architecture, literature, politics, religion, and science.

It was a day of individualists. Personal ambition vied with intellectual curiosity and religious zeal as driving forces for the age. The guiding spirit of the period is known as "humanism." It reaffirmed the dignity and capacity of man. After centuries during which most of the sense of continuity with the ancient cultures of Greece and Rome had been lost, and many men had no knowledge of the noble achievements of their species, a rediscovery began. The improvement in civil order that we have mentioned led to

awakening knowledge, more education. The renewed consciousness
of the heritage of man became a new pride in man, a new energy,
a new confidence and expectation of things to come.

We would expect such a wonderful age to produce a theatre
without equal since the Greeks. Painting, sculpture, the beginnings
of music as we know it today, architecture, politics, science, literature, poetry, philosophy—all these things flourished. Yet the Italian
Renaissance produced no comparably distinguished, enduring
drama. The popular comedy with which this chapter is concerned
was remarkable but created nothing permanent in itself. The other
form of theatre practiced in courtly circles was peculiarly artificial
and concerned with values and effects essentially not dramatic. The
sharp and, in the West, unprecedented division between a popular
theatre and a formal theatre of an aristocratic class is somewhat like
the difference between kabuki and *noh* in ancient Japan.

We must take a look at the formal theatre. In 1508 a man named
Bernardino Prosperi wrote a letter to a friend describing the courtly
entertainment he had seen while on a visit to a certain duke:

> . . . what has been best in all these festivities and representations
> has been the scenery in which they have been played, which
> Maestro Peregrino, the Duke's painter, has made. It has been a
> view in perspective of a town with houses, churches, belfrys and
> gardens, such that one could never tire of looking at it, because
> of the different things that are there, all most cleverly designed
> and executed. . . .

The court theatres were chiefly a spectacle, a display for the
eyes, an exhibition of technical ingenuity in creating illusions. To
meet the vogue for scenic lavishness the stages of Renaissance
theatres were disproportionately big compared to the auditoriums.
The tail was wagging the dog.

Such elaborate spectacles were enormously expensive, though, as
Prosperi's letter shows, the courtly audiences considered them the
best part of the show. These stage sets were solid architectural con-
structions, like some of the sets built on motion-picture lots.

A scene might show, in receding perspective, a long street lined with varied buildings, towers, spires, archways, and bridges; glimpses of docks or vistas of trees. Added to architectural features were such wonders as artificial, moving clouds, some carrying gods and goddesses; there were thunder-and-lightning storms, flowing water, cages of animals or singing birds, and surprisingly inventive anticipations of modern stage lighting techniques. Bowls of wines or other colored liquids, like apothecary jars in old-fashioned drugstores, were placed before lights to produce the effect of the colored films, or gelatins, the stage electrician uses with his lights today to give varied and changing hues to a scene.

This was all very well in its way, but Prosperi was far too optimistic in his belief that "one could never tire of looking at it." One could tire all too soon when the plays were dull and overpowered by their backgrounds. As one of the best of modern drama critics, John Mason Brown, remarked about a lavish but dramatically weak production on Broadway, "the audience got tired of looking and began to wish there were something to listen to." The poetry of the court plays was flowery and heavy in a warmed-over imitation of classic style. The acting was stiff and pompous, for there cannot be live acting with dead material. To liven things up, interludes of an uninhibited bawdy nature were inserted into the plays, but such trimmings cannot substitute for dramatic vigor.

The most prominent literary figures contributing to the court drama were Renaissance names distinguished for other work: Lodovico Ariosto, Pietro Aretino, Niccolò Machiavelli, and Giovanni Boccaccio. These men did not give their finest efforts to the stage, and what they gave—perhaps more fairly, what was asked of them—was not sufficient. What talented writer would want to compete with mechanical clouds as a secondary attraction?

The chief contribution, if such it should be called, of this period of staging, was the introduction of the familiar "picture-frame stage," as we know it today, enclosed by the arch called *proscenium*, meaning "in front of the scene." Even the proscenium was a form

of confinement to the stage, a kind of artificial barrier between
players and audience. The most advanced staging of our time has
discarded it in favor of the ancient platform stage or the arena, the
so-called "theatre-in-the-round."

Pastoral dramas were the principal entertainment in the court
theatres. Derived from Greek mythology, the plays dealt in sentimental poetry with stories of nymphs, dryads, shepherds, shepherd-
esses, the god Pan, satyrs, and other such beings. They were
manipulated for happy endings or else were a sentimentalized,
melodramatic pseudo-tragedy. Different as the backgrounds are,
they had something in common with the Hindu idyllic drama.
They were pretty enough but did not offer very robust entertainment. The leading pastoral playwright was the poet Torquato
Tasso.

Though pastoral plays sometimes were performed indoors, they
began a vogue in Italy for outdoor garden theatres. In the warm
season, gardens were a pleasing and logical setting for such drama.
Every large estate had its carefully landscaped, well-tended stage,
often decorated with fountains, using ornate wrought-iron gates, or
corridors of boxwood or other ornamental shrubbery for entrances
and exits.

The enduring theatrical invention of the high Renaissance in
Italy was grand opera. Late in the sixteenth century a group of
scholars, poets, and musicians began to gather regularly at the
house of Giovanni Bardi for classical musical studies. They had
rediscovered the fact that music had played an important part in
ancient Greek drama. They jumped to the conclusion that all
Greek drama must have been spoken or sung to music. Although
no one knows to this day what Greek music was like, Bardi and his
friends set about imitating what they thought it might have been.
In 1597 two of the members created the first opera, *Dafne*, composed by Jacopo Peri with a libretto (literally "little book") by
Ottavio Rinuccini. Although the word opera simply means "work,"

the name has clung particularly to this musical-dramatic creation. Like *Dafne*, the other works composed by Bardi's group clung to the pastoral stories that were the vogue.

To look ahead a little at the evolution of this art form, we must pass over the work of Monteverdi, the first major composer, in the sixteenth century, to the Scarlattis, father and son, in the seventeenth. Each of them introduced changes which shaped the form of Italian grand opera as we know it today.

Monteverdi worked principally in dramatic recitative, in which words are recited or declaimed against the instrumental background. He brought more melodic variety to the form. After him, the Scarlattis created the style of the true *bel canto* aria, or "air for beautiful singing," which led to the flowering of melody in the romantic operatic tradition. Italian opera has remained identified with this style ever since.

Opera spread throughout Europe, and many nations have made great additions to music drama. It is so much a field in itself that we cannot consider it at length here, but we must remember that it is a significant wing of the theatre, combining all the elements we have ever seen in the theatre, and constantly reminding us by its conspicuous difference from real life that the essence of theatre is make-believe.

The unique genius of Renaissance theatre was in the popular comedy, generally called the *commedia dell' arte*, or sometimes the *teatro dell' arte*. It began in the streets and was later taken indoors, called even into the court theatres that needed its gusty life. The *commedia* began to flourish around 1560. Earlier we called it a descendant of the Roman comedies, especially of the form in which they had been presented by the *atellanae*, the provincial players of Rome. Whatever the line of descent, the new comedy surpassed its origins, for possibly nothing quite like the *commedia* has existed before or since.

Like all such entertainments having folk origins, the comedy began as amateur performances for special occasions and then, becoming popular, went professional.

The first important figure of the comedy is Angelo Beolco, known as *Il Ruzzante*, the joker. His career began about 1502. Beolco was an actor-playwright said to have used Paduan, Bergamask, Bolognese, Venetian, and Tuscan dialects as well as Latin, Spanish, and Greek. Rustic humor characterized his plays. In one of *Il Ruzzante's* comedies a peasant declares to his sweetheart: "But what sweetness, what joy to me to die at thy dear hands, my beautiful Fiore; for thou art dearer to me than my oxen."

Soon the formal playwright in the style of Beolco disappears from the *commedia*. Extensive improvisation takes the place of a play script. On a wall or curtain behind the scenes is pinned a sheet containing a *scenario*, or outline of the story, the order of entrances and exits, and perhaps certain principal comic speeches or punch lines. The actors glance over this guide sheet and then follow the impulse or inspiration of the moment in spinning out the scene on stage.

It is not total improvisation, for the members of the company have been over the performance countless times. It is second nature to them, but except for the basic features of the plot and the sure-fire lines they never play it twice alike. This is the beginning of what is still called ad lib dialogue, an abbreviation of *ad libitum*, or "at liberty." It is to speak as you like, to say what comes into your head; in our own time it is considered the mark of the most gifted and resourceful comedians, but it takes an experienced actor to keep up with such a fellow player.

As the occasion, or the particular town, or some notable topical event suits, the players introduce new dialogue or action. They are rough-and-ready fellows who also play a variety of wild tricks upon one another on stage. The comedy is broad farce, of the kind also called "slapstick."

"Slapstick" comedy is exactly what the name implies. The actor carried a split flat stick, like a split lath, which had a springing

Commedia dell' arte player. *New York Public Library Theatre Collection*

action that made a good loud whack. Whenever he made a joke
at the expense of another character he would proceed to pound
the victim lustily and noisily by way of rubbing in the point. This
is still done in low burlesque comedy, or farcical films of the Laurel
and Hardy or Abbott and Costello type, when the leading comedian may hit his "stooge" over the head when he cracks a joke.
Pie-throwing comedy is in the same tradition. In the uninhibited
commedia of the streets, catering to peasant tastes, the throwing
of garbage or worse filth pleased the crowd.

Sometimes instead of the slapstick an inflated bladder was used
for the same purpose. Jonathan Swift borrowed this idea. In the
third voyage of *Gulliver's Travels*, on the island of Laputa which
floats in the air, the learned men all carry bladders; they are so
absorbed in their own thoughts that if one should wish to com-
municate with another he must beat him about the head with a
bladder to get his attention.

Companies of players became more important than individuals
in the *commedia dell' arte*. The earliest and greatest of the companies was *I Gelosi*—the Jealous Ones. Their name was taken from
their motto, *Virtu, fama ed onor ne fer gelosi*: "We are jealous of
virtue, fame, and honor," a slogan which accords a bit oddly with
the tone of their art.

The *Gelosi* were the first of the comedians to be taken up by
the nobility and the courts, to be brought indoors. They attained
high honors and popularity in Italy and began the practice, followed by others after them, of touring outside Italy, carrying the
tradition and influence of the *commedia* all over Europe. They
played in Paris, Poland, Spain, and Germany.

Flaminio Scala was director and stage manager of the company,
and it was he who drew up and posted the scenarios for the
performances. This was all that remained for a time of the function
of the playwright.

The star performer of the *Gelosi* was Francesco Andreini, a man
of reckless, adventurous temperament. The Andreini family was

outstanding in the *commedia*. Isabella Andreini, aside from being the troupe's leading actress, was one of the belles of the age. Her death marked the beginning of the decline of the *Gelosi*.

Giovanni Battista Andreini, their son, became director of another famous company, the *Fedeli*. His was a typical minor Renaissance career. He led a wild, immoral life and created many bawdy plays, but finally he wrote a religious drama, *L'Adamo*, thought by some to have been a partial source of inspiration of Milton's *Paradise Lost*, and afterwards retired to spend the rest of his days in a monastery.

Other great companies, the *Uniti* and the *Confidenti*, also toured extensively, particularly in France.

The tours made the influence of the *commedia* far-flung indeed. Shakespeare was writing when the comedy still flourished. No less than eight of his plays—not all of them comedies—have roots to some degree in the *commedia dell' arte* and in the earlier Roman drama through this channel. *The Comedy of Errors, Romeo and Juliet, Othello, All's Well That Ends Well, Love's Labour's Lost, The Merry Wives of Windsor, The Taming of the Shrew,* and *The Two Gentlemen of Verona* all come in part from this source. Several have Italian settings and Italian phrases are sprinkled thoughout them.

As we shall see later, an equal influence was exerted upon the French playwright Molière, who saw performances of the *commedia* and helped himself to the rich material he saw there, refining it with his own genius as Shakespeare did.

The comedies had a stock form, though, as we have seen, nothing ever conformed absolutely to a set rule. The manager, who laid out the basic scenario, was called the *corago*, which suggests a link to the term *choregus* by which the Greeks called the leader of the chorus.

Each actor had his own *zibaldone*, a kind of commonplace book. It was a storehouse of lines, phrases, speeches for all occasions, humorous or tragic (the *commedia* did present melodramas). It was a handbook, a dramatic dictionary, to help him elaborate a situation before going on stage. It would help him to dig up something fresh to enliven an old routine. It contained all the tips, hints, and sure-fire tricks which he had jotted down throughout his professional life. Many old-timers today, left over from the heyday of American vaudeville and burlesque shows, can show one or more battered "gag books," or "blackout books" (so called because at the end of each skit the stage lights are momentarily blacked out, instead of lowering a curtain) which are the same as the *zibaldone* —collections of the stock-in-trade of low comedy.

The plays used conventional characters, who in turn wore conventional costumes and masks. The richness and variety came from within—new twists to old business and a resourceful wit to renew the dialogue.

First there were the old men, *Pantalone* (Pantaloon, from whom came the baggy-pants costume), and *Il Dottore de Bologna* (The Doctor of Bologna, or the Professor of Baloney). At one time they might be rivals; at another, fellow conspirators. Inevitably one or both of the old men was pursuing the young heroine of the piece, or else one of them was married to her and either being betrayed or suffering jealous doubts of her fidelity and striving to keep her securely locked up away from all risk.

Then there was the Captain, *Il Capitano,* or at full length, *Capitano Spavento dell' val Inferno* (Captain Spavento of the Valley of Hell). He is descended directly from the mock soldier, the *Miles Gloriosus* of Roman comedy. He was a loudmouthed, blustering, bragging, swaggering fool and a coward to boot. *Spavento* means "fear" or "fright" and a double meaning is possible in that he boasts of the fear he inspires, but is in fact easily frightened. Often he was called the Spanish captain because Italy was militarily dominated by Spain in the sixteenth century, but he might be identified with any nationality the players wished to ridicule. His stock business was to recite his mighty and valiant deeds, and then to bolt and run in terror if confronted by a mouse, hearing an unexpected noise, or meeting a threatening gesture. Captain

Parolles in *All's Well That Ends Well* is a considerably refined and subtle modification of *Il Capitano.*

Then followed the roster of outrageous rogues and servants, the prime tricksters of the comedy who made miserable the lives of the old men and the captain. They had various names according to the locality, the company, or the actor: *Arlechino* (Harlequin), *Brighella, Burratino, Cucurucu,* or *Coviello.* They were buffoons, utterly mad and often malicious. They were called *zanni,* from which we get the modern word "zany" for someone or something a little mad or irresponsible. Ed Wynn, Laurel and Hardy, the Marx Brothers, or Jerry Lewis are zanies of our time.

Then there are the lovers—essential, if somewhat standardized, characters: *Leandro, Lelio, Flavio,* or *Ottavio,* in love with *Isabella, Lucinda,* or *Florinda.*

Scaramuccio, swashbuckler and charlatan, a role created by Tiberio Fiorelli of Naples, is the prototype of the later, romanticized *Scaramouche* of French comedy.

These are universal types, extraordinarily persistent and endlessly varied or recombined while essentially the same. You encounter them frequently today, not only in theatrical variations on stage, television, and film, but in many other media—especially the comic strip. One of the oldest "funny paper" features still goes on, *The Katzenjammer Kids,* or sometimes *The Captain and the Kids.* Under his low German coloration the Captain is a blend of *Pantalone* and *Capitano Spavento* in one. His friend, "der Inspector," is *Il Dottore de Bologna.* The terrible "kids" themselves are juvenile-delinquent *zanni.*

Most of the standard characters of the *commedia* had some comic specialty—a monologue—that was an expected part of the show. Certain of the great speeches of Shakespeare's immortal Falstaff are of this nature, in their way, especially his famous discourses on honor and on wine drinking.

Pantalone, the querulous, harassed old man, had his *consiglio,* or list of complaints and abuses, which he never failed to relate at length in the midst of numerous interruptions and torments. He might come onto the stage, alone, mumbling to himself: "Drat that Brighella! Rogue! Scoundrel! He has not only failed to purchase the chickens for my supper but has brought home and prepared pork! He knows perfectly well I can't eat pork! Can't touch a mouthful! Teeth won't stand it! Wretch! And that's another thing, the rascal! He should have fetched Florinda here, this very minute! Letting my wife roam all over the town, at such an hour! He knows my orders! Let me get my hands on him! Just let me give him a good drubbing! Villain! I shall know how to deal with him! Watch me! . . . . Hey! Ouch! Who did that? . . . ." at which point we will assume that Brighella, rascally subject of the denunciation, has slipped slyly onto the stage and administered a resounding kick to the old man from behind, then immediately disappeared. A moment later he will reappear to demand, indignantly, who has dared to molest his master.

The Captain had his *Bravura Spagnola* ("Spanish boasting," another sign of Italian resentment of Spanish domination), his long-winded brag about his exploits in battle or love.

Another stock speech is *Il Dottore's tirata della giostra*. Literally this could be "tirade of the merry-go-round" inasmuch as it goes on and on and roundabout. It is chiefly a list of ridiculously big words, supposed scientific discoveries, and phony medical terms.

A fine example of the *tirata* occurs in *The Man Who Married a Dumb Wife*, an old *commedia* plot in a version for the modern stage by the nineteenth century French writer Anatole France. Leonard has had his wife cured of dumbness. Now she talks so much that he wishes to have the surgeon make her dumb again. Master Simon, the doctor, says that this is impossible but offers another solution.

MASTER SIMON

We have medicines to make women speak; we have none to make them keep silence.

LEONARD

You haven't? Is that your last word? You drive me to despair.

MASTER SIMON

Alas, young Honour! (*He advances to the center, claps his hands for attention, and declaims.*) There is no elixir, balm, magisterium, opiate, unguent, ointment, local application, electuary, nor panacea that can cure the excess of glottal activity in woman. Treacle and orvietano would be without virtue, and all the herbs prescribed by Dioscorides would have no effect. . . . I can cure you at once, and for all time, of your wife's verbal hypertrophy, by means of cophosis.

LEONARD

By cophosis? What is cophosis?

MASTER SIMON

'Tis what is vulgarly called deafness. Do you see any disadvantages in becoming deaf?

[*He then further explains*]

Cophosis, vulgarly called deafness, may be brought about in several ways. It is produced either by etorrhea, or by sclerosis of the ear, or by otitis, or else by anchylosis of the ossicles. But these various means are long and painful.

LEONARD

I reject them . . . I reject them absolutely!

MASTER SIMON

You are right. It is far better to induce cophosis by means of a certain white powder which I have in my medicine-case; a pinch of it, placed in the ear, is enough to make you as deaf as Heaven when it's angry, or as deaf as a post.

And thus Leonard's predicament is ended.

The actors of the *commedia* also made lavish use of *lazzi*, or *faux pas*, slips, blunders, falls, somersaults, trippings, and other such

comic accidents. It is the comedy of the slip on a banana peel—
essentially the upsetting of dignity.

Typical comedy situations are built around episodes such as the
servants, Brighella and Arlechino, conspiring to persuade Pantalone, their master, that his breath smells and that he will therefore
never be able to win Lucinda—a point which would be much re-
inforced by modern TV commercials. On this pretext they talk the
old man into letting them pull all his teeth, a performance under-
taken with much violent buffoonery and loud cries of anguish.

In another case, Pantalone and the Doctor may be in love with
Isabella, who, in turn, loves and is loved by Leandro. Brighella and
Arlechino separately inform first Pantalone and then the Doctor
that Isabella will meet him after dark in a secret place. Each one
is told that he must come disguised as a woman and must not
speak a word, in order not to compromise Isabella. At the appointed time the Doctor and Pantalone encounter one another at
the trysting place, disguised as women. Each takes the other for
Isabella and attempts to woo her, keeping silent as instructed. The
result is a great deal of none too delicate comedy before the two
old men realize the hoax.

The life of these rambling players, in spite of its outward show
of glamor, had its hard realities. The average permanent company
was made up of seven men and three women. In the main, possibly excepting the three most famous troupes, they led wretched,
haphazard lives. They never knew security. They were dependent
for support upon patronage and whim. Briefly they might ride
high, with honors, jewels, or money lavished upon them by some
patron. At another time it was equally likely that they would be
driven out of a town by some nobleman whose anger they had
incurred.

Life within the companies was turbulent. The moral character
of the actors and actresses was anything but high, as a rule. The
Church sometimes attempted to clamp down on them and some-

times they were driven out of rural communities because of the looseness of their women. Frequently there was no restraint whatever either in their performances or their private lives. Prostitution might be part of the profession of a poor actress; and pimping, of an actor.

The romantic aspect of the *commedia* was captured in tragic form, centuries later, in Leoncavallo's opera, *I Pagliacci* (*The Clowns*), one of the staples of the operatic stage, famous for its heartbreaking tenor aria, *Vesti la giubba*. The betrayed clown, Canio, about to kill himself from grief, orders himself to dress for his role, and dies with the cry of *ridi, Pagliaccio* . . . "laugh, clown, laugh. . . ."

The *commedia*, vigorous as it was, had no lasting forms with which to preserve itself. That it had no playwrights was once its unique distinction, but finally became its extinction. There was no farseeing intelligence or artistry to keep its level above the depths of vulgarity toward which, lacking such guardianship, it tended to slip.

There were no roots of character or organization by which it could be nurtured. It was such men as Shakespeare and Ben Jonson in England and Molière in France who gave immortality to the *commedia* by preserving and improving its materials in their own lasting works touched by personal genius. On its native soil, the *commedia* passed from spiciness to sordidness and on to downright degradation until it died a melancholy, lingering, ignominious death. The comedy was ended.

Elizabethan stage

Chapter 7

A Race of Giants:
The Elizabethans

LEAVING THEATRE matters for a moment let us suppose ourselves
unseen spectators at a sinister and tragic event all too fatally non-
theatrical. We betake ourselves in imagination to a tavern owned
by Eleanor Bull, in Deptford, a district in the southeast suburbs

112

of London, in the county of Kent, at the great bend of the Thames. It is the thirtieth of May 1593.

Here four men have met in the late morning and stayed through the afternoon, sometimes walking outdoors in the mild spring weather. In the late day they take supper in a private room. One of these men is Christopher Marlowe, twenty-nine years old, a brilliant poet who has won Elizabethan audiences with a series of plays, each of which the modern theatre would call a hit. The others present are Ingram Frisar, who seems to have been host to the party, Robert Poley, and Nicholas Skeres. All are well off—more so than Marlowe. Though they have some standing in society there is something dubious about all of the poet's companions, either in personal morals as with Poley, political intrigue, or both.

All four have had ties with the Walsingham circle, the influential group that formed around Queen Elizabeth's powerful secretary of state, Sir Francis Walsingham, and his younger cousin, Thomas, the latter of whom was friend and patron of Marlowe. All four have been involved at one time or another as spies in the espionage system of Sir Francis. Allen Dulles, former director of the United States Central Intelligence Agency, in *The Craft of Intelligence,* credits Walsingham with organizing one of the earliest complex espionage systems in history.

Sir Francis had died some three years earlier. Have these four met to talk of secret matters related to their spying for the late secretary? Are current political conspiracies involved? Is there any connection, as some have speculated, with charges of heresy—a mask for political matters—that are even now brought against Marlowe?

None of this is certain though speculations have been elaborate. All we can say is that in this room at Deptford a quarrel breaks out. The ever impetuous Marlowe snatches for a dagger Frisar is wearing. Frisar wrestles for it, the other two leap in, and perhaps in the accident of struggle, two inches of the steel penetrate Marlowe's eye. Shakespeare's only serious rival lies dead in a tavern

brawl, whether spontaneous or provoked. He lies buried in Deptford Churchyard close to where he died. Frisar and the others
were brought to book but acquitted quickly of any charges for
this death on grounds of self-defense.

We can borrow some lines, out of context, from Shakespeare
and find them appropriate to Marlowe's wasteful death:

> O, what a noble mind is here o'erthrown!
> The courtier's, soldier's, scholar's eye, tongue, sword:
> The expectancy and rose of the fair state,
> The glass of fashion and the mould of form,
> The observ'd of all observers,—quite, quite down!

This ending is not out of harmony with the pattern of the playwright's life. Christopher Marlowe was born in 1564, also the year
of Shakespeare's birth, when nature appeared prodigal with genius.
He was the son of a shoemaker and leather worker in the cathedral
town of Canterbury. With something of irony, religion first appeared likely to be the shaping force of his life. After his earlier
schooling in the King's School, Canterbury, he went up to Corpus
Christi College, Cambridge, on a scholarship intended only for
those who were to take holy orders. Not only did he fail to carry
out this intention, but even before his Cambridge days were over
he had begun to disappear from the college on mysterious missions
connected with activities as an English spy on the Continent.

Many companies of players came to Canterbury. Also the
schools Marlowe attended were well known for dramatic activities. These influences awakened his love for the theatre he served
so well but so briefly. It is a pity he could not have given himself
wholly to this career, as did Shakespeare. The drama of a personally adventurous, dangerous life absorbed him too much.

In the nine years of his life past twenty he was poet-playwright
extraordinary, poetic rival to the more slowly developing Shakespeare, political plotter of questionable ethics, associate of noblemen and people in power. He was involved in a fracas leading to

the death of a man but with the others escaped the gallows on a
plea of self-defense. He was arrested, jailed, and occasionally placed
under bond to keep the peace.

He was the intimate of many of the outstanding men of Queen
Elizabeth's time in various walks of life. He knew the men of the
theatre, the scientists and philosophers, the skeptics and poli-
ticians. He was a friend of Sir Walter Raleigh and Sir Philip
Sidney. He shared lodgings with another popular playwright,
Thomas Kyd.

The year 1593 was a tense one in English politics. Elizabeth was
watchfully suspicious of conspirators. Heresy in religious doctrine
was a charge conveniently used to cloak a variety of suspicions and
many persons were imprisoned or beheaded for it. A warrant for
Marlowe's arrest on charges of heresy had been issued a short
while before the stabbing at Deptford. He was vulnerable to such
a move for he was known to have dabbled in witchcraft and speculated on other occult matters.

Four plays represent the roster of his mature dramatic works.
Tamburlaine the Great is a stirring, bravura tale of one of the
ancient conquerors from the east; it is in two parts, in effect being two plays, of epic proportion. *Edward the Second* is a moving,
sensitive English historical play containing some of his finest
writing. *The Jew of Malta,* a grim but popular melodrama, has
some links with the later *Merchant of Venice.* Shakespeare was
not guilty of plagiarism, for the plots of the plays differ greatly.
Also Shakespeare mellowed the tone into romantic comedy even
though the near-tragic figure of Shylock dominates the story. It
was the practice of the time for playwrights to borrow freely and
rework one another's materials. The stories were regarded as a
common stock and the question of merit and individual stamp
lay in what each man did with them.

Greatest of Marlowe's plays, still alive and widely performed on
the English-speaking stage to this day, is *The Tragical History of
Doctor Faustus.*

Let's go to the Red Bull Theatre, one of the less elegant show places of Elizabethan London, and see a performance of *Doctor Faustus*. By turns it will be comical and terrifying, swift moving and filled with wonderful effects. As we learn from a writer of the period who saw just such a performance of the play, ". . . indeed a man may behold shag-haired devils run roaring over the stage with squibs [firecrackers] in their mouths, while drummers make thunder in the Tiring-house [dressing rooms back- or below-stage], and the twelve-penny hirelings make artificial lightning in their Heavens!"

What we are watching is the story of the excessively ambitious scholar, Faustus, tempted by his craving for universal knowledge and unlimited worldly power. He sells his soul to the devil in return for these gifts. His learning in the dread art of black magic has taught him how to effect this transaction.

Alone in a grove, he performs mystic incantations within circles of smoke and fire. Then appears the devil Mephistophilis, a great demon of only somewhat less power than mighty Lucifer himself, the Prince of Hell. His appearance is as a dragon so horrible that Faustus cannot endure to behold him. By his magic spell he commands Mephistophilis to go and return in the appearance of a Franciscan friar.

After much deliberation and discussion with the cunning fiend, and urgings for and against by his good and bad angels, Faustus finally commits himself to the fatal decision and signs the hellish contract with his own blood. That very blood so loathes the act that it congeals and he cannot write with it; Mephistophilis, with sardonic appropriateness, liquifies the blood with a fiery coal. Here is the dreadful document:

> On these conditions following. First, that Faustus may be a spirit in form and substance. Secondly, that Mephistophilis shall be his servant, and at his command. Thirdly, that Mephistophilis shall do for him and bring him whatsoever. Fourthly, that he shall be in his chamber or house invisible. Lastly, that he shall appear to the said John Faustus, at all times, in what form or shape so-

ever he please. I, John Faustus, of Wertenberg, Doctor, by these presents, do give both body and soul to Lucifer, Prince of the East, and his minister, Mephistophilis; and furthermore grant unto them, that twenty-four years being expired, the articles above written inviolate, full power to fetch or carry the said John Faustus, body and soul, flesh, blood, or goods, into their habitation wheresoever. By me,

JOHN FAUSTUS

At the end of the twenty-four years—a more swiftly passing time than he could have imagined—having journeyed throughout the world and gratified his every wish for wealth, power, knowledge (but not wisdom), and pleasure, Faustus faces the hour at which he must fulfil his end of the contract by surrendering body and soul. The tragic irony of this bitter bargain is that all the vast powers for which he had contracted have been thrown away, wasted, on vain frivolities. This tells us something profound about the limitations of human nature. The same point is made, more playfully, in the common three-wishes motif of fairy tales. You will find they are almost always wasted. This circumstance causes the chief and not easily avoidable dramatic weakness in Marlowe's play, the fact that the central portions do not match the power of the beginning and the ending.

Now Faustus is consumed by terror. Urged on by his few friends, he hopes vainly to save himself by an eleventh hour repentance. It will not avail. The clock strikes eleven. Faustus in anguish begins the great speech commencing:

> Ah, Faustus,
> Now hast thou but one bare hour to live,
> And then thou must be damned perpetually.
> Stand still, you ever-moving spheres of Heaven,
> That time may cease, and midnight never come;
> Fair Nature's eye, rise, rise again and make
> Perpetual day; or let this hour be but
> A year, a month, a week, a natural day,
> That Faustus may repent and save his soul.

He continues his plea for mercy in a crescendo of agonized dread and remorse. The clock strikes the half hour. He finds no hope. He suffers. In a theatrical compression of time the clock now strikes twelve.

> *O, it strikes, it strikes! Now, body, turn to air,*
> *Or Lucifer will bear thee quick to hell.*
>   *(Thunder and Lightning)*
> *O soul, be changéd into little water-drops,*
> *And fall into the ocean—ne'er be found.*
>   *(Enter Devils)*
> *My God! my God! look not so fierce on me!*
> *Adders and serpents, let me breathe awhile.*
> *Ugly hell, gape not! Come not, Lucifer!*
> *I'll burn my books! Ah, Mephistophilis!*
>   *(Exeunt Devils with Faustus)*

So it ends, the ancient story of the man who gained the whole world at the loss of his immortal soul. The Elizabethan performance was filled with explosions of fireworks and countless tricks of jugglery and sleight of hand. In the 1930's, under the auspices of the Federal Theatre Project, Orson Welles, himself in the role of Faustus, produced and directed the play on Broadway with great success.

However, the natural inheritors of the Elizabethan tradition are the English. In 1962, in London, there was a memorable production of *Doctor Faustus* by the Old Vic Company. It had all the gusto and pageantry of Marlowe's own stage. As in the description from the period, quoted above, there was such a running of roaring shag-haired devils about the stage with squibs in their mouths, such a conjuring of spells with flashing and smoky explosions, that the nostrils seemed full of hellish smoke. Those in the first two or three rows, at intermission, found their clothes sprinkled with a sooty powder ash.

From high niches to stage right and left, Faustus' good and evil angels, respectively, exhorted him to their own purposes. In a characteristic comic scene one of the learned doctor's clownish servants appeared and confided to the audience:

> O this is admirable! Here I ha' stolen one of Doctor Faustus' conjuring books, and, i' faith, I mean to search some circles for my own use. . . .

As he went about this "roaring piece of work," uttering incantations, a fierce fiend sprang up beside him, frightening him out of his wits and curing him of ambitions for wizardry.

Once when Faustus thought of repentance, great Lucifer himself appeared in red and gold flamelike splendor to threaten him against breach of contract. The final scene of terrible retribution, when the devils swarmed from Hell to carry away their struggling, screaming victim, was reminiscent of the Hell Mouth of the miracles, for a gaping mouth seemed to open up in the very wall of the doctor's study, lurid with flame and smoke.

This Faustian theme of selling one's soul to the Devil is one of the profound motifs by which men have dramatized their perpetual struggle of choice between good and evil. It has received many varying treatments and we will meet it again when we come to the theatre of Germany.

Who can guess what Christopher Marlowe might have achieved had he not met so untimely an end? As it was, he did not reach the maturity and mastery of the finest work of Shakespeare, after him. What a stimulus two such rivals might have exercised upon each other had their careers run on in parallel. His friend and fellow writer Thomas Nashe called Marlowe "one of the wittiest knaves that ever God made," adding "His pen was sharp pointed like a poniard; no leaf he wrote on but was like a burning glass to set on fire all his readers." He left us some exalted passages in the blank verse that was the special dramatic medium of Elizabethan England. Ben Jonson, in a famous commemorative poem to Shakespeare, also praised "Marlowe's mighty line," a phrase that has echoed ever since to the playwright's lasting honor.

Now let us trace the links between the English religious plays and the theatre of Marlowe. England began her own Renaissance around 1500, some two hundred years after the beginnings of that revitalizing in Italy. Here it cannot be called actually a rebirth in the sense of the Italian culture which sprang up directly upon the ruins of Rome. This was really the time when England first realized her powers and potential splendors as a nation. As we mentioned in the last chapter, it had required the discovery of the Americas to reveal England as a power strategically situated to command the new spheres of trade and colonization.

In our day it is hard for us to imagine the significance of the discovery of two of the major continents of the world, to imagine our conceptions of geography being revolutionized by half a world suddenly heaving itself out of the seas, so far as our previous knowledge of it went. Yet only by attempting to grasp the emotional reaction and the challenge created by such events can we understand the people of Elizabeth's island kingdom.

People who actually knew Shakespeare must have set foot on the shores of America. Some of them may have seen the writer himself as actor, perhaps putting in an afternoon as the ghost of Hamlet's father.

King Henry VIII, Elizabeth's father, about whom Shakespeare wrote one of his last plays, committed England to her new destiny by building a British navy capable of challenging Spain, which had dominated the seas until then. England's first great rival for world power lost the contest at last in Elizabeth's reign when the huge Spanish Armada was destroyed by battle and storm. The power struggle then returned to what Shakespeare's chronicle plays often portrayed in its earlier phases, an intermittent duel between England and France, in which occurred alternate periods of friendship and bitter enmity.

After the appearance of nonreligious elements in the miracles, clearly observable in *The Second Shepherd's Play*, the development was swift. Two wholly secular comedies appeared. The first was Nicholas Udall's *Ralph Roister Doister*, an undistinguished comedy based on Plautus. This was followed by *Gammer Gurton's Needle*, which some believe was written by William Stevenson and others by Bishop Still, a folksy play about the furor over a lost needle which finally is found in the breeches of a manservant.

The first tragedy was *Gorboduc*, or *Ferrex and Porrex*, by Sackville and Norton. It was the bloody story of the struggle between two brothers for a throne, similar in many ways to the conflict between Eteocles and Polyneices, the Theban brothers, sons of Oedipus, which we discussed in the Greek drama.

A landmark among the early secular tragedies—more properly called a melodrama—was *The Spanish Tragedy*, or *Hieronimo Is Mad Again*, by Thomas Kyd, written in 1592. It is a particularly gory revenge play in the course of which ten characters lose their lives violently. It was one of the most persistently popular plays of the Elizabethan period, for all its many melodramatic excesses and faults. It held the stage well past the Elizabethan period. Samuel Pepys, in his famous diary, speaks of going to see *Hieronimo Is Mad Again* in 1668. He considered the play "a bad one" (which it is) and chiefly remarks on his vexation at being cheated of a shilling by the doorman.

We remember Thomas Kyd as one who roomed and worked together with Christopher Marlowe in the same quarters for some years. It was Kyd who gave the evidence, under torture, that resulted in the last warrant issued against Marlowe.

The other forerunners and contemporaries of Shakespeare are too numerous for all of them to be talked about adequately. They were minor talents, though some might have been more prominent if they had lived in an era less overshadowed by genius. The best known of the other men were John Lyly, George Peele, Robert Greene, Thomas Lodge, and Thomas Nash.

In 1576 the first public theatre in London was opened by James Burbage, the foremost actor of his time and head of a company of players sponsored by the Earl of Leicester. Almost immediately others sprang up in competition and the secular English theatre was launched.

Although theatres enjoyed the patronage of wealthy noblemen, even of the queen herself indirectly, puritanical opinion was strong enough so that theatres were barred from the city proper. They were built in the less reputable part of town, on the east side near the Thames, known as Shoreditch. It is still somewhat of a slum. Later Bankside, on the south bank of the Thames in Southwark, became the principal site of theatres and bull- and bear-baiting pits.

Elizabethan theatre architecture was not planned systematically but grew out of a combination of influences. Its most famous and developed form was like a large, puffy doughnut. A "wooden O" was Shakespeare's term for it in the prologue to *Henry V*. It was lined within by several stories of nearly circular tiers of seats or boxes. The playing space was a platform of which an "apron" projected out into the auditorium, flanked by the audience on either side. Farther back was the inner stage, across which a curtain could be drawn in order that scenes or persons might be "discovered," that is, suddenly disclosed, or else put in readiness while action progressed on the forestage. Above the inner stage, also curtained, was a second level, used for such purposes as the balcony scenes in *Romeo and Juliet*, or King Richard's address to the besieging nobles at Flint Castle in *Richard II*. Yet higher still were levels housing musicians, or stagehands to raise or lower objects, and above all a place for setting off blank cannon shots. This design for playing was marvelously resourceful as we can see when we observe the many changes of scene and place in Shakespeare's plays.

This interesting stage combined elements of the inn yards, which long served as the sole theatre for strolling players, and the rings for bull-, bear-, or cock-fighting. From the latter arenas also comes the term *pit*, sometimes given to the ground level where the rabble could stand for the cheapest admission while quality folk occupied the various tiers of seats. One of the earliest theatres, the Red Lion, was made over from an inn of the same name.

There has been argument about the kind and amount of scenery used on these stages. Certainly it was not limited to signs reading, "This is the Forest of Arden," or to spoken lines in the texts of the plays identifying and describing the scenes. It is unlikely that the zestful and ingenious Elizabethans would have failed to improve on the ingenious stagecraft of the miracle plays.

The Bankside "wooden O" theatres were not roofed and the shows could be rained out. Plays usually began at about two o'clock in the afternoon. Of course there were no vast architectural stage sets such as those in the court theatres of the Italian Renaissance, yet there was some painted scenery. Small trees were set up for forest scenes, or the Birnam wood episode in *Macbeth*. Costumes were elaborate and as we've already seen they used tricks entailing fireworks, thunder and lightning machines, smoke and steam effects, trap doors, acrobatic feats, and sleight-of-hand illusions. Bladders of "blood" and in extreme cases sacks stuffed with the entrails of animals were used to make murders or battle scenes more graphically effective. A bladder would be used, for instance, to stain the toga of Julius Caesar when he was stabbed. The most famous of the theatres, the Globe, owned by the company in which Shakespeare was a partner, burned to the ground in 1613 from sparks resulting from cannon fire, heralding the entrance of the king, Henry VIII, in a play that may not have been Shakespeare's. Sir Henry Wotton, who was present, described the burning jestingly in a letter:

> Now King Henry making a masque at the Cardinal Wolsey's house, and certain chambers [small cannon] being shot off at his entry, some of the paper, or other stuff, wherewith one of them was stopped, did light on the thatch [of the roof], where being

Reconstruction of Globe Theatre. *British Travel Association*

thought at first but an idle smoke, and their eyes more attentive to the show, it kindled inwardly, and ran round like a train [fuse], consuming within less than an hour the whole house, to the very grounds. This was the fatal period of that virtuous fabric, wherein yet nothing did perish but wood and straw, and a few forsaken cloaks; only one man had his breeches set on fire, that would perhaps have broiled him, if he had not by the benefit of a provident wit put it out with bottle ale.

All the companies in their several theatres, the Globe, the Swan, the Rose, the Fortune, and the Red Bull, competed to attract the public. On the day of a performance a flag was flown at the top of the theatre to advertise the event. Elizabethans loved the theatre and the public came in great numbers and all classes, even those who had the minor inconvenience of crossing the river in the boats of the watermen.

William Shakespeare, who stands as the greatest playwright in the English, and any other, language, was born in April 1564, at Stratford-on-Avon. The Shakespeares and his mother's family, the Ardens, were old and honest names on the land about Warwick-shire. John Shakespeare, the father, was a glover and wool dealer who prospered and made other investments in business and land. Also he held important civic offices in Stratford, such as bailiff and chief alderman. He had a wish to rise to the status of gentleman and acquire a coat of arms for the family, an ambition realized only in his old age with the help of his son, William, who had won some reputation, considering that he had started merely as a player. John is buried in Holy Trinity Church, Stratford, as are William and most of that worthy family who never forsook their deep roots in the town beside the Avon.

In Stratford's grammar school William received a sound education—one which was sufficient understructure for his unparalleled mastery of the language, even though he never went to one of the great universities as did the unfortunate Marlowe.

Young Shakespeare may have taught school in Warwickshire. Tradition says he got in a minor scrape for poaching. He married Ann Hathaway, who was several years older. He was attracted by the companies of players who performed often in Stratford. Around 1587 he went to London, perhaps as a recruit in one such company, and his lifelong commitment to the theatre had begun. Ann stayed behind in Stratford and raised their children, Hamnet and Judith—the boy later died. Shakespeare had not abandoned his family. Stratford is not far from London. He returned often, spent

William Shakespeare (*portrait by Ely Palace*). *British Travel Association*

summers there at times, writing, and at last retired there to live in New Place, the handsomest property in town, which he bought. He had become modestly wealthy, his earnings as a playwright contributing a share of his income. A bigger portion, however, came from his partnership in that flourishing producing company, originally the Lord Chamberlain's Men and later, after James I succeeded Elizabeth, the King's Men.

Before he was a playwright he was an actor, presumably a good one, for he rose in the company and the esteem of his fellows. The plays extensively reflect his knowledge of acting and the high standards he held for the craft, as in Hamlet's instruction to the players.

Marlowe, though the same age, had a head start on him, had made his own fame and been killed while Shakespeare's career was still in its early phase. These were the years when he wrote his narrative poems and the autobiographical sonnet sequence which is the most famous in English and about aspects of which scholars continue to debate. He began to tinker and mend other men's plays. Elizabethan companies bought plays outright and owned them entirely, as a rule. They would hire other men to alter or improve them if they wished. Shakespeare's three *Henry VI* plays—his earliest—undoubtedly contain remnants of other men's work, though for all their relative crudity, the Shakespearean hand is unmistakably evident in them at flashing moments.

At the height of his powers he outdoes even his mighty Greek predecessors. He is unique as being equally the master of brooding tragedy, sparkling comedy, tender love stories, and historical chronicles. He is not just an occasional revival but an always vital presence in every season of the modern theatre. His are still the great roles by which actors and actresses are measured.

He advances no philosophy that we can surely call his own. All kinds of views find eloquent voice among his characters. Male or female, young or old, king or peasant, soldier or priest, villain or saint, man of action or of contemplation, he goes to the heart of their natures. With justification he has been called the man who knew everything, who understood everything.

The magnificence of his poetry is blended with the firmness of his structural sense and the canniness of his stagecraft. Clearly he never gave much thought to preserving the texts of the plays. It is to two of his partners and fellow players in the King's Men, who survived him, John Heminges and Henry Condell, that we are indebted immeasurably for the First Folio edition of the plays which they published as a memorial to him—one of many evidences that he was much loved—in 1623, several years after his death.

Ben Jonson, a younger man, fellow actor, and rival playwright of whom we shall say more later, contributed a poem to the prefatory matter of the Folio. It is a remarkable tribute from one professional to another, rising above all jealousy: "To the Memory of My Beloved the Author, Mr. William Shakespeare, and What He Hath Left Us." It says in part:

> *Soul of the age!*
> *The applause, delight, the wonder of our stage,*
> *My Shakespeare, rise! I will not lodge thee by*
> *Chaucer or Spenser, or bid Beaumont lie*
> *A little further to make thee a room:*
> *Thou art a monument without a tomb,*
> *And art alive still while thy book doth live,*
> *And we have wits to read and praise to give.*

>   . . . . .

> *I should commit thee surely with thy peers,*
> *And tell how far thou didst our Lyly outshine,*
> *Or sporting Kyd, or Marlowe's mighty line.*
> *And though thou hadst small Latin and less Greek,*
> *From thence to honour thee, I would not seek*
> *For names, but call forth thundering Aeschylus,*
> *Euripides, and Sophocles to us,*

. . . . .

Triumph, my Britain; thou hast one to show
To whom all scenes of Europe homage owe.
He was not of an age, but for all time!

. . . . .

Nature herself was proud of his designs,
And joyed to wear the dressing of his lines,

. . . . .

Yet must I not give nature all; thy art,
My gentle Shakespeare, must enjoy a part:
For though the poet's matter nature be,
His art doth give the fashion; and that he
Who casts to write a living line must sweat
(Such as thine are) and strike the second heat
Upon the Muses' anvil, turn the same,
And himself with it, that he thinks to frame,
Or for the laurel he may gain a scorn;
For a good poet's made as well as born.
And such wert thou!

. . . . .

Sweet swan of Avon, what a sight it were
To see thee in our waters yet appear,
And make those flights upon the banks of Thames
That so did take Eliza and our James!

Shakespeare used every resource of his theatre. He knew its limitations and when to face them candidly and call on the audience to supply its always essential contribution of imagination to the experience of drama. This theatre always acknowledged that what was afoot was a play in the presence of an audience. Characters addressed themselves directly to the spectators in many speeches, and so did the playwright himself, as in the prologue and many other times throughout the play the Chorus—a single actor—speaks for the author in *Henry V*:

O for a Muse of fire, that would ascend
The brightest heaven of invention,
A kingdom for a stage, princes to act,

. . . . .

But pardon, gentles all,
The flat unraiséd spirits that have dared
On this unworthy scaffold to bring forth
So great an object. Can this cockpit hold
The vasty fields of France? Or may we cram
Within this wooden O the very casques
That did affright the air at Agincourt?

. . . . .

Piece out our imperfections with your thoughts.

. . . . .

Think when we talk of horses that you see them
Printing their proud hoofs i' the receiving earth.
For 'tis your thoughts that now must deck our kings,
Carry them here and there, jumping o'er times,
Turning the accomplishment of many years
Into an hourglass.

This captures the very essence of what happens in theatre and of the part which the audience must supply which, if withheld, would make theatrical communication impossible. Drama is perhaps more effective when its theatrical nature is frankly acknowledged than in all those modes of so-called realism which try to pretend that they are life itself.

Shakespeare's powers of characterization range with assurance over kings and clowns, from the noble, tormented Hamlet, to the raving, broken Lear, to the robust, incomparable Falstaff of the *Henry IV* plays. Sir John—plump Jack—Falstaff seized the popular imagination from his first appearance and has not relinquished his hold on it in four hundred years. Tradition says that *The Merry Wives of Windsor* (which Verdi later made into the opera

Falstaff) was written to please Queen Elizabeth who had asked Shakespeare to show her the fat knight in love. He has a lesser cousin in Sir Toby Belch, of *Twelfth Night*, with his shrewd challenge to puritanism: "Dost thou think, because thou art virtuous, there shall be no more cakes and ale?"

We must not slight the great roles for women. Rosalind in *As You Like It*, Olivia in *Twelfth Night*, are gaily womanly, tender, and perceptive. Katherine is the termagant of *The Taming of the Shrew*, softened and gentled at its end. Beatrice brings the tart tongue of wit to *Much Ado About Nothing*. Portia's is the resolving wisdom in *The Merchant of Venice*.

The gallery is immense. In the tragedies his women range from the pathos of gentle Cordelia, in *King Lear*, to her savage sisters. Lady Macbeth stirs us first to horror in renouncing the natural attributes of her womanhood, then to pity in her remorse. Perhaps most challenging to an actress, Shakespeare caught the height of self-destroying yet wildly splendid passion in his Cleopatra.

Hamlet is a work of such unique fame that the traditional peak of ambition for every actor is to play its brooding hero. He is what the theatre calls a "fat" role—a man suddenly confronted by a terrible duty. He is called upon to revenge the murder of his father and to right a wrong against the state. This obligation is a burdensome secret, supernaturally revealed to him, and possibly—fearful thought—a trap set for him by some devilish delusion.

Prince Hamlet, who shoulders this burden, is a reflective, complex young man. Moreover, he is in love, and his personal happiness will be engulfed in the great charge laid upon him. The closest ties link the central figures of the tragedy—it is no clash of strangers, but involves father, mother, uncle, and the girl whom Hamlet loves.

To Shakespeare's audiences *Hamlet* was one of their chief delights, a revenge play like Kyd's *Spanish Tragedy*, bathing the stage in blood before it was finished. There were many revenge plays, highly successful, but there were not many playwrights like Shakespeare. To the gory, violent formula he brought the dimension of genius. The play soars above the standard products of its kind. It satisfies the tastes of both the excitement seeker and the contemplative man who looks beneath the action.

Hamlet is caught in multiple conflicts: with the object of revenge, with his own complicated inner nature, and with evil itself. As a result, this play has held audiences and readers since it first appeared, inspiring diverse stage interpretations and critical studies. Hamlet is a universal image of a man divided within himself, hesitating on the brink of unavoidable decision.

In *King Lear,* unquestionably one of the greatest and the most deeply pessimistic of his plays, Shakespeare harrows our hearts with the tragedy of the old king, maddened and undone by his own follies, and broken cruelly on "the rack of this tough world." Yet there, too, he summed up his wisdom of human life, character, and growth in the words,

> *Men must endure*
> *Their going hence, even as their coming hither:*
> *Ripeness is all.*

It is the old wizard of the stage, speaking in the voice of the wizard Prospero, in almost the last play and one of the most fancifully original, *The Tempest,* who seems to be summing up his own career and the mystery of the theatre he served:

> *Our revels now are ended. These our actors,*
> *As I foretold you, were all spirits and*
> *Are melted into air, into thin air:*
> *And, like the baseless fabric of this vision,*
> *The cloud-capp'd towers, the gorgeous palaces,*
> *The solemn temples, the great globe itself,*
> *Yea, all which it inherit, shall dissolve*
> *And like this insubstantial pageant faded,*
> *Leave not a rack behind. We are such stuff*
> *As dreams are made on, and our little life*
> *Is rounded with a sleep.*

Maurice Evans as Hamlet. *Vandamm Collection of the New York Public Library Theatre Collection*

The plays remain fixed stars in the firmament of world theatre. Grand operas have been based on them—most notably Verdi's *Otello* and *Falstaff*, and Benjamin Britten's *A Midsummer Night's Dream*. Sir Laurence Olivier has made superb films of *Henry V*, *Hamlet*, and *Richard III*. A notable British television achievement, widely shown in the United States as well, was *An Age of Kings*, a consecutive cycle of eight historical plays from *Richard II*, through *Henry IV, V*, and *VI*, to *Richard III*. The visual flexibility, the mobility of film and television are well adapted to Shakespeare, yet in whatever media he is cast, it is the stage with the living presence of the actor that is his supreme domain. The principal commercial theatres of New York and London see a procession of productions. Regular repertory seasons ranging through all the plays are established in many places, the best known of which is the Royal Shakespeare Company's Memorial Theatre in Stratford-on-Avon, where the swans to which Jonson likened the playwright swim proudly in the waters flowing beside the place of his birth, his burial, and his living art. Other companies dedicated to Shakespearean production are London's Old Vic, and the companies that perform on replicas of Elizabethan stages at Stratford, Ontario, and Stratford, Connecticut. In recent years, free open-air productions of Shakespeare plays in Central Park have been sponsored by New York City and private grants.

Busily active during Shakespeare's lifetime, working with him, and some continuing after he was gone, were Beaumont and Fletcher, John Webster, John Ford, and Thomas Middleton.

Thomas Dekker deserves special mention for his *The Shoemaker's Holiday*. A genial comedy, it is also of some social significance in that it celebrates the rise of the class of merchants, traders, and craftsmen. It shows how Simon Eyre, the "mad shoemaker of Tower Street," a hearty, winning man, attains the high office of Lord Mayor of London. It shows an heir to a title, who has become a shoemaker voluntarily, winning the hand of a middle-class girl against the opposition of his noble uncle. Side by side is the story of the lame but valiant apprentice who keeps his pretty wife against the competition of a nobleman. It is a refreshing gallery of lively characters, chief of whom is Simon Eyre himself, with his constant refrain of "Prince am I none, yet am I Princely born!" who captures the respect of the King of England himself.

The dramatist who ranks next after Shakespeare and Marlowe is Ben Jonson. He was the son of a bricklayer and for a time worked at his father's trade. He had a good education and prided himself on his knowledge of the classics. His early life was marked by literary quarrels, in one of which he killed a man in a duel for which he served a term in prison. As the Elizabethan theatre faded into another and lesser era he acquired favor in royal circles as author of many masques, pastoral pageants like those of Italy, which became a vogue in court and garden theatres. On such displays he worked closely with the architect and stage designer Inigo Jones. Yet the writing of masques was not the true vehicle for Jonson's genius. In his best vein he was a critic of human nature and excelled as a writer of somewhat bitter comedies. They are satirical and sharp in contrast with the gay and graceful spirit of Shakespeare's.

Jonson's *Volpone, or The Fox,* is a scathing exposure of human greed, which is both immensely funny in its mocking way and horrifying in its merciless revelation of baseness. The rich, avaricious Venetian, Volpone (The Fox), aided by his wily servant Mosca (The Fly), pretends that he is dying. He tricks his greedy acquaintances, Voltore (The Vulture), Corbaccio and Corvino (The Crows or Ravens), into giving him costly gifts of gold and jewels, each one in the expectation of soon becoming heir to all of Volpone's wealth. By playing one against the other, the two plotters lead them to appalling excesses of currying favor. One would-be heir disinherits his son in Volpone's favor, another offers him his wife. It is then given out that Volpone has died and the hopefuls are confounded by a will making Mosca his heir. Mosca seizes the advantage, tries to keep up the pretense of Volpone's death to keep all for himself, but brings the house of cards down on the heads of the whole unsavory crew. As the names of the characters show, it adapts an animal fable to human terms. Its link to the *commedia* is obvious.

Jonson often used the device of summarizing his plot, at the beginning of a play, in an acrostic of its title, thus:

V   olpone, childless, rich, feigns sick, despairs,

O   ffers his state to hopes of several heirs,

L   ies languishing: his parasite receives

P   resents of all, assures, deludes; then weaves

O   ther cross plots, which ope themselves, are told.

N   ew tricks, for safety, are sought; they thrive: when, bold,

E   ach tempts the other again, and all are sold.

Volpone holds the stage well and is done often in the modern theatre. Other of Jonson's best plays are *The Alchemist; Epicene, or the Silent Woman;* and *Every Man in His Humour.*

Then the English theatre experienced a brief eclipse. In the years following Elizabeth's strong reign, political and religious struggles wracked England and the Puritan party won a bitter civil war, beheading King Charles I and setting Oliver Cromwell at the head of state for some years as Lord Protector. With a bitterness equal to the denunciations of Tertullian in early Christian Rome, they suppressed the theatre. In 1642 every public theatre in England was closed, awaiting the liberation that came a few years later with the restoration of the monarchy under King Charles II. In due time we shall see the gay theatre that flourished then.

Chapter 8

The Theatre

of France

Molière. *French Cultural Services*

WE ARE in a rather dark hall, wide, long, and low-ceilinged. There seems to be no one about and we might as well be in a barn for all we can see in the dim light. But wait! Here comes someone with a lit taper. He begins to light the candles of the chandeliers, now resting on the floor, and to hoist them up to their proper places over our heads. As one after another are raised, we and the others who have begun to arrive are able to get a proper look at our surroundings.

At the end of the hall is a deep stage, curtained just now, which will also be lit by candles when it is time for the performance to begin. Along the walls are two tiers of boxes to be occupied by persons of rank. The central floor, where we stand, is like the pit of the Elizabethan theatre, though the place resembles it in no other way. The greater number of the audience, probably the

137

truest lovers of the theatre, will stand, or sit on benches, here. Over in the corner is a table for wines, fruits, and pastries which will be vended by young girls when the audience has arrived.

This is the Hôtel de Bourgogne, the first, and for many years the best, theatre in Paris, or in all of France for that matter, in the first half of the seventeenth century. You may see a re-creation of the preparations just described, and also the beginning of an actual performance, if you see or read the first scene of Edmond Rostand's popular play, *Cyrano de Bergerac.* The slow coming to life of the dark hall, the arrival of the enthusiastic fans who can hardly await the start of the drama, the lighting of chandeliers, the flirtations of the girls who sell the sweetmeats, the pranks of the page boys who fish for wigs from the upper tier of boxes, all are pictured by Rostand. Then arrive the dandies, fashionably late, the persons of rank, or possibly royalty, perhaps even His Eminence Cardinal Richelieu, the real power in France, and a patron of the theatre who writes for it himself, after a fashion, as we shall see.

Though the scene is re-created in a romantic play, it is true to the period. There was also a real Cyrano de Bergerac in this early day of the French theatre. Little is known about him except that he was a soldier and eccentric, a minor poet and playwright. In addition to plays, he actually wrote a fantastic book about a journey to the moon which is mentioned and becomes the occasion of a scene in the play. He owes his immortality less to himself than to the beloved character Rostand made of him in the freedom of creative imagination.

This early theatre, the Hôtel de Bourgogne, was established by the first theatrical organization in France, the *Confrérie de la Passion,* or Brotherhood of the Passion. The Brotherhood was a band of trade-guild members and artisans who, as we remember, had taken over the production of miracles and mysteries. They carried their activities beyond the days of the purely religious plays and became part of the general European movement toward a secular drama. More interesting to us than any of their producing activities is the forecast of what we might call the strictly business exploitation of the theatre.

Early in the fifteenth century, well before nonreligious drama yet amounted to anything, the influential Brotherhood obtained a theatrical monopoly in Paris. They had a royal grant permitting them to control and claim the profits from any and all public theatrical performances in the city.

The Brotherhood ceased actually producing plays in 1548, for its members were tradesmen and artisans who could not compete in time or talent with the developing class of professional actors. But the Brothers were shrewd enough to maintain their organization and use its privileges. The Brotherhood of the Passion conducted the first extensive business in theatrical real estate. Today on Broadway a theatrical real-estate firm may own several theatres and lease them to producing managers, thus operating a profitable theatre business that has no connection with the art of the theatre at all. The Brotherhood of the Passion not only owned the Hôtel de Bourgogne. They also controlled for a while the general license to put on plays publicly. Such a comprehensive privilege could not be maintained for long in the hands of any one group, but they managed to keep their hold on the Bourgogne Theatre until 1710.

Touring companies of the *commedia dell' arte* had helped to spread the nonreligious theatre in France. Even after French theatre was firmly established Italian players continued to visit Paris every season and tour the provinces. They did not always come in dignity as ambassadors of art, but frequently as attractions hired by quack doctors to draw crowds. The sight of a large crowd in a public square, watching the rollicking players and remaining to hear the persuasive harangue of the medicine vendor, or mountebank, was common. Early America later knew this as the medicine show, where quacks often employed Indians or blackface minstrels as their attractions.

The first important acting company leased the Hôtel de Bourgogne in 1610 and began operations under the name of the King's Players, by royal permission. It was headed by an actor named Valleran Lecomte and largely supplied with plays by a skillful playwright, Alexandre Hardy, whose plays began the development of a peculiarly French mode of drama based on a narrow imitation of classical models, especially the tragedies of the Roman Seneca.

No one who has read Alexandre Dumas' swashbuckling romance, *The Three Musketeers*, will ever forget Cardinal Richelieu. That crafty, brilliant arch-villain who waged relentless war upon the dashing d'Artagnan and his three henchmen, Athos, Porthos, and Aramis, possessed a genius for statesmanship far beyond the limits of his fictional portrait. It was Richelieu, not the king, who ruled the France of Louis XIII.

His Eminence was a patron of the arts, particularly the theatre. Stage-struck himself, amid all his burdens of state he found the time to write, or at least plan, plays and supervise their production in a beautiful ballroom theatre which he built in his palace in 1641. His stagecraft did not match his statecraft. He maintained what was probably the first staff of ghostwriters in the history of the theatre. He would sketch the main outlines for a play and deliver it to one of his writers to expand and complete, he himself perhaps touching up the final draft to his taste. The finished product, of course, was credited to the Cardinal though everybody knew about his stable of writers.

An unknown playwright, finding it difficult to gain recognition, might have his play sponsored by the Cardinal if His Eminence were allowed to tinker with it, "improve" it, and share in the billing. There is a splendid episode in *Cyrano de Bergerac*, in which Cyrano, unable to get his plays performed, nonetheless spurns the offer of production by such means, preferring to have his play produced on its own merits, in his own name, as he had written it, or not produced at all.

At one time the Cardinal's literary retainers were a group known as "the five poets." One of the younger of them was a former lawyer from Rouen named Pierre Corneille who had given up the practice of law out of love for poetry and the stage. His outward appearance was not winning and his personality was of a proud and bristly sort; he was not the man best suited to do literary chores under another's name. Sometimes he annoyed the Cardinal by departing from his outlines and following his own ideas.

Corneille's first play, *Mélite*, had been produced in 1629, when he was twenty-three, by the Théâtre du Marais. The Marais had not been in operation very long before this brilliant young playwright came to them. It was a lucky chance for both. It was no easy task for the Marais to set up in competition with the established King's Players of the Hôtel de Bourgogne. The theatre in which Corneille launched his career was a converted indoor tennis court, as were many of the early theatres of France, except the Bourgogne. The shape of the courts, with their boxes for spectators, was easily adaptable to theatrical purposes by the building of a shelflike stage across one end.

In 1636 the Théâtre du Marais excited Paris and all of France by the production of Pierre Corneille's most famous play, *Le Cid*. The story of *The Cid* (from the Arabic *"el seyd,"* the lord) was taken from a heroic legend of Spain in the eleventh century, which found an early form in the *Poema del Cid* of the twelfth century, and many works after it. A lavish and popular motion picture was made from this ancient story in recent years. Corneille's highly formalized poetic treatment delighted his audiences and made *The Cid* the most successful French play of its century.

Rodrique, a young Spanish nobleman, is in love with and is loved by Chimène, daughter of a prominent family. The course of love runs smoothly until a chance circumstance and the Spanish code of honor complicate matters. Chimène's father quarrels with Rodrique's father and strikes the older man. Rodrique, acting as honor compels him to do, challenges Chimène's father to a duel and kills him. The Spanish code now calls for Chimène to take vengeance by demanding her lover's death. Rodrique, overcome by the hopelessness of the situation, is inclined to commit suicide. His father persuades him to seek the more honorable course of dying in battle. But even in this Rodrique is frustrated—one never seems to get killed when one wishes. At the head of a small force he repels a Moorish invasion and instead of dying becomes the hero of Spain. Though Chimène still loves him, she must continue to try to achieve his death to avenge her father. The king tells her to appoint a champion and arrange a duel, upon the condition that she must marry the winner. Rodrique is willing to allow himself to be defeated, but Chimène, unable to hold out any longer, admits her love and begs him to win. Naturally he does so and they are united. That is where Corneille ended his version, though there is considerably more elaboration to the Spanish story.

Now the remarkable part of this, as Corneille presents it, is that *it all takes place in twenty-four hours!* Someone called it "the most crowded day in all recorded time."

The reason for this ridiculous and artificial compression lies in the strict and rigid rules that governed seventeenth-century French drama. The writing of tragedy was restricted by narrowly defined requirements of "unity" of time, place, and action. These unities were supposedly in imitation of the Greek drama. They were more truly the invention of the court dramatists of the Italian Renaissance, exaggerated still further in France and falsely attributed to the Greeks through a misapplication of Aristotle's analysis of Greek tragedy in his *Poetics*. Indeed, this style of *tragédie pathétique*, as it was called, was more influenced by the tragedies of the Roman Seneca than by the Greek dramatists who had enormously greater simplicity and vigor.

The Cid was a tragicomedy, as the French called a serious play with a happy ending. According to the prevailing rules all the action of a tragedy or tragicomedy had to take place within twenty-four hours, preferably with no changes of scene but at least with as few as possible, and it had to be cast into five acts. No violence was permitted on stage. (How different from the Elizabethans with their blood and thunder!) The chief characters had to be either noble or divine. To cap it off, the dialogue had to be written in strictly prescribed forms of rhymed verse.

The unevenness of Corneille's extensive works, the contrast between his best and lesser plays, the nature of the petty carping about technicalities with which critics and rivals harassed him, all suggest that his genius suffered from the restrictions of the dominant style. What might he have given us had he enjoyed the broad freedom and scope of Shakespeare's stage, which French aristocratic taste considered crude and vulgar?

The popular success of *The Cid* roused professional hostility and set off one of the hottest controversies in the history of French literature. Cardinal Richelieu was irked by the independent fame of one of his hired poets. He condemned the play severely, insisting that the unities were not sufficiently observed in spite of the grotesque compression Corneille had forced upon the story. It was said that the story itself was not suitable for the tragic stage. The French Academy, then and since regarded as the highest arbiter of the arts, censured him and delayed for more than ten years the playwright's own admission to membership in its august circle.

Corneille could only bow before the tempest. Outwardly, peace was preserved between himself and the Cardinal, whose patronage was essential. Yet the tension between the man and the conventions of his stage were such that he later withdrew from the theatre for some five years before resuming work again.

His brother Thomas, twenty years younger, was also a playwright of skill, but not of genius. The brothers were devoted to one another and lived in attached houses. Tradition is that a panel could be opened between the houses and that the greater brother, less adroit at verses, would sometimes open the panel and call to Thomas to furnish him a rhyme.

In spite of quarrels and rivalries, Corneille was widely considered to be the leading French dramatist of his day—an age which included two other playwrights of genius, one of whom may be said to have worn better, at least in terms of the world theatre. Corneille also wrote comedies, though his tragedies were more celebrated. Among the foremost of his works after *The Cid* are plays on Roman classical themes: *Cinna, Horace, Sertorius,* and *Polyeucte,* the latter a story of conflict between early Christianity and pagan Rome.

The chief contender with Corneille for honors in tragic drama was a younger man, Jean Racine. He did not chafe against the rigidly conventional form; indeed, he found it congenial and carried it to perfection of its kind. Also, though he could be savagely sharp-tongued in quarrels, he had the gift of ingratiation and could play the subtle games of courts and cliques. He remarked once that the blunt Corneille wrote verses "a hundred times more beautiful" than his own but that he, Racine, made himself agreeable.

He was orphaned early, raised by pious grandparents, and well educated with the aim that he might enter the priesthood. His temperament was worldly, however, and he had a taste for high living. He went to Paris and made the acquaintance of distinguished men in the literary and theatrical world, including the famous writer of rhymed fables, La Fontaine, and the great comedian, Molière. It was Molière's company, although best known for comedy, that gave the young dramatist his first opportunity and produced two of his early plays, *La Thébaïde* and *Alexandre.* Neither was very good and Molière lost by the venture. Racine, however, had got a start. He allowed *Alexandre* to be played also by Molière's rivals at the Hôtel de Bourgogne and gave his further plays to that company. Molière considered this an act of ingratitude and it ended the friendship between the men. Yet it should be added, in fairness to Racine, that as we shall see shortly, Molière's troupe simply was not distinguished for tragedy and was not the best company for the developing career of a brilliant young tragic dramatist.

One of Racine's best-known plays is *Phèdre,* based on the Greek drama like so many of his others. It is the tragedy of Phèdre, second wife of the hero Theseus, king of Athens. In her husband's prolonged absence she falls in love with Hippolytus, his grown son by his first wife. The tormented queen confesses her love but is spurned with horror by Hippolytus. Soon after, Theseus returns. Phèdre's loyal maid, fearing that the youth might denounce her mistress, seeks to protect her by accusing Hippolytus of making advances to Phèdre. Theseus angrily banishes the young man. Shortly afterward the youth's chariot horses, terrified by a sea monster, bolt, and Hippolytus is dragged to his death. Too late, Theseus learns of his son's innocence and the guilty, remorseful Phèdre slays herself. This much of the story is like its Greek original, the *Hippolytus* of Euripides. Racine, making a concession to the French temperament, threw in an added love interest between Hippolytus and a captive princess.

Like all of Racine's work, the play is written in fluent and beautiful verse, but is so completely formal that it lacks a sense of real life and vigor. The speeches are long and the movement slow. Yet it is a style well liked in France and Racine continues to hold a place on the French stage and many actresses have made triumphs as his poetically talkative heroines. But the plays have not had wide popularity outside of France as this is not a theatre of universal appeal.

In a typical passage from *Phèdre,* Hippolytus is declaring his love to Aricia, a captive princess. He has long been silent and apparently indifferent, but now he bursts forth:

> *I have said too much*
> *Not to say more. No prudence can resist*
> *The violence of passion. Now, at last,*
> *Silence is broken. I must tell you now*

The secret that my heart can hold no longer.
You see before you an unhappy victim
Of hasty pride,—a prince who begs compassion.
For I was long the enemy of love.
I mocked his fetters, I despised his captives,
And while I pitied these poor, shipwrecked mortals,
I watched the storms, and seemed quite safe on land.
And now I find that I have such a fate,
And must be tossed upon a sea of troubles.

It is only fair to say that Racine's skillful and formalized verse loses its true character in translation.

Though Racine had courted favor with some, he also had enemies. They spoiled the success of his *Phèdre*, boycotting it in favor of an inferior play of the same name by a less able writer. This may have contributed to Racine's decision to leave the theatre, which he did more definitely than Corneille had done. In the last twenty years of his life he turned from his worldly ways back to the Church and wrote little except for a sequence of religious *Confessional Sonnets,* which were brought to light and published only recently, and two religious plays, *Esther* and *Athalie,* which rank among his best work.

The careers of Racine and Corneille reflect the amount of intrigue and maneuvering for position that characterized the court-dominated theatre of France in their day. Though Racine had been a jealous rival of Corneille he rose to a moment of high grace and magnanimity on the occasion of Thomas Corneille's taking Pierre's seat in the Academy after the older brother's death. Racine, in a famous speech, paid eloquent and moving tribute to Corneille's genius.

In spite of the distinction of the two essentially tragic dramatists, Jean Baptiste Poquelin, who later called himself Molière, is the greatest figure of French seventeenth-century theatre, the one whose work has reached farthest and lasted longest outside his own country. When Molière is played today—as he is constantly—it is not as a museum piece but as living comedy.

Molière was born in Paris in 1622, the son of Jean Poquelin, one of the official upholsterers to King Louis XIII. It was the consuming ambition of Jean Poquelin that Jean Baptiste should follow him in what he regarded as this high place. The boy was well educated but his training was not neglected in that craft which had been pursued by several generations on both sides of his family. For a short time during his restless youth he followed his parent's wishes, availing himself of the privilege of succession to the royal appointment which his father had purchased for him at considerable cost.

Yet the destiny of Jean Baptiste was not for upholstery. There is a tradition that the house in which he lived as a child had sculptured decorations of monkeys in an orange tree, and was known accordingly as *la maison des singes* or house of the monkeys. The monkey was also a symbol of comedy. There are other factors more likely than that pleasing coincidence to have shaped the course of Jean Baptiste's life.

He had unusual opportunities to see theatre of all kinds. A family friend had important rank in that ancient *Confrérie de la Passion* which, as we've seen, owned the Hôtel de Bourgogne. That gave the boy access to a box, and Jean Poquelin also had a box at a theatre noted for comedy, so Jean Baptiste saw not only French comedy and tragedy but the Italian comedians as well. In addition, during his school and college days he became fascinated by the study of the classic dramatists, taking with particular enthusiasm to the comedies of Plautus and the earlier Greek comedians. Some say that at college he was a fellow student in philosophy of the historical Cyrano de Bergerac who also pursued the theatre as a branch of his diverse career.

The young upholsterer became seized with the ambition to become an actor. He broke with his distressed father, relinquished the upholsterer's needle and his right of succession to the royal appointment (he would get a different one, some day), and sought the companionship of actors, which was regarded as a step downward for a good bourgeois youth. His acquaintance with the theatrical family Béjart helped further his aims. In company with the Béjarts and some others the young man, as yet little more than an apprentice at his new profession, ambitiously founded a company which they called, with more enthusiasm than modesty, the Illustre Théâtre. The Illustrious Theatre belied its name and was a disastrous failure. Creditors could not be paid. Their building was closed and young Poquelin, as the nominal head of the company, spent a few dismal hours in debtors' prison. In spite of this fiasco, the great Comédie Française, still an honored institution of the French stage, likes to claim its descent not only from Molière but from the short-lived Illustre Théâtre.

Jean Baptiste was released when his associates argued persuasively that they could never earn the money to pay off their debts if their leader remained in prison—a philosophy few debtors' courts honored in the long, melancholy history of such institutions. In spite of his bitter disappointment at his son's choice of career, the elder Poquelin, being a loving father, came forth with financial aid, an act which it is pleasant to say the son was able to return in kind years later. Now, with several of his associates of the Illustre Théâtre, "the little upholsterer," as some of his friends then called him, took to the road with a troupe of traveling players. In the meantime, Jean Baptiste Poquelin was now left behind forever, for the young man followed the custom of the day and assumed a professional name: Molière.

It was twelve years before he attempted a return to Paris. In the meantime much happened. Molière became a seasoned player. He rose to be head of the company he had joined and the troupe flourished, attracting distinguished patronage and making a good bit of money. His debts were paid and he was on good terms again with his father, who now was convinced that Molière knew what he was doing and that all was for the best. Most important of all the developments of these years, Molière had begun to try his hand at playwriting and had dashed off some light farces which had been unusually popular wherever the troupe had played.

At last, in 1658, the company decided to make a fresh assault upon Paris. By some careful wire-pulling they managed to get themselves appointed players to the king's brother, the young Duke of Anjou. Slightly to their consternation they were instructed to give their first performance at the Royal Palace, before the king himself, now Louis XIV, *le Roi Soleil*, the Sun King, the Grand Monarch who set his stamp on an era.

Molière had not yet learned that he was first and foremost a comedian. Believing that they must perform something suitable to the dignity of the occasion the company decided to present a tragedy, the *Nicomède* of Corneille. Tragedy was not their true talent, particularly in comparison with the polished tragedians of the Hôtel de Bourgogne who were still the king's own players. Members of that company were in the audience.

When the play was over it was evident that they had not succeeded very well; all could sense the awkwardness of the situation. Perhaps they would be dismissed curtly and have to return to the provinces forever. Hastily Molière stepped forward and bowed to the king. With that grace which was one of his distinguishing gifts, he apologized for their presumption in overreaching themselves and with their cruder, rustic talents, performing tragedy not only before the king but in the very presence of his own gifted tragedians. The mistake arose from their nervousness and their zeal to do the right thing, which sometimes leads one to do the wrong. Now that they had been heard so patiently, might they implore the king's permission to play a little farce of Molière's own which had been popularly received in the provinces—probably for lack of anything better.

Louis XIV seems to have sensed quickly the rare qualities of Molière. He received graciously the unnecessarily humble apology—

the performance had not been *that* bad—and gave the requested permission.

Molière and his fellows galloped into the little farce of *The Doctor in Love* (it has not survived) with such verve and abandon, such spontaneity of comedy as Paris had not seen before. The relative failure of *Nicomède* was forgotten. Molière had won his second battle with Paris.

The rest of his career was triumph upon triumph. By the king's favor he inherited Richelieu's beautiful little theatre in what was now called the Palais Royal. In time his company supplanted the Hôtel de Bourgogne as the King's Troupe. Richelieu's successor, the equally brilliant statesman, Cardinal Mazarin, favored him highly. The king himself maintained a consistent loyalty of favor toward the great actor-playwright. Louis did him the rare honor of dining with him privately, and was an admiring, perceptive patron throughout his remaining career. Molière's success and the esteem he enjoyed at court made a vast improvement in the social status of actors.

Molière virtually invented what is called "high comedy," or the comedy of manners. In English it finds its closest match in some of the comedies of the Restoration theatre which we shall discuss later although they overlap Molière's work in time. His plays stand back a little from their subject matter and view it with the mind more than with the emotions. They are intellectual comedies, scintillating with a brilliant Gallic wit to which translation finds it hard to do justice. He used many of the standard plots of the *commedia dell' arte*, raising them high above their old levels by the penetration of his intellect and his own richness of comic invention and characterization.

One of his most delightfully complicated plots is found in *L'École des Femmes* (*The School for Wives*). Arnolphe, a crabbed elderly man, is the guardian of young and pretty Agnes. It is his intention to marry her, and he keeps her closely guarded within his house. During Arnolphe's brief absence on a journey a young man named Horace sees Agnes, courts her, and wins her love. But Agnes cannot escape her guardian.

Arnolphe returns. Now it happens that Horace, who has not met the old man before and does not know his house, is the son of one of Arnolphe's close friends, who has given him a letter of introduction. Horace meets Arnolphe on the street, makes himself known, and before long has confided in Arnolphe, telling with glee of his love for the closely guarded girl and his intention to steal her out from under the nose of her guardian. Arnolphe is furious but is smart enough to keep silent. He says he will help Horace if given his complete confidence.

In the meantime, Arnolphe sharply scolds Agnes and instructs her to throw stones at any suitor who may appear beneath her window. Agnes obeys and throws a stone at Horace, but she has wrapped a lover's message around it first. Horace arranges an elopement.

Meeting Arnolphe, he unfolds his plan eagerly and confesses that he does not know where to take Agnes for safekeeping when he has smuggled her from her guardian's house. Arnolphe is enraged but conceals his wrath. He owns another house and he tells Horace that he may bring his sweetheart there and that he will look after her for him. Horace is delighted. He proceeds to steal Agnes away from one of Arnolphe's houses and take her straight to another, giving her over unwittingly to the keeping of the very man from whom he has stolen her.

The vexed Arnolphe prepares to marry her without further risk or delay. But Horace's father arrives. It is revealed that Horace and Agnes have been betrothed unknowingly since childhood. Arnolphe relinquishes his hopes and all ends happily.

One of Molière's finest plays, running close after the brilliant *Le Misanthrope* for top place, is *Tartuffe*. We can note in passing a familiar irony. *The Misanthrope*, which time has confirmed by general acceptance as his greatest play, was too subtle and advanced for its age and so was one of the least successful. *Tartuffe*, for differ-

Scene from Molière's *Le Misanthrope. French Cultural Services*

ent reasons, could not be played freely in Molière's lifetime. It is a scathing attack upon unscrupulous religious hypocrites, of whom there were then quite a number in Paris. Characters were drawn bluntly and in some instances recognizably from life. The play was filled with such explosive potentials that the king himself, even though he liked it, could not afford to permit its public perform- ance for fully five years after it had been played privately at court. Even the private showing had been toned down somewhat.

Tartuffe, a rascally hypocrite, has ingratiated himself with Orgon, a wealthy businessman. Orgon believes him to be a model of goodness and piety. By degrees Tartuffe utterly dominates his household, living richly on Orgon's money, running the affairs of everyone in the family, and even making advances toward Orgon's wife. Only the women of the household, the wife and the maid, know Tartuffe for the unscrupulous pretender that he is. Orgon is so completely under his spell that he thinks Tartuffe lives like a saint and an ascetic, all evidence to the contrary. When Orgon returns from a journey he inquires about his wife's health. The maid, Dorine, says, "She suffered from such nausea, she couldn't eat a thing all day." Orgon: "And how about Tartuffe?" Dorine: "He crammed down two partridges and a leg o' mutton for sup- per." Orgon: "Poor man!"

Orgon extravagantly praises Tartuffe to his brother, Cléante.

ORGON

> If you only knew him, dear brother! He is a man who—well— he is a man! His converse has weaned me away from all earthly love—and I could see my brother, children, wife, and mother all die before my eyes and never shed a tear. . . . The very first time I saw him, at church, I felt the presence of a godly man. He was kneeling—on both knees—and praying so fervently that he drew the eyes of the entire congregation . . . When I left the church, he ran before me to offer me the holy water at the door . . . And when I gave him money, he distributed a part of it to the poor . . . I asked him to come to my house—it was

an inspiration from heaven—and from that day on, everything has been well with us . . . he even watches over the virtue of my wife. He seems to be six times as jealous of her as I am . . . You have no idea how scrupulously pious he is. Why, the other day I heard him censure himself for having killed a flea.

CLÉANTE

Brother, you're mad.

ORGON

And you're an atheist!

Orgon becomes estranged from his family; attempts to betroth his daughter to Tartuffe; disinherits his son; makes Tartuffe his heir; deeds his house and property to him and reveals to him certain secret papers that would incriminate a friend politically. Finally he is persuaded to hide under a table while Tartuffe talks with his wife. When Orgon hears the hypocrite declare his love for his wife he is disillusioned at last. But Tartuffe holds such power, by now, that he threatens to turn Orgon out of his own house and even have him imprisoned. Only the intervention of the king, leading to Tartuffe's imprisonment for fraud, saves the day.

One of Molière's slighter but merriest comedies is *Le Médecin Malgré Lui* (*The Physician in Spite of Himself*). It is the story of how Sganarelle, a woodcutter, is palmed off unwillingly as a physician and made to treat a supposed case of dumbness in a young girl. He discovers that the young lady is actually shamming because her father stands in the way of her marriage with her sweetheart. Sganarelle manages to straighten matters out for the young couple and apparently effects a wonderful cure.

In a consultation with Géronte, the young lady's father, occurs another example of the *tirata della giostra*, or mock-scientific gibberish, we talked about in the *commedia dell' arte*.

SGANARELLE

I am of the opinion that this impediment arises from some certain peccant humors. Peccant . . . that is to say . . . a . . .

a . . . peccant. For, as the vapors exhumed are formed by a certain exhalation of circuitous . . . a . . . you understand Latin?

GÉRONTE

No.

SGANARELLE

What, you don't understand Latin?

GÉRONTE

No.

SGANARELLE

Carborias influxorium arci thrumbi thantrat. . . .

GÉRONTE

Ah, why didn't I study and learn things when I was young?

SGANARELLE

So these vapors, passing from the left to the right side, come into contact with the lungs . . . Latin *armyan* . . . Hebrew *polyglum* . . . and from there they proceed immediately to the . . . please follow me more attentively.

GÉRONTE

I am.

SGANARELLE

And have a certain malignity by a . . . pay attention to me now.

GÉRONTE

I am paying attention, Monsieur.

SGANARELLE

Which is always caused by a sharpness of these, and the concavity of the diaphragm . . . *nequaquam in uterque imibus.* And for these reasons your daughter is dumb.

GÉRONTE

No one could possibly argue better. But, Monsieur, what do you think should be done?

SGANARELLE

I suggest that she be put immediately to bed, and take plenty of bread and wine.

GÉRONTE

Why, if you please?

SGANARELLE

Because this wonderful combination often produces speech.

Sganarelle is rewarded with a heavy purse, although he protests, "I do not practice for money. I am not a mercenary physician." But actually he finds the whole business so profitable that he determines to give up woodcutting and continue to be a quack doctor.

Molière himself was a brilliant actor of comedy and always appeared in his own plays. In the three we have discussed he appeared respectively as Arnolphe, Orgon, and Sganarelle. His interpretations were celebrated. It is said that he acted with an incredible vigor, in constant, swift movement, with a riotous comic play of face and gesture. His rather awkwardly set head was poised between hunched shoulders, his hands were eloquent, his voice ringing every change of comic effect that could be squeezed from a scene.

He died in the best troupers' tradition. Although desperately ill in the last stages of tuberculosis, he insisted upon appearing for a performance of his play *Le Malade Imaginaire* (*The Imaginary Invalid*). He had written that sharp satire of self-indulgent sham sickness while suffering himself from actual mortal illness—the detachment of comic genius carried to its height! He barely got through the performance, collapsed immediately afterward, and was carried to his home where he died within an hour or so at the age of only fifty-one.

It was then a strict rule of the Church, even in a notoriously loose age, that an actor must renounce his profession before he could receive the last rites for the dying. Molière refused to renounce his proud calling until the very end. Then, it is said, scornful priests refused to come when called and before one could be brought Molière had died. For that reason this great, humane man, this glowing, scintillating genius who had showered a permanent glory upon the theatre and literature of his nation and the world, was buried without religious ceremony, possibly in unconsecrated ground, for the site of his grave never has been found.

Perhaps two elements helped to lift Molière's achievement so much above his contemporaries in the theatre. Like Shakespeare, he was a skillful actor, working in all aspects of theatre craft. Also, comedy was not bound by the confinements of form that limited Corneille and Racine. Molière's art, again like Shakespeare's, was free in form, untrammelled in scope, to grow and develop as genius guided it. In his own person, Molière is said to have been rather grave and melancholy, a paradox frequently seen in gifted comedians.

Another major career, in this case devoted only partly to the theatre, was that of François Marie Arouet, called Voltaire, who lived from 1694 to 1778.

This man's fame as a philosopher, political writer, and satirist has overshadowed his activity in the theatre. Yet Voltaire, by his amazing energy and force of personality, for a time was literally the dictator of the French stage. Although he spent years in exile because of his political writings, nonetheless in his old age in Paris he was the most famous living man of French letters. In his eighties he received triumphant acclamation at the opening of his last play, *Irène*. It was not very good and someone remarked caustically that it was not so remarkable that so old a man had written so bad a play as that he had written any play at all. The same could be said of the last plays of another aged man, George Bernard Shaw, many years later.

Voltaire's plays were not without merit, yet his general influence was of greater importance than his actual dramatic writings. Oddly enough the man who was more advanced in scientific and political thought than any other of his generation, and who was one of the major prophets and forerunners of the French Revolution, was the most hidebound adherent to the rigid restrictions of French classic drama. His own plays were confined by them and he enforced them sternly in his critical verdicts on the plays of others. He even undertook French adaptations of Shakespeare in which he tried vainly to break that giant to fit the narrow frame of French style, much like the mythical Procrustes who chopped off or stretched out all guests to fit his bed exactly.

Perhaps Voltaire's best single theatrical achievement was to banish from the stage the foppish noblemen who infested the very playing space itself during performances. This annoying custom was said to have started with the great success of Corneille's *Le Cid* when the lack of enough seats in the auditorium led to the placing of extra chairs around the sides and back of the stage for the accommodation of persons of rank—an improvised anticipation of theatre-in-the-round. These fops and dandies became extremely insolent at times and did not hesitate to walk about the stage or make sneering comments while the play was in progress. Voltaire used his influence and prestige to end the practice.

The last of the great men of this general era of the French theatre is Pierre Augustin Caron de Beaumarchais, who lived from 1732 to 1799. He was the son of a watchmaker and practiced the trade himself. He became watchmaker to the king and invented improvements in clock mechanism which brought him a good bit of wealth and prominence. He obtained a patent of nobility and took the titular name of Beaumarchais. During the American Revolution he befriended the cause of the hard-pressed colonists and spent much time, energy, and money in arranging shipments of arms and ammunition to the struggling Continental armies.

His political activities aided the advance of the onrushing French Revolution—an event of altogether a different nature from what might be more accurately called the American War for Independence. When the savage French Revolution occurred, Beaumarchais, like many other of its theoretical idealists, narrowly escaped the guillotine himself in the Reign of Terror. Finally, having seen the Revolution come and degenerate into a monstrous horror, worse than the evils it had been meant to cure, he died in 1799.

His two most famous plays, upon which his lasting fame rests, are *The Barber of Seville* and its sequel, *The Marriage of Figaro*. *The Barber* is a gentle and innocent enough comedy, rather more in the *commedia dell' arte* vein than otherwise. It follows a familiar pattern in which the wily and lighthearted barber, Figaro, enables Count Almaviva to woo and win Rosine from her closefisted and severe guardian who had intended to marry her himself and claim her fortune.

The significance of the play doesn't lie in the plot but in the subtle shadings of characterization, situation, and dialogue by which the noble or wealthy characters are shown to disadvantage in comparison with the simpler, but cleverer and more honest persons of lesser rank.

The real political thrust came in the sequel, *The Marriage of Figaro*, produced in 1784, a time when the cauldron of revolution had nearly come to boil. In this play Beaumarchais takes the selfsame Count Almaviva, who had been the romantic hero of the earlier play, and turns him into a contemptible figure. Figaro is about to be married to a maid in waiting of the countess. Almaviva, by unscrupulous tricks, attempts to prevent the marriage and secure the girl as his mistress. After a tough battle of wits the wily Figaro triumphs and the play ends happily. The revolutionary significance of the play again lay in its scathing exposure of the corruption of the aristocracy, contrasted to the supposed virtues of the lower classes, a romantic generalization that reality seldom supports with such simplicity. The play caused a riot when it was first performed and was banned by the tottering government of Louis XV.

Both plays, their once topical political implications forgotten, are well loved and widely performed today in the magnificent operatic versions which have been made of them: *The Barber of Seville* by Rossini and *The Marriage of Figaro* by Mozart.

After Beaumarchais comes a long period of relative decline in the French theatre, in the sense that no new, distinguished drama was created for some time. French acting and production techniques flourished, but it will not be until the latter half of the nineteenth century that we will turn again to a vital period of French drama.

Lope de Vega. *The Bettmann Archive*

Chapter 9

Spanish Cape and Sword

In 1588 a vast fleet of Spanish warships approached the English coast. It was the boastfully named Invincible Armada, sent by King Philip II of Spain to crush, once and for all, the English nation which was rapidly and seriously threatening the superiority of Spain on the oceans and in the new world of the Americas.

161

The English calmly, but surely a little tensely, awaited it on what Shakespeare called

> *This fortress built by Nature for herself*
>
> .   .   .   .   .
>
> *This precious stone set in the silver sea,*
> *Which serves it in the office of a wall,*
> *Or as a moat defensive to a house,*
> *Against the envy of less happier lands. . . .*

It is said that the British naval commander, Admiral Drake, played at bowls on the sandy beach, waiting for word that the hostile fleet had been sighted. Such was the attitude with which the English awaited the approach of the most formidable naval force which, at that time, had ever been launched.

The tide of history ran against the king of Spain. The fateful elements, followed up by English sea strength, doomed the splendid Armada. A great storm burst upon the Spanish fleet, sinking many ships, driving others aground, hurling them upon one another and tangling them. After the storm, the English fleet swept down upon the scattered remnants of the Armada and all but wiped it from the sea. So much for invincibility.

Only a straggling handful of vessels escaped the havoc. One of these, the *Juan,* managed to slip past the watchful English warships. It sailed north and circled entirely around the British Isles, managing at last to head safely toward its distant home port. On board the *Juan* an undisturbed young poet, whose loss would have altered the history of Spanish theatre, worked serenely at his long narrative poem, *The Beauty of Angelica.* The narrow escape of his vessel was not important enough to distract him from his writing.

The poet's name was Lope de Vega. When he reached home again he settled down to give his full attention to his chief occupation of playwriting. Having seen him safely through this perilous naval expedition we shall jump to very nearly the end of his long career, and go to the theatre to see one of his plays.

In spite of the terrible defeat of the Armada, Spain had only begun to slip from the summit of her glory. She did not yet realize that England was destined to complete the task of shattering the Spanish empire and curbing her might on the seas.

The theatre in Madrid to which we go is in the form of an enclosure called a *corral*. It is rather like the early inn-yard theatres of England. The apron of the stage projects out into the auditorium; boxes are ranged along the sides. There is a pit in the center for standing spectators.

As we enter we see cards announcing the performance. The advertisement is simple—consisting only of the words: "*Es de Lope* . . . It is Lope's," for Lope de Vega is now the most popular author of the Spanish theatre and people will flock to see anything of his.

The play, one of his later works, is called *El Mejor Alcalde el Rey* (*The King the Greatest Alcalde*, or *The King Is the Greatest Judge*). The Spanish office of *alcalde*, which might be bestowed upon more than one man in a village, was something of a combination of mayor and judge.

The story is simple. Sancho is a young peasant—a peasant insofar as he is humble and poor, although his family had been of a higher class at one time. He loves and is loved by Elvira, daughter of the wealthy farmer Nuño. He seeks Nuño's blessing on their marriage and receives it cordially. But Nuño urges the young man to obey the formal custom of the country and also seek the permission of Don Tello de Neira, young feudal lord of the region. Sancho does so reluctantly. Don Tello and his sister are cordial to the young petitioner. Tello gives his consent to the union and confers a rich gift of cattle upon Sancho, adding the further great honor of saying that he and his sister will attend the wedding themselves that very evening.

When Don Tello arrives for the wedding he sees Elvira for the first time and is so overcome by her beauty that he determines to have her for himself. Abruptly he orders the postponement of the wedding. He is obeyed to the dismay and disappointment of all. That same night Tello has Elvira abducted and carried to his castle.

Sancho and Nuño come to the castle to demand Elvira's release. Although his sister pleads with him to come to his senses, Don Tello angrily has the father and suitor whipped out of the house.

In desperation, Sancho goes to the court of the King, Alfonso VII, who is renowned for his justice and his interest in the troubles of the common people. He is so angered at the injustice done to Sancho that he writes an immediate order, in his own hand, for Elvira's release. Triumphantly armed with this, Sancho returns to Tello's castle.

The young lord, meanwhile, has been spurned by Elvira. When Sancho brings him the King's order he is filled with blind rage.

DON TELLO

> Out of my palace on the instant, and look you linger not within my lands, or I will have you done to death with clubs! What? To come to me! . . . . If I have taken your wife, you knave, know I am who I am, and I reign here and here I do my will, as the King does his in Castile. My forebears never owed this land to him. . . .

Tearing up the King's letter he again has Sancho and his faithful companion Pelayo thrown out of the castle.

Sancho returns to the King with an account of what has happened. The King is angered.

KING

> *Offended sore*
> *At the cruelty, mad violence and rage*
> *Of Tello, here we take upon ourselves*
> *In our own person to do chastisement.*

The King comes secretly to Nuño's home and together with all the wronged persons goes off to Tello's castle. In the meantime, Tello, enraged at Elvira's rebuffs, has taken her by force. The King presents himself to Tello, pretending to be a royal messenger. Tello is insolent and defiant.

KING

How does he differ from our lord the King
Who comes for him?

DON TELLO

Wide worlds to me . . . .
. . . . Unless the King
Against me come with iron bond and brand,
No power throughout the world shall stay my hand!

KING

I am the King, thou slave!

Tello is humbled. The King ignores his pleas for mercy, sentences him to death, ordering that he first must make the wronged Elvira his wife. Then, he proclaims, when Tello has been executed, Sancho shall marry the happily widowed Elvira and have half of Tello's lands for himself.

Such is the story of *The King the Greatest Alcalde,* one of the best of Lope's plays. It is also one of the most important because of the political significance of its plot.

As well as its central dramatic content it contains some of Lope's warmest humor and characterization of peasant life. The simple but loyal Pelayo, at the beginning of the play, tells Nuño and Sancho that he thinks Elvira is really in love with him.

PELAYO

As she was coming out of the house yesterday, Elvira called to me: "Hello, Pelayo! Your pigs are fat."

NUÑO

Well, what did you answer?

PELAYO

Amen, like the sacristan.

NUÑO

You did? But what do you make of this?

PELAYO

Don't you see she loves me, and this is the way she takes to let
me know that she wants to marry? . . . . Sancho, you know
what tricks these lovers feign. To have a rich and pretty woman
say to a poor fellow fresh as flowers of Spain, "Your pigs are fat"
—would she not mean, I pray, she'd like to marry somehow
with that man?

Lope Félix de Vega Carpio, known to literature simply as Lope
de Vega, was born in Madrid in 1562, just about two years before
the birth of Shakespeare. He was to live considerably longer than
the great Elizabethan, dying in 1635 at the age of seventy-three.
His parents were peasants from the *vega*, or valley, of Carriedo.
This humble origin contributed to his superb characterizations of
peasants and pictures of their life.

Lope himself lost no time in leaving his background behind him.
No ordinary peasant in spirit or intellect, he was to become a
symbol of the Golden Age of Spain, fabulous in his accomplishments and his complex personality. He had a touch of our old
acquaintance, *El Capitano*, the Spanish Captain, except that Lope
de Vega was no bluff, no caricature of his qualities, but truly the
master of "cape and sword," romantic lady-killer, soldier, playwright, and finally priest.

Lope entered the theatre early but long remained an adventurer
and soldier of fortune as well. He accompanied a successful military
expedition to the Azores. Much later, again interrupting his theatrical career, he sailed with the Armada, as we've seen.

In his prime he dominated Spanish letters and theatre as
supreme arbiter, much as Voltaire did in France. His prestige was
so great that his lowly origin was forgotten and he moved among
noblemen nearly as an equal. Though he minimized his plays by
comparison with his poems and novels (an evaluation history has

reversed) he regarded himself as having virtually founded and shaped the Spanish theatre and felt that he had shown the way to all who might come after him.

He added an ironic touch to his violent and colorful life by entering a monastery and finally becoming a priest of the Holy Inquisition. No doubt he was as vigorous in religion as he had been in his other activities, but it is certain that the step made little difference in his habits of life and action. His later years were saddened by the death of his son and other family griefs. In his struggles of the spirit he whipped himself sometimes until blood spattered the walls of his cell-like room. He embodied the temperamental extremes of the Spanish spirit.

As a playwright Lope had a splendid influence insofar as he wrote as he pleased. He recognized no rules and did not hesitate to develop or extend his plays as his purpose suited. He kept the Spanish stage as free from choking restrictions as the Elizabethan stage, which in many respects ran parallel. No foothold ever was gained in Lope's time for the narrow classicism which had taken hold of the French theatre and unquestionably limited it.

Statistically Lope de Vega is the most fascinating man in the history of the theatre. The simple facts of his career are staggering. Some say he wrote more words than any other man who ever lived. Be that as it may, he is credited with eighteen hundred full length secular plays and over four hundred religious one-act plays called *autos*. Naturally to write so much he had to work at extraordinary speed. Lope himself said, "more than a hundred of my comedies have taken only twenty-four hours to pass from my brain to the boards of the theatre." Some of his friends claimed to have seen him write five full length plays in two weeks. Some three or four hundred of these many plays survive today.

Lope's contemporary, the great novelist Cervantes, whose *Don Quixote* is the glory of Spanish literature, called him "the Monster of Nature," and wrote of him: "He filled the world with plays written with purity of style, the plot conducted with skill, in number so many that they exceed eighteen hundred sheets of paper [not to be confused with the eighteen hundred plays written by Lope; Cervantes wrote this in Lope's mid-career]; and what is most wonderful of all that can be said on the subject, every one of them have I seen acted or heard of their being so from those that have seen them; and though there have been many that have attempted the same career, all their works together would not equal in quantity what this single man has composed."

Aside from this huge accumulation of plays he wrote twenty-one volumes of assorted prose, poetry, novels, and essays, including such widely different works as *The Triumph of the Faith in Japan*, a critical treatise on *The New Art of Writing Plays*, and a partly autobiographical novel in dialogue, *Dorotea*.

His plays varied in subject matter and style. He was skilled in many ingenious forms of verse. He wrote tragedies, comedies, tragicomedies, and religious plays. Many were of the romantic, swashbuckling type which came to be known as *capa y espada*, or "cape and sword" plays. One of his dramas, undistinguished, has the ambitious title, *The Discovery of the New World by Christopher Columbus*.

Lope de Vega is a good example of the truth that bulk is not enough and that quantity cannot substitute for quality. Apparently Lope singlehandedly wrote more plays than the entire body of Elizabethan dramatists together. Yet when we compare Lope's eighteen hundred full length plays with Shakespeare's thirty-seven it is Lope who diminishes in the comparison. He wrote too much too hastily. He had not the profound human understanding, the compassion, the poetic genius, the universal qualities overcoming boundaries of language and time that are Shakespeare's. Lope de Vega never has commanded a significant place on the English-speaking professional stage, for all the statistical fascination of his unique and energetic career.

One of Lope's major works is *La Fuente Ovejuna* (*The Sheep Well*). Though it is the superior of the two, it has much in com-

mon with *The King the Greatest Alcalde*. We have talked earlier
about feudalism in the Middle Ages. It was impossible to picture
in a few words the real nature of feudal power and the kinds of
resistance to it that developed. These two plays of Lope's illuminate
the matter.

In Spain the king, supported by a strong Church, was seeking to
centralize power in the monarchy instead of allowing the country
to remain a collection of petty states ruled by tyrannical local lords.
Lope supported the monarchy and the Church. It was good politics
to write sympathetically of a revolt of the peasants so long as they
revolted against the feudal lords and appealed for ultimate justice
to the king. It is this circumstance that makes *La Fuente Ovejuna*
seem more revolutionary than it really is.

In *The King the Greatest Alcalde* Alfonso was represented as the
benevolent higher power to whom persons mistreated by feudal
lords could appeal for justice. Lope had the same intention in *La
Fuente Ovejuna*, but this time, though he achieved his purpose, he
worked so well that he touched greater depths than he supposed
and his play is not without applications to the political life of times
long past the feudal society of the Middle Ages. The spirit of Lope's
play could be applied against a king as well as against independent
lords.

The people of the village of Fuente Ovejuna are cruelly abused
by their lord. He caps a series of outrages by kidnapping and attempting to violate the daughter of an *alcalde* of the village, just as
she is about to wed her own betrothed—so far we see Lope almost
repeating himself.

The outraged people storm the lord's castle and kill him. This
is an appalling act for the downtrodden peasants of Spain to perform. The king's own judge arrives to investigate. Although he puts
many villagers to the torture and cross-examines all of them relentlessly, men, women, and children alike will give but one answer to
the question of who killed the lord: "Fuente Ovejuna," the village
itself as a single entity. The judge must either hang no one or wipe

out the entire town. The king is so impressed by the courage and heroism of the villagers, who firmly proclaim their loyalty to him, that he pardons them all and takes the village under his personal protection.

In the cross-examination scene the judge is out of sight but we hear him clearly. The villagers listen anxiously to each succeeding answer.

JUDGE

Old man, I seek only the truth. Speak!

FRONDOSO

An old man tortured?

LAURENCIA

What barbarity!

ESTEBAN

Ease me a little.

JUDGE

Ease him. Who killed Fernando?

ESTEBAN

Fuente Ovejuna.

LAURENCIA

Good, father! Glory and praise!

FRONDOSO

Praise God he had the strength.

JUDGE

Take that boy there. Speak, you pup, for you know! Who was it? He says nothing. Put on the pressure there.

BOY

Judge, Fuente Ovejuna.

The king and queen of the play are that Ferdinand and Isabella known to every American for their backing of Columbus.

Pedro Calderón de la Barca. *The Bettmann Archive*

Lope de Vega was seventy-three years old when he died. He had been the most popular playwright in Spain. With his death a change came and for a time his name was eclipsed by that of another man, Pedro Calderón.

The Spanish theatre in its Golden Age, as they themselves considered this to be, shared the exuberance of the climactic peak of the country's history. Spain had liberated herself from a long bondage to the Moors and turned back the tide of Mohammedanism which had threatened Europe from the north coast of Africa.

For a long time Spain controlled the New World, with the impetus of the advantage it had gained by sponsoring the Italian visionary, Columbus, when no one else would listen to him. Even after the setback of the loss of the Armada, Spanish explorations and settlements in America prospered. The story of the conquistadores is fascinatingly mixed, blending greatness, heroism, and piety with equal parts of greed, cruelty, and hypocrisy. It is against the general background of this age that we view the Spanish theatre and consider the one important man who came before Lope and others who were his contemporaries or lived on after him.

Lope de Rueda, who lived from 1510 to 1565, nearly a century before Lope de Vega, really founded the Spanish drama though it was the later Lope who established and molded it. Lope de Rueda was at first a gold-beater, one who beats and flattens the fine, thin sheets of the metal used in gold-leaf applications. He became an actor and then a playwright, working in homely Spanish terms but almost entirely on the model of the *commedia dell' arte* observed from the Italian companies that toured Spain. Most of his plays were short comedies called *pasos*, meaning incidents or skits. Later writers used this form for interludes between the acts of longer plays.

Miguel de Cervantes Saavedra, born in 1547, is the greatest literary genius of Spain though he is not of major importance in the drama. Cervantes was long a soldier, living a dangerous and painful life. He was captured by Algerian pirates and held prisoner for five years before gaining his release when his captors finally realized he was not a person for whom a great ransom could be obtained. His plays were not bad, they simply were not his natural medium and lacked genuine inspiration. Free of petty jealousy, he was quick to realize the superiority in drama of the younger Lope de Vega and, as we have seen, wrote lavish praise of his accomplishments. Yet Cervantes' novel, *Don Quixote*, riotously but compassionately laughing at human folly, creating figures as heartwarming as they are ludicrous, as admirable as they are befuddled, offers more to the reader than all the works of Lope put together.

Another of Spain's major playwrights was Gabriel Téllez, born in Madrid in 1571, who wrote under the name of Tirso de Molina. He was a priest and monk of the Order of Mercy (many of whose priests accompanied Cortés and other of the conquistadores) and wrote its official history. He was the author of more than four hundred plays, with what we recognize as typical Spanish proliferation; only some eighty survive, of which the best are fine indeed. His chief work, *El Burlador de Sevilla* (*The Libertine of Seville*), brings on stage for the first time that classical rake, Don Juan. The character of Don Juan Tenorio, based to some extent upon a real person, has persisted in literature and drama ever since. Mozart wrote an operatic masterpiece about him under the Italianate form of his name, *Don Giovanni*. Richard Strauss made him the theme of a tone poem. Byron wrote a lengthy satirical poem about him, and Molière, Rostand, and the modern George Bernard Shaw are among the many others who have written plays about him.

Another figure of this Golden Age was Mexican-born Juan Ruiz de Alarcón who was educated in Spain and spent most of his life there. He probed individual character much more deeply than Lope. His *La Verdad Sospechosa* (*The Suspicious Truth*) is considered one of the great plays of character in Spanish drama. Corneille made a French adaptation of it called *Le Menteur* (*The Liar*). Alarcón's other best-known play is *El Tejedor de Segovia* (*The Weaver of Segovia*).

The closest theatrical rival to Lope de Vega was Pedro Calderón de la Barca. He was the last of the important playwrights of the Spanish theatre's great age and it was appropriate that he should have been born at the turn of the new century, in 1600. Unlike Lope, who had sprung from peasant stock, Calderón was of the nobility. His talents showed themselves at an extraordinarily early age and his first play, *The Chariot of Heaven,* was written before he was fourteen. Through his abilities and social position he was made official playwright and master of revels in the court of Philip IV and also won knighthood.

Like Lope he was a soldier who saw action in several campaigns. Once more like Lope he became a priest, in 1651. Religion colored his plays more than Lope's, and some of them are shadowed by the harsh and confining attitudes of the Spanish Inquisition, then at its height of power.

Calderón is credited with one hundred and twenty-one plays. Compared to Lope's record this seems slight but the quality of his work was more even. Most of his plays were in the *capa y espada* manner, of which he was a master. Yet to some tastes his style is marred by the ornate manner which the Spanish call *conceptismo* because of which Calderón is less pleasing to read than Lope.

A good example of his work is *El Príncipe Constante* (*The Constant* [or perhaps the *Unyielding*] *Prince*), a military play about the Portuguese wars with the Moors.

Don Fernando, a Prince of Portugal, is the defender of the town of Ceuta on the Moroccan shore opposite Gibraltar. It had been captured from the Moors by his father. Don Fernando and his brother Don Enrique are attempting to make further conquests.

They are defeated by the Moorish forces and Don Fernando is taken prisoner. Although the Moors starve him and treat him with great cruelty he remains unyielding and refuses to give up Ceuta to them. Finally he dies. His ghost guides a revenge party against the Moors, who are then defeated. Throughout this general story runs a romantic subplot about a Moorish princess and a Moorish commander.

The tone of the play can be seen in a passage from one of Don Fernando's speeches of defiance to the hostile king—one hundred and sixty lines long in all:

> *Art thou a diamond? then by*
> *Thy own dust make deadliest poison,*
> *Weary thyself out in wrath: but I,*
> *Though I suffer greater torments,*
> *Though I greater rigours see,*
> *Though I weep still greater anguish,*
> *Though I go through more misery,*
> *Though I experience more misfortunes,*
> *Though I more hunger must endure,*
> *Though my poor body have no covering*
> *But these few rags; and this impure*
> *Dungeon be still my only dwelling,*
> *All for the faith my soul derides;*
> *For it is the sun that lights me,*
> *For it is the star that guides!*
> *It is the laurel that doth crown me;*
> *No triumph o'er the Church thou'lt have;*
> *O'er me, if you desire it, triumph:*
> *God will my cause defend and save,*
> *Since it is his for which I struggle.*

The last line alludes to his refusal to surrender Ceuta because it contains a church.

After he became a priest Calderón continued to write for the stage, including many *autos sacramentales* (literally "sacramental acts"), plays dealing with the mystery of the Mass. In spite of his piety and his appointment as honorary chaplain to King Philip IV, some of his *autos* were condemned for heretical tendencies by the rigid and suspicious Inquisition.

Even though, after Lope's death, Calderón eclipsed his fame on the Spanish stage for some years, he is inferior to Lope for the very smoothness and bombastic eloquence that made him so popular with his own audiences. He does not have the sometimes magnificent simplicity of Lope at his best. Calderón's manner was stiff, leaning more in the direction of the French *tragédie pathétique*.

When Calderón died at the age of eighty-one, apparently in self-chosen poverty, there was no one left to succeed him in his tradition. The glory of Spain was waning. The bullfight became the popular entertainment. Spain has not been felt as a major force in world drama for many years, though she has had some able modern playwrights, such as Jacinto Benavente, Martínez Sierra, and Garcia Lorca.

Hans Sachs. *German Information Center*

Chapter 10

The Theatre of Germany

THE SCENE is a meadow on the bank of the river Pegnitz, outside
the town of Nuremberg. The high spires and steep roofs of the
town can be seen in the background. Great preparations are under
way. Gaily colored tents have been erected, housing refreshments
of all kinds. Crowds of burghers with their wives, apprentices of
various trades, people young and old stand, or are seated, around

177

the tents. Barges come continually up the river and discharge passengers to swell the crowd. Processions from the trade guilds parade with flags and pennants, singing gay songs.

Dominating the scene is a large, flag-bedecked platform on which a few people have begun to gather. The occasion is to be the song contest of the Mastersingers of Nuremberg. At last the Mastersingers themselves march forward and the prominent members of the guild take their proper places on the great platform. From among them steps a kindly, bearded man. The assembled people catch sight of him, and before anything can be said, burst into a mightly acclamation and homage.

> *Hail Sachs! 'T is Sachs!*
> *See! Master Sachs!*
> *Sing all! Sing all! Sing all!*
> *'Awake! draws nigh the break of day:*
> *I hear upon the hawthorn spray*
> *A bonny little nightingale;*
> *His voice resounds o'er hill and dale.*
> *The night descends the western sky*
> *And from the east the morn draws nigh,*
> *With ardor red the flush of day*
> *Breaks through the cloud bank dull and grey.'*
> *Hail, Sachs! Hans Sachs!*
> *Hail, Nuremberg's darling Sachs!*

With this fanciful scene we have bridged the large gap of time which we must cover in this chapter. The figure of Hans Sachs, poet, playwright, musician, and cobbler of Nuremberg, first master of the German stage, is here re-created at the hands of Richard Wagner, the extraordinary music-dramatist who followed him by approximately four centuries. The spectacle we have described, with its homage to Sachs, is from the beginning of the last scene of Wagner's comic opera, *Die Meistersinger von Nürnberg* (*The Mastersingers of Nuremberg*).

In the thirteenth and fourteenth centuries, Germany was active in the production of religious plays, the miracles and mysteries. Another form of entertainment of a courtly kind was found in the *Minnesingers*. These were roving minstrels who flourished in Germany. They were chivalric knights and minnesong was a knight's tribute to his mistress. Their natural places were the feudal courts and they traveled from one to another with their songs and ballads.

Mastersinging, which developed in the fourteenth century, was the expression of the growing burgher, or citizen, class of the Renaissance in Germany. The burghers were the merchants, tradesmen, and skilled artisans who were becoming increasingly important in public life.

Versecraft, or mastersinging, became a recognized trade and guild. The founder of the guilds and schools of the mastersingers was Heinrich Frauenlob von Meissen, who died in 1318. The organizations grew and became influential.

It should be understood that to belong to the guild of mastersingers was by no means as simple as belonging to a glee club or choral society today. The mastersingers did not gather together just to sing songs. It was long before the age of the printed song, and songs were either circulated by tradition or not at all. The mastersingers wrote their own songs and the music to accompany them. The formal rank of "Master" was given only to those who excelled as poets and musicians. To qualify as a Master one had to compose new melodies as well as new words for old tunes.

The mastersingers believed that this study of song and verse would improve the standards of youth and be uplifting generally. Unfortunately, human nature being what it is, they entangled themselves with elaborate rules and restrictions which grew out of the pompous self-importance of many of the smug, prosperous burghers. Wagner satirized this aspect of the guilds in the comic figure of Beckmesser.

The various ranks within the guild ranged from Scholar to Master. There were two kinds of singing: *Freisingen*, or free-singing, in which anyone could take part, and *Hauptsingen*, or principal-singing, which was competitive among the members of the guild. Through victory in the competitions members could gain advancement in rank.

The song contests were scored by a marker. This was a judge who kept track, on a slate, of the various faults or violations of the rules committed by the singer. Such things as unsingable phrases, clipped words, bad rhymes, lines too long to be sung with a single breath, and so on, were considered faults. There were thirty-three classified faults in all. In the contests a singer was allowed a leeway of seven faults. If he exceeded this number he was held to be *versungen und verthan*, "outsung and outdone."

Youthful newcomers, aspiring to membership in the Mastersingers Guild, were coached and trained by the older members. Sometimes the guild would maintain a regular school.

Hans Sachs was born in Nuremberg in 1494, two years after the discovery of America. As a boy he was apprenticed to a shoemaker and in his youth traveled for a year around Germany, as a journeyman at his trade, in a tradition known as the *Wanderjahre*, literally the "wanderyear."

The little town of Nuremberg was a surprisingly active place, for one of the great trade routes of Europe led through it. Accordingly, with his scholarship and the many aspects of life which he had an opportunity to witness, Hans Sachs developed into a man of broad vision and great wisdom.

In time he became the head of the Nuremberg Guild of Mastersingers. He wrote more than four thousand songs (*Meisterlieder*) and two hundred short plays, together with a large number of pamphlets. Many of these works have survived. The lyrical song which Wagner includes in the people's homage to Sachs possibly is one of them. Wagner was well acquainted with Sachs's works and must have drawn considerable inspiration from them. Part of the sources for Wagner's *Tannhäuser*, *Tristan und Isolde*, and *Parsifal* are plays by Sachs dealing with these three stories.

Most of Sachs's plays are simple and hearty. The best remembered are his *Fastnachtspiele*, which were Shrovetide plays. They were performed on platform stages usually in the open air. Occasionally churches, taverns, or private houses might be the scene of a performance. They were played wholly by amateur actors and Sachs is said to have directed and acted in his own plays.

One of the best of them is his brief *Death in the Tree*, which is like an abbreviated morality play. The characters are a Hermit, a Bully, a Cynic, and a Coward.

A Hermit chances to discover a sack of gold coins in the hollow of a tree. Though he is tempted for a moment, he rejects the gold and hastens away, lest it should corrupt and further tempt him.

THE HERMIT

No, not one penny will I take,
But, as though Death himself, full-cry
Were after me, I'll turn and fly!

Along come the Bully, the Cynic, and the Coward, who are thieves. They sit down to discuss their plans. While they talk they see the Hermit in the distance. They seize him, thinking that he may have a hoard of gold sewed up in his cloak. They ask him why he had been slinking so stealthily through the woods. The Hermit replies:

I have seen Death within that tree!
It is from Death so fast I flee,
So let me now in safety fare,
And do you of the tree beware!

Though the Coward objects, the Bully and the Cynic slay the Hermit and then decide to investigate the tree about which he had made such a fuss. To their delight they find the bag of gold.

They agree to eat before dividing the spoils. Lots are drawn and the Coward departs with a little money to buy food and bring it back to them. In his absence the Bully and the Cynic decide to murder him for he had been terrified by the Hermit's dying curse and they fear he may betray them. Besides, there will be so much more gold for each of them.

When the Coward returns with the food and drink they fall upon him and kill him in spite of his pleas for mercy. Then they settle down to eat and soon are gripped by a terrible agony. The Coward had poisoned the food he brought, intending to secure the gold for himself. As he dies, the Cynic says:

> *The ancient sage in frock of grey*
> *Spake but the truth when he did say*
> *That dismal Death made here his den,*
> *For to destroy poor mortal men.*

The story may have been influenced by Geoffrey Chaucer's "The Pardoner's Tale," from *The Canterbury Tales*, which it resembles, though it was old when Chaucer used it. The theme and plot motif of three men all destroyed by mutual treachery and greed after finding a treasure are ancient and persistent. You will meet many modern variations on this tale. One of the best known and most popular is the film *The Treasure of the Sierra Madre*.

Another side of Sachs's talent is shown in the little farce called *The Wandering Scholar from Paradise*. A farmer's wife misunderstands the words of a wandering scholar, who had said he was from Paris, and believes him to be from Paradise. She begs him for news of her first husband who has been dead about a year. The scholar is bewildered at first but then sees an opportunity and seizes it. The good woman describes her former husband:

WIFE

When he went down to the grave he had on his blue hat and his shroud, none too good a one. In truth he had nothing else on him.

SCHOLAR

Why, good dame, I know him well. He goes about without hosen or shoon [stockings or shoes], and with no shirt, just as he was laid in the grave. When I saw him last, he wore an old faded blue hat, and was wrapped in a winding sheet. When the other souls feast and make merry, he hasn't a farthing to do the like, save what they give him of their charity. Upon my word he has a sorry time!

In great distress the woman gathers up a bundle of clothing and some money and gives them to the scholar, begging him to take them to her husband:

Say that next time I will do better still by him. He shall never lack for money. So go your road, and set him free from poverty. Ah me! He was a simple man, homely and honest. Of the two I always liked him the best!

When the scholar has gone the woman tells her second husband what she has done. He is furious at the hoax and mounts a horse to pursue the scholar. But the scholar comes by, disguised as an old man, just as the second husband is about to start. He says that he has seen the scholar leave the road and take to the swamps, and advises the husband to pursue him by foot. The husband sets out angrily, and as soon as he is gone, the scholar rides off on his horse.

When the disgruntled husband returns he is enraged to find his horse gone. His wife misunderstands the situation again and praises his generosity in giving the horse to the scholar to make the journey back to Paradise easier for him. The husband has just concluded that he can save face by accepting this version of the story when he discovers that his wife has told the whole village about the matter and finds they are a laughingstock.

In the comic opera of which Wagner has made Hans Sachs the leading figure, the composer mocks the stodginess of the Mastersingers and their narrow rules. It is the story of a young knight named Walter von Stolzing, who seeks admission to the Guild of Mastersingers. Pogner, one of the Masters, has offered the hand of his daughter Eva to the winner of the coming song contest. Walter loves Eva and his desire to belong to the Guild is in order that he may take part in the contest for her. He sings for the Guild members but commits so many faults that Sixtus Beckmesser, the crochety marker, covers the slate with marks. Walter is rejected by the Guild.

Hans Sachs, who is wiser and more tolerant in his judgments, has perceived a real talent in the young man, even though he does not conform to the rules of the Mastersingers. He takes him under his wing and coaches him in perfecting the beautiful song which Walter had prepared for the contest.

In the meantime, Sachs allows the rascally Beckmesser, who has determined to win Eva for himself, to take the words of Walter's song which he has found written on a piece of paper in Sachs's shop. At the contest, as Sachs had foreseen, Beckmesser makes a ludicrous failure of trying to sing Walter's poem to his own bad music which it does not fit. Sachs steps in quickly and persuades the Masters to let Walter sing the song as it should be sung. Walter does so, to his own lovely melody, and is rewarded by both Eva's hand and membership in the Guild.

In *Die Meistersinger* Wagner satirized in the persons of the Mastersingers the music critics of his own time who were hostile to the new musical forms which Wagner had created. There actually was a Sixtus Beckmesser living in Sachs's time, but instead of being the buffoon which Wagner chose to make him, he was second only to Sachs in his talents and prominence as a Mastersinger.

Sachs died in 1576. The true tradition of the Mastersingers had reached its peak in his time and then declined. The changing social order of Europe became too complex, too subject to bitter and prolonged warfare, for such a gentle communal art to flourish.

After the decline of mastersinging, the theatre of Germany was limited for a long time to comedy of the lowest order, a most degraded form of the *commedia dell' arte*. The popular clown of these entertainments was a buffoon character called *Hanswurst,* which would mean, in English, something like Henry Sausage. Side by side with the *Hanswurst* of the German theatre was a Dutch comedy character known as the Pickleherring. No entertainment without one or the other of these low comedians could hope for much success. They crept into the titles of serious plays. A tragedy would be billed with a long, descriptive title, winding up with the addition, "with Hanswurst." A typical comedy of the period was called *A Schoolmaster Murdered by a Pickleherring; or the Bacon Thieves Nicely Taken In*. There was little merit of any kind, and nothing lasting, about these farces.

The German stage was also constrained by the strong influence of French dramatic style. German dramatists were much in awe of French critics for a good many years until the dawn of a new life for the German theatre early in the eighteenth century.

The rescue was begun by a courageous, brilliant woman, Carolina Frederika Neuber, an actress and the manager of her own company. She did not hesitate to produce plays which ran against the critical vogue. Her whole career was a long battle with the die-hards of French-style *tragédie pathétique* on the one hand and a struggle against the vulgar tradition of Hanswurst on the other. One of the most important things that Carolina Neuber did was to encourage the theatrical ambitions of a young man named Lessing, with whom a new era in German drama arrived.

Gotthold Ephraim Lessing was born in 1729. He was attracted to the theatre and began writing plays quite early in his youth. He despised the formal French theatre and was quick to see the brilliance of Carolina Neuber and to make a professional ally of her. He shocked the German theatre with his first important play, *Miss Sara Sampson*. The play was not remarkable in itself, but it dared to place ordinary, middle-class people on the stage in situations as commonplace and realistic as everyday life. This was the greatest possible revolt against the stuffiness of the theatre of classical imitation, with its dull, high-flown verse and its divine or noble characters. A howl went up from critics but Lessing and those who were quick to follow him were not to be silenced. The theatre of classical revival in the French manner was on its way out.

Soon Lessing followed the serious *Miss Sara Sampson* with a charming and popular comedy, *Minna von Barnhelm*. Minna held the German stage for many years. In the meantime, Lessing was making another important contribution to the theatre. He had become the most distinguished critic and theorist of the drama since Aristotle, a truly impressive distinction.

In 1767 a progressive German National Theatre was founded in the city of Hamburg. Its life was brief, two years only, but its impact on the theatre of its time was immense. The best actors of Germany were associated with the enterprise and plays of many kinds were produced, even some in the old French manner.

Lessing was invited to become playwright to the theatre but declined, choosing instead the position of official critic. In this post he produced an important work: a volume of his collected reviews of the productions of the National Theatre throughout its two years of existence. It was more than passing journalism, for these reviews expressed the ideals of the National Theatre and Lessing's own ideas about the drama. The collection was published under the title of *Hamburgische Dramaturgie* (*Hamburg Dramaturgy*). It remains important to theatre scholars to this day. He laid down the basis of modern playwriting and, among other things, held up Shakespeare to German playwrights as a model of living drama.

In one of the essays of the *Hamburg Dramaturgy* the story is told of a man who had attended a five-act tragedy. At the end of the play the heroine died a tearful death. "But of what did she die?" asked the mystified man, unable to see any real logic in the ending of the play. "Indeed," was the reply, "she died of the Fifth Act!" For in truth, as Lessing said, the Fifth Act was a terrible disease that carried off many a character in his prime.

In the monarchist Germany of Lessing's time there occurred a wave of anti-Jewish feeling similar, though less frightful in its consequences, to the anti-Semitism of Nazi Germany under Hitler. Lessing was a man of the broadest liberal thought and had long been the intimate friend of a kindly Jewish thinker and philosopher, Moses Mendelssohn. Lessing's friendship for Mendelssohn was made the excuse for many bitter attacks upon him so that, late in his life, Lessing answered these prejudices with a noble play, *Nathan the Wise.*

The story of *Nathan the Wise* takes place in Jerusalem during the Third Crusade. Saladin, the great commander of the Saracens, has his palace there. Nathan, called the Wise, is a wealthy and benevolent Jew of Jerusalem.

A young Knight Templar, a German soldier captured by the Saracens, saves the life of Recha, Nathan's adopted daughter. When Nathan is told of this by Daya, Recha's Christian companion, he seeks out the Templar to thank him. The Templar, however, is so scornful of the Jew that he does not wish his thanks.

In the meantime, Saladin sends for Nathan, who comes to his presence.

SALADIN

You call yourself Nathan?

NATHAN

Yes.

SALADIN

Nathan the Wise?

NATHAN

No.

SALADIN

The people call you so?

NATHAN

Perhaps. But who knows what wisdom is?

SALADIN

A truce to modesty. Let's to the point.

NATHAN

You want my goods? My gold?

SALADIN

I want your wisdom. . . .

The Sultan then asks Nathan which is the true religion, that of Christian, Mohammedan, or Jew? Nathan answers in a parable.

A certain family possessed a ring which had been passed down from generation to generation to the favorite sons. The ring had the power of enabling its owner to win the love of God and man. But there came an owner who had three sons whom he loved equally. He sent the ring to a skillful goldsmith and had two identical copies made, so exact that no one could tell which of the three rings was the original. The man gave one of them to each of his sons.

After their father's death the three sons fell to quarreling and fighting among themselves as to which one possessed the only true ring. Finally they appealed to a wise judge who advised each one to believe his to be the genuine and original ring. Thus, each of them would win the love of God and man. So it should be, concludes Nathan, with the religions of Christian, Mohammedan, and Jew.

Saladin is greatly struck by Nathan's wisdom and is further pleased when Nathan voluntarily offers to place his gold at the Sultan's disposal.

But a complication arises. The young Templar has been told that Nathan's foster daughter was a Christian orphan whom Nathan has reared in the Jewish faith. The penalty for such an offense is death at the stake. Believing that he must save her soul, the Templar reports the matter to the Christian patriarch of Jerusalem.

Thus a threatening web is drawn around Nathan. It is broken when Nathan at last reveals a strange complication which had been brought about in the confusion of religious massacres years before, when many identities had been mixed up among refugee children. It is proved that Nathan's ward, Recha, is the sister of the Templar, who, himself, is actually the nephew of the Sultan Saladin. Thus it is found that the supposedly divided groups of Christians, Moslems, and Jews are closely bound by ties of blood and gratitude. The play ends on a note of broad racial and religious tolerance.

Lessing died in 1781, two years after writing *Nathan the Wise.* He never saw his play upon the stage, for the spirit of the time was hostile to it. It remained for the great poet-dramatist Goethe to produce it some years later at the court of Weimar. The play is less important as a drama than as a noble plea for tolerance. No better tribute could be paid to it than the fact that it was barred from the stage in Hitler's Germany.

Johann Christoph Friedrich von Schiller, a man with the soul of a poet, had the misfortune to be born into a military tradition. He was the son of a stiff, stern military surgeon of the small army of the Duchy of Württemberg. He toed the line with military strictness under his father's discipline and was then hustled into a military academy. After a miserable period of training he was permitted to change his course enough at least to follow in his father's way, and he too became a military surgeon attached to the army of Württemberg.

He was not happy in this career, for all his efforts to adapt himself to it. He had a habit of writing in his spare time and it soon developed that this interfered with his duties. He was ordered curtly to cease his literary activities. When he failed to obey this command he was arrested and put into military prison. Somehow he managed to escape, taking refuge for a long time in the home of a friend. Thus, as a fugitive, and already in ill health, he launched in earnest upon a brilliant career as a poet and dramatist.

Always liberal of mind, he was at first almost a revolutionary. His first play, *The Robbers,* is one of his most famous and was written during his army service. It is the story of a man cruelly wronged by his brother, who takes refuge with outlaws in the forests of Germany. In Robin Hood fashion the outlaws are pictured as more moral in their way of acquiring wealth than the prominent respectable citizens who are piling up great fortunes through unscrupulous practices.

Schiller had a remarkably productive career, especially considering that he struggled for many years in a losing fight against the tuberculosis that finally caused his death. One of his best-known nondramatic works is the *Ode to Joy* which Beethoven set to magnificent music in the last movement of his Ninth Symphony. The play *Don Carlos* dealt with a hero of Spanish history and was made into a fine opera by Verdi. German history provided the material of a trilogy, *Wallenstein. Mary Stuart* dramatizes the tragedy of Mary, Queen of Scots, who lost her head, literally, in a dramatic power struggle with Queen Elizabeth.

Schiller's last play was *William Tell,* the well-known story of the hero of Switzerland and his remarkable feats of archery. William Tell, a proud and independent man, refuses to bow to the publicly displayed cap of the tyrant, Gessler, who rules Switzerland with a harsh, merciless hand. Seized for his insolence, Tell is ordered by Gessler to demonstrate his famous skill by shooting an apple from the head of his own son. Tell does this successfully, but later he slays the tyrant as the people of Switzerland rise in revolt.

Schiller wove a romance into this story, characteristically, for he had the true spirit of the romantic theatre that was just beginning to flower throughout Europe. His *William Tell* has been made into an opera by the composer Rossini who, as we mentioned, also made an opera from Beaumarchais's *The Barber of Seville.*

Without question the outstanding genius of German letters is the poet, dramatist, novelist, philosopher, statesman, scientist, art critic, soldier, and financier, Johann Wolfgang von Goethe. We may well repeat Napoleon's eloquently simple tribute to him, "*Voilà un homme!*" translated slangily as, "What a man!"

Goethe was born at Frankfort-on-Main in 1749. He studied law at the University of Leipzig but a legal career was not sufficient to employ his great gifts.

The new, romantic period in the German theatre was launched by his early play, *Goetz von Berlichingen,* a strangely contradictory work. In its sweep and vitality it has an almost Shakespearean flavor. It is the story of a famous robber baron of the Middle Ages. He is presented as a hero struggling for freedom and independence against the power of the Holy Roman Empire. Thus, Goethe, in his romantic attempt to beat the drum for the independent spirit, worked himself into the curious position of writing a play which seemed to be a defense of the feudal system— which, of course, did have its due place in the evolution of our Western society.

His many plays and novels, as well as other assorted works of prose and poetry, would place him in the first rank of letters even if he had never written his immortal *Faust.*

In about 1775, Goethe was invited to the liberal court of the young Duke of Weimar. He accepted, and for the rest of his life held sway over an unequaled and versatile cultural center. At Weimar he wrote and supervised the production of plays. In addition, he received distinguished visitors from all over the world, took responsibility in many practical political and administrative problems, and conducted scientific research.

His masterpiece, *Faust,* was begun in his youth and occupied from time to time almost his entire mature life. It is the distillation, finally, of all his accumulated experience and wisdom; the finishing touches were put to the second part just before his death, in 1832, at the age of eighty-two. The scope of this work is so great that it is quite impossible to examine it closely here.

Goethe in his study dictating to his scribe (from a painting by J. J. Schneller, 1831). *The Bettmann Archive*

The philosopher-poet refined and extended the already notable conception of Christopher Marlowe until, in its second and less theatrical part, it seems to include the world.

Part one is a straightforward story and a practical play for the stage. It begins with a prologue in Heaven, which is a paraphrase of the first part of the Book of Job, that wonderful biblical drama.

SAYS GOD TO SATAN, IN JOB,

> Hast thou considered my servant Job? for there is none like him in the earth, a perfect and upright man, one that feareth God, and turneth away from evil.

In *Faust:*

THE LORD

Know'st Faust?

MEPHISTOPHELES

The Doctor Faust?

THE LORD

My servant, he!

The same bargain is struck in both cases. The Lord, at Satan's challenge, gives him permission to make a test of the man. In *Faust* the interview ends with the somewhat sophisticated Mephistopheles, alone upon the stage, remarking:

> *I like, at times, to hear the Ancient's word,*
> *And have a care to be most civil:*
> *It's really kind of such a noble Lord*
> *So humanly to gossip with the Devil!*

When Mephistopheles makes his bargain with the aged Faust it is not for the simple twenty-four years of Marlowe's play. Mephistopheles is to serve Faust until:.

FAUST

> *When thus I hail the Moment flying:*
> *"Ah, still delay—thou art so fair!"*
> *Then bind me in thy bonds undying,*
> *My final ruin then declare!*

In short, when he no longer looks more eagerly for that which is yet to be than for that which is, then Satan may collect the debt.

Faust becomes young again. With Mephistopheles he travels about, enjoying every kind of earthly pleasure. He has a love affair with a simple girl, Margaret (Gretchen), whom he betrays, and for whose downfall and death he is responsible. Mephistopheles expects to capture the soul of Margaret, too, but the purity of her love for Faust, so cruelly betrayed by him, causes her to be saved. As the first part ends, Faust has not yet found that wonderful moment of existence to which he could really wish to cling.

The second part of *Faust* is a long, profound philosophical poem, not a viable stage play, even though it is cast into five acts. In it, Faust has moved on from a superficial sensual plane. He tastes every form of intellectual and worldly power but still fails to find the moment for which he seeks so eagerly. Mephistopheles has almost despaired of his bargain. At last, having lived through to a second old age—he is just turning one hundred—the weary, world-sated Faust takes an interest in a vast project to reclaim land from the sea; an undertaking which will be of no profit to him, personally, but which will bring great good to countless numbers of people. Here, to his astonishment, in this disinterested and socially constructive occupation, Faust finds truly profound happiness, is willing to arrest the moment—and so dies. So noble has been his new self-realization through selflessness that Mephistopheles is deprived of the soul of Faust, who, like the unfortunate Margaret of the first part, is also redeemed. Margaret's forgiveness is an additional contribution to his salvation and she is among the blessed spirits who escort his soul into Heaven. Mephistopheles is frustrated and further tormented by the sight of the Heavenly Beings in bliss from which he is excluded by his own will.

As Angels are bearing the soul of Faust, they sing:

> *The noble Spirit now is free,*
> *And saved from evil scheming:*
> *Who'er aspires unweariedly*
> *Is not beyond redeeming.*
> *And if he feels the grace of Love*
> *That from On High is given,*
> *The Blessed Hosts, that wait above,*
> *Shall welcome him to Heaven!*

Thus Goethe has reached beyond the tragedy of Marlowe's

Faustus, who wasted all he had bought so dearly, and shows that even the presumably damned soul may win redemption by growing into interests and desires beyond its own gratification. The aged Goethe had lived through to a wisdom not possessed by the rash, youthful Marlowe who, ironically, as an unbeliever, could yet chart only a man's damnation and not find again the possibility of his salvation.

Goethe's *Faust* is a monument of German literature. On rare occasions both parts have been performed, after much cutting and careful adaptation to solve the production problems of part two. There are a number of notable Faust operas, all largely derived dramatically from Goethe's part one. Gounod's *Faust* is one of the favorites on the operatic stage. Others include the colorful *Mefistofele* of Boito, and *The Damnation of Faust* by Berlioz.

A lamentably early death cut off a talent of great promise in Georg Büchner, who was born in 1813 and died at the age of twenty-four. Because he took part in the revolutionary movements that were beginning to trouble Germany he had to flee from his birthplace, the Duchy of Hesse-Darmstadt. At twenty-two he received a degree and a post as lecturer at the University of Zurich, in Switzerland.

Two years before his death he wrote the play by which he is best remembered, and which shows that he may have had some second thoughts about revolutions, even when the provocations to them are great. The play was *Danton's Tod*, or *Danton's Death*. It is an impressive portrait of a liberal idealist horrified by the violence and bloodshed of the French Revolution which he had labored to bring about. Danton, not extreme enough to satisfy the aroused people or the ruthlessly fanatical revolutionary, Robespierre, is swept to his own death. It was a fate the grim Robespierre himself met not long after.

In general composers do not come within the frame of this

book, but we should give a little more attention to Richard
Wagner, whose *Die Meistersinger* we have discussed at some
length already. He brought about great changes in the form of
opera, calling his creations music-dramas. One of them, *Parsifal*
(a variation of the Percival of the King Arthur stories), he called
a "Consecrational Festival Play."

In moving beyond the traditional forms of opera Wagner
brought a new vigor to the musical stage. He was at the center
of fierce musical controversy and tempestuous human encounters
throughout his life. In his works he abandoned the pattern of
recitative, interrupted every so often for a grand display aria, duet,
or quartet. Wagner's music-dramas are tightly organized and move
with music and text so woven together in the conception of the
whole fabric that many people thought his operas were without
melody. That was a mistake, for they contain some of the noblest,
most beautiful music ever written, offering all the display of the
human voice that the most accomplished singer could desire—
perhaps more, for he is relentlessly demanding upon his singers,
giving them long roles, with great vocal range, and compelling
them to sing against the competition of massive orchestral
volume.

His earliest audiences were sometimes shocked, and rebelled
against his unfamiliar style. Mark Twain satirized Wagnerian
music in his *A Tramp Abroad,* and it may have been he who remarked, "Wagner's music is not as bad as it sounds." Some critics
denounced him and Wagner often answered back. Yet one perceptive music critic in England, who was to become a great playwright later in his career, acclaimed Wagner's genius—George
Bernard Shaw, in a little book called *The Perfect Wagnerite.* For
many years, now, Wagner has been among the most popular of
all composers to world-wide opera audiences.

He was born at Leipzig in 1813, which was also the year of the
birth of the short-lived Georg Büchner. Wagner was the son of
a minor police official. He studied at the University of Leipzig
and began his musical career as a conductor.

Again like Büchner, he embroiled himself for a while in revolutionary politics before settling for revolutionary music. Because of some participation in the uprisings of 1848 in Germany he had to spend many years in exile. He lived in Italy and France until finally, his fame as a composer having spread, he was invited to the town of Bayreuth and given a generous pension by King Ludwig of Bavaria. At Bayreuth Wagner established a superb musical center, comparable to Goethe's cultural center at Weimar.

Unlike most operatic composers, Wagner was a poet of ability and wrote the librettos himself for all his major works. He also wrote extensively on the theories of drama, music, and stagecraft. At Bayreuth he built the first modern theatre structure, the *Festspielhaus*, which has a sloping, fan-shaped auditorium, with no balcony, in which the stage is visible from all seats—thus the first "modern" theatre is surprisingly classical.

It is a rich musical-theatrical experience to see Wagner's music-dramas as well as hear them. Simply to listen to recordings is to miss more of their full dimension than would be the case with many other operas.

His most extraordinary achievement is the vast tetralogy, *Der Ring der Nibelungen* (*The Ring of the Nibelungs*). It took him twenty years to complete, yet its unity and consistency of tone and style in no way show the variations or changes that might be expected over so long a span.

In the first of the four operas, the relatively brief *Das Rheingold* (*The Rhinegold*), the secret treasure of the Rhine Maidens is stolen by the Nibelung (dwarf), Alberich, and made into a wondrous magical ring. Wotan, chief of the gods, calling upon the aid of Loki, the mischievous fire spirit, steals the ring from the Nibelung. The opera is filled with the thunderous tread of giants, the magic feats of dwarves and gods, and culminates in the building of the great palace of the gods, Valhalla.

Die Walküre (*The Valkyrie*) pursues the story of the slow-moving ruin which the stolen ring brings upon the gods. It contains the desperate lovers, Siegmund and Sieglinde, who are the

Richard Wagner. *The Metropolitan Museum of Art, Gift of Frederick Loeser, 1889*

parents of the hero Siegfried; the sinister hunter, Hunding, who is their undoing, and the defiant Valkyrie, Brünnhilde, who dares to disobey the commands of her father, Wotan. For this she is left sleeping, on a mountain top, bereft of her godhood but surrounded by a protective ring of magic fire.

In *Siegfried*, that fearless youth penetrates the fire and awakens Brünnhilde from her sleep, making her his wife. The young hero has first mended his father's broken sword, slain the dragon Fafner, and had encounters with a mysterious Wanderer, who is Wotan in disguise.

The cycle comes to a majestic close in *Die Götterdämmerung* (*The Twilight of the Gods*). Here the vengeance of the ring is complete. Hagen, half dwarf half man, the crafty son of Alberich, slays Siegfried by a treacherous spear-thrust in the back. Brünnhilde mounts her horse and rides into the flames of her husband's funeral pyre. The Rhine waters rise, Hagen is drowned, and the Rhine Maidens regain the ring which is rightfully theirs. In the meantime, Wotan, who has long realized that such an end must come, has had faggots piled about Valhalla. Ignited by the sparks from Siegfried's funeral pyre, the great palace burns, and the gods with it, perishing through their own errors, leaving man responsible for himself and his world.

A major aspect of Wagner's music-dramas was his invention and extreme development of the leitmotif—a musical figure or theme, specifically identified with a particular character, object, or idea. These leitmotifs always accompany direct appearances of their subjects and are also introduced indirectly as reminders, references, or associations. This device enhances both the meaning of the drama and the intricacy of the music; familiarity with them— easily acquired—makes for the richest understanding and appreciation of Wagner's music.

His other masterworks include *The Flying Dutchman, Tannhäuser, Lohengrin*, and the passionate drama of love and death, *Tristan and Isolde*.

A scene from a Bayreuth performance of Wagner's *Tristan und Isolde*. *German Information Center*

After Wagner's death, Cosima, his widow, began to hold annual Wagner Festivals at Bayreuth, interrupted only by wars. These attract music lovers from all over the world and are a pilgrimage to some as to a shrine. The composer's descendants still continue to constitute a priesthood of his cult. His son, Siegfried, took over the direction of Bayreuth after Cosima's death. In turn, his sons, the composer's grandsons, Wieland and Wolfgang Wagner, still share the direction of the festivals.

Eighteenth-century stage. *The Bettmann Archive*

Chapter 11

England's Merry Comedies

A KING of England lost his head; lost it grimly by the executioner's axe. Such a thing happened only once in English history and it befell the strong-willed King Charles I, who was not wise as a ruler but was brave as a man. He died well, in regal dignity, so that as Shakespeare said in *Macbeth*,

> Nothing in his life
> Became him like the leaving it.

This was that King Charles whose head crept so persistently into all the writings of the lovable but slightly addled Mr. Dick, who will never be forgotten by anyone who reads *David Copperfield*.

202

From 1642 to 1660 the theatres of England were dark, closed by the stern censorship of the Puritans who were also the force behind the political revolution. Oliver Cromwell ruled England, under the title of Lord Protector, for some five years. Like his role as field general that won him the nickname "Ironsides," this power was not wholly of his choosing, but he found himself swept into it by the course of events and his undoubted abilities. When he died the reaction was swift and the Puritan regime outlasted him by very little.

Another Stuart, the son of the beheaded king, ascended the throne as King Charles II. The era of this event is known as the Restoration. Back from France, where they had shared the exile of the man who was now king, came the whole courtly troupe of cavaliers—fops, dandies, sports, men of fashion and high birth, wits and rakes—and their womenkind, too.

Charles II was no tyrant, as his father had been charged with being, nor had he the special strength and integrity of the late king. He was a man too preoccupied with his own pleasures, including those of gay and witty company, to practice statecraft very diligently. He had numerous children by a host of mistresses, but had no legitimate heir, so on his death he was succeeded by his brother James II, who was forced from the throne three years later in another revolution in 1688. That was the end of the royal line of Stuart; the throne was next held by William of Orange and his wife, Mary, who was the daughter of James II, thus preserving some sense of succession.

The era of the Restoration was eventful in more ways than the political. Like all the great cities of the time, London was struck by devastating plagues periodically. One of these was ended, in 1666, by the great fire which left most of Tudor London in ashes. The plagues, the fire, the political upheavals, the manners and morals of the time are captured in many writings, especially such intimate ones as the famous diaries of Samuel Pepys and John Evelyn.

There is no denying that the Restoration era was an age of frivolity and moral laxness in courtly circles. The court set represented one extreme—the Puritans represented another. Society at its best has always managed to find a reasonable mean between such extremes. Even in Restoration England, at various levels of society, there were decent, busy people who were neither dissolute nor Puritanical.

The cavaliers, with all their faults, were a scintillatingly witty lot, amusing to contemplate from a distance. Moreover, as we shall see, they left us a notable literary-dramatic heritage in the comedy of manners that was a by-product of the way they lived.

When English theatres were reopened in 1660 the staple plays still were those of the Elizabethans: Shakespeare, Jonson, and the lesser lights But several major changes had taken place in taste. First of all, the newly revived theatre was for some time almost wholly the entertainment of the cavaliers and the fringes of their set. It did not have the broad audience of Elizabethan times; its standards were determined by a smaller and more uniform group. Cavalier taste had been influenced strongly by the time of exile in France. They brought back with them a taste for the French imitation of classicism, a desire for perfection of an accepted form more than for vitality of human representation. They did not wholly reject their Elizabethan heritage, but they had decided that those plays were crude and needed to be revised and adapted to the newer vogue. The principal effect of this was felt in tragedy.

There was a change in staging also, of which the beginnings had been seen already, before the Puritan revolution, in the courtly masques, poetically formalized and elaborate in pageantry, which Ben Jonson and others had written, and for which Inigo Jones made lavish scenic designs and devices. The great poet John Milton wrote a masque called *Comus.* The Restoration theatre began to use extensive scenery and strove more and more to please and astonish the eye.

The art of acting was adapted to the new styles in drama, especially in the mannered comedies, but the biggest change in this respect was the admission of women as players on the English stage for the first time.

The early Restoration comic dramatists pursued a cult of the amateur. The playwrights would not dream of carrying their work so far as to be considered professional. We see many instances in which a courtly playwright would win increased esteem by his work, perhaps receive some benefit of place or appointment, and promptly cease writing altogether. It was a point of honor and status to preserve one's amateur standing. To set about writing plays in earnest, as if one wanted to earn money, or as if there were any possible fame more desirable than being a gentleman of the court, just was not done. These writers were uniquely contemptuous of literary reputation.

Their plays were written to entertain a particular class, by men who were themselves of that class, and the whole point of the game, with reasonable allowance for theatrical exaggeration, was to show the audience a mirror in which it would recognize itself precisely. Thus for all the stylization, Restoration comedy does reflect the manners and morals of the period accurately, as the other writings of the period, including letters and diaries, show clearly. Perhaps it was some note of grace that the courtly set laughed at themselves. But there was no pretense of reform.

The earliest of these fashionable amateurs was Sir George Etherege, known to his friends as "Easy Etherege." He started the vogue in 1664 with *The Comical Revenge; or Love in a Tub*, a play which combined prose comedy with a heavier dramatic part in heroic rhyme. This was followed soon by *She Would If She Could*, which was altogether comedy. His next work, *The Man of Mode*, is considered the best of his plays, although it has no plot and is instead a study of character. Like many of these amateur plays, it drew caricatures which the audience could recognize readily. The title identifies the play as a satire on man-

ners and the character of Sir Fopling Flutter is supposed to be
a self-portrait of Etherege. Like those who followed him, he shows
an unmistakable influence of Molière, without the great French-
man's genius or professionalism. Characteristically, Etherege
ceased writing after *The Man of Mode* to devote himself wholly
to fashionable living.

William Wycherley, who was nicknamed "Manly" Wycherley,
was a comic dramatist of much greater talent though none the
less a devoted amateur. His first play to be produced was *Love in
a Wood*, acted in 1671. He claimed to have written it while a
very young man, before even his Oxford days—a boast which later
opinion does not credit because of the worldliness and skill of
certain of its scenes. It won for him one of the typical rewards for
which the Restoration playwrights most hoped—the favor of the
Duchess of Richmond, one of the mistresses of King Charles II.

His other plays are *The Gentleman Dancing-Master, The Country Wife*, and *The Plain Dealer*. *The Country Wife*, one of the
most ribald of his comedies and still much played, is about the
harassments of Pinchwife, who tries to keep his young bride, Mrs.
Margery Pinchwife, fresh from the country, from being corrupted
by the fast set of the town.

Wycherley's early education was in France, where he moved
in the smart *salons* which Molière had satirized sharply in *Les
Précieuses Ridicules* (*The Ridiculous Poseurs*). Poor Wycherley,
whose plays were so liked, had the worst of luck in playing the
fashionable game. He met and married secretly a wealthy, widowed noblewoman of the court—a match he expected to bring
him all he desired in means and position. But when the news was
out it angered the king. Wycherley lost all place at court, became
involved in lawsuits and debts when his wife died, was imprisoned
for a time, and suffered a general blight of expectations.

William Congreve is the finest of the Restoration comic playwrights and is in the latest group of those who properly bear that
name. He was twenty-three, in 1693, when his first play, *The Old*

Bachelor, was performed. He wrote three more: *The Double Dealer, Love for Love*, and *The Way of the World*. The latter is his best work. A perfect mirror of its time and class, it carries the comedy of manners to a polished perfection unmatched until the work of Sheridan, seventy-five years later.

Sir John Vanbrugh, who was also a distinguished architect, wrote several popular plays, including *The Provok'd Wife* and *The Provok'd Husband*. George Farquhar turned from being an army officer to being an actor, and then to the writing of plays. In a fairly large output that yielded him little financial reward, the best are his two last plays, both still stageworthy, *The Recruiting Officer* and *The Beaux' Stratagem*.

Thus far we have emphasized comedy. Two figures are important as reflecting the taste in tragedy in the Restoration drama. We have noted already that a French influence had made itself felt in English taste, and that though the Elizabethan plays were still popular, it became the fashion to revise and "improve" them.

The most influential English literary figure of the Restoration era—a professional—was John Dryden. The theatre was only one of his interests, though he wrote both comedies and tragedies. He was the foremost critic, and as such a setter of standards. He was both poet laureate and court historiographer; biographies and histories and a great translation of Plutarch were among his works.

Marriage à la Mode is the foremost of his comedies. Much the best of his tragedies is *All for Love; or the World Well Lost*, an adaptation to the new taste of Shakespeare's *Antony and Cleopatra*. For a long time it supplanted its great original on the English stage. It simplifies the dramatic line and concentrates upon the latter part of the story. On its own premises it is a play of some merit.

Dryden's other tragedies tended toward grossly exaggerated absurdities in the heroic vein. Samuel Johnson, who was as much the literary dictator of the eighteenth century as Dryden was of the seventeenth, speaks, in his *Lives of the Poets*, of Dryden's "seeming determination to glut the public with dramatic wonders, to exhibit in its highest elevation a theatrical meteor of incredible love and impossible valour, and to leave no room for a wilder flight to the extravagance of posterity."

With his great literary gifts, Dryden possessed also the grace of self-criticism. He knew that Shakespeare's greatness lay beyond the taste of this latter time and said of him, in his *Essay of Dramatic Poesy*: "He was the man who of all modern, and perhaps ancient, poets had the largest and most comprehensive soul. . . . He was naturally learn'd; he needed not the spectacles of books to read Nature; he looked inwards, and found her there."

In his poetic *Epistles*, in the one addressed to the playwright Congreve, he says of the Elizabethans:

Theirs was the giant race before the flood.

                    .   .   .   .   .

Our builders were with want of genius curst;
The second temple was not like the first.

Elsewhere he spoke savagely of the general tone of the era of which he himself was so prominent a part:

O gracious God! how far have we
Profan'd thy heav'nly gift of poesy!
Made prostitute and profligate the Muse,
Debas'd to each obscene and impious use,
Whose harmony was first ordain'd above
For tongues of angels, and for hymns of love!
O wretched we! why were we hurried down
    This lubric and adult'rous age,
    (Nay, added fat pollutions of our own)
    T' increase the steaming ordures of the stage.

It is surprising to find such sharp words about the worst vices of the Restoration stage from a man who was one of its ornaments, and no Puritan. Yet the Puritan spirit itself was not voiceless. In 1698, Jeremy Collier, a high churchman and not a Puritan in the

sectarian sense of the word, published a bitter pamphlet called
*A Short View of the Immorality and Profaneness of the English
Stage,* with Congreve and Vanbrugh singled out among many as
particular targets. Dryden's earlier testimony is further evidence
that there was a case to be made. Collier's attack may have had
some small restraining influence, but there was no question at this
time of the suppression of the theatre. Forceful suppression is an
unfortunate and seldom successful way of dealing with the excesses
of the arts. A high standard of professional and public taste is their
chief safeguard, but there are times—and we live in one of them
at present—where these are not easy to maintain.

The other chief writer of tragedies in the late Restoration
theatre was Thomas Otway, who turned to writing after an unsuccessful attempt at acting. He wrote both comedies and tragedies, but his finest achievement is in three tragedies of substance
and dramatic power: *Don Carlos* (a subject Schiller later used in
the German theatre), *The Orphan,* and *Venice Preserved.*

Another much admired tragedy was *Cato* by Joseph Addison.
It seems dry and sterile to us today, unlike the famous Sir Roger
de Coverley papers, the delightful essays its author wrote with
Sir Richard Steele, for their periodical, *The Spectator.*

The appearance of women on the English stage was one of
the notable aspects of the era. We do not meet them solely as
actresses. Mrs. Aphra Behn, who served Charles II as a spy in
Antwerp during wars in Holland, is one of the earliest women to
gain prominence in English letters. She wrote poems, novels, and
a considerable number of plays, and also had much influence as
a personality in theatre circles.

The novelty of actresses, instead of boys, playing women's parts
was a gain for the stage—if not always for public morals. Among
numerous actresses, the most celebrated—or notorious, as Jeremy
Collier would have put it—was "pretty, witty Nell" Gwyn. Her
career embodied both the hardship and worldly glamor of the age.

She was born of the lowest origins in the alleys of London, possibly within an echo of the Drury Lane Theatre of which she became a bright star. She was an orange seller in that famous theatre before she trod its stage in triumph. She moved through her time like a glittering comet, beloved of audiences, and a favorite mistress of the king, by whom she bore two sons, one of whom was made Duke of St. Albans. She could not read, but was taught her lines. Charles, who died before her, is said to have charged his brother James, "Don't let poor Nelly starve." Nell died of a stroke at the age of thirty-seven.

What we have discussed thus far as the Restoration theatre progressed into another brilliant period of English letters in which professionals supplanted courtly amateurs again. The eighteenth century was the time when Samuel Johnson held sway as what Tobias Smollett, the novelist, called the "great Cham [Khan] of literature." It was full of shining figures, including Alexander Pope, James Boswell the biographer and diarist, and those early masters who shaped the English novel, Henry Fielding, Daniel Defoe, Tobias Smollett, and other gifted writers whom we shall consider. This period is sometimes called the Augustan Age in allusion to the apparent peak of Roman glory under the emperor Augustus, appropriate both to the heights of excellence reached and the strong revival of classical models.

Kindly, soft-spoken Oliver Goldsmith, like several great later dramatists (and also like his contemporary Jonathan Swift, famed for *Gulliver's Travels*) was born in Dublin (in 1728) and educated at its Trinity College. When he came to England he was hired by a bookseller and earned his living as a literary hack. He happened to meet Dr. Johnson and win his good will, and by this acquaintance moved in the highest literary circles of London. Soon he earned his right to remain in such company by his fine novels, plays, essays, and poetry. His long poem, *The Deserted Village*, and his novel, *The Vicar of Wakefield*, would have made his reputation lasting even if he had not written two fine comedies.

The first of these, *The Goodnatured Man*, was not received as well as it deserved, which hurt the always sensitive Goldsmith greatly. He was compensated by the immense success of *She Stoops to Conquer* which remains a lively, lasting staple of the English comic stage.

She Stoops to Conquer; or the Mistakes of a Night is a gentle comedy, far different in tone from those of the Restoration stage. It has been said aptly that the Restoration playwrights were strong in wit but deficient in humor. With Goldsmith, true humor, warmly blended with sentiment, came back to the stage.

A young man named Marlow, who is on his way with some reluctance to lay formal suit to the hand of Miss Hardcastle—it is an arranged match, the two have never met—is tricked into believing that her father's house is an inn. He proceeds to treat the dignified Mr. Hardcastle as though he were merely an impudent and eccentric landlord, orders the servants about, and generally takes confident possession of the establishment. The confusion and consternation resulting from this mistake are vast. Hardcastle nearly has a stroke from rage and indignation. On the other hand, Miss Hardcastle, the object of Marlow's suit, has been wary of him because of a reputation he has had for excessive bashfulness and modesty. Perceiving his error, she takes advantage of the situation by pretending first to be a barmaid, then a poor relation of the family. In this humble guise she truly conquers Marlow. When the mistakes of the night have been unraveled and old Hardcastle's indignation appeased by understanding, all ends happily and a planned match turns out to be true love.

In the course of the first meeting between Hardcastle and Marlow, the young man and his traveling companion, Hastings, have persistently treated Hardcastle as an innkeeper, otherwise ignoring him. "Such a brazen dog sure never my eyes beheld!" Hardcastle says of Marlow, aside. The two young men call for "the bill of fare." When the perplexed Hardcastle obliges by producing a list of the items they are to have for dinner more trouble is brewed.

MARLOW

[*Reading*]

For the first course, at the top, a pig and pruin sauce.

HASTINGS

Damn your pig, I say.

MARLOW

And damn your pruin sauce, say I.

HARDCASTLE

And yet, gentlemen, to men that are hungry, pig, with pruin sauce, is very good eating.

MARLOW

At the bottom, a calve's tongue and brains.

HASTINGS

Let your brains be knock'd out, my good Sir; I don't like them.

MARLOW

Or you may clap them on a plate by themselves, I do.

HARDCASTLE

[*Aside*]

Their impudence confounds me. . . . This may be modern modesty, but I never saw anything look so like old-fashioned impudence.

Goldsmith, "Nolly," as his friends called him, was generally popular, beloved for his gentleness by most, yet by some others held in a certain contempt for it. The age was hardly gentle, even if more restrained than that of Queen Elizabeth. During the years of his success as a writer he earned some money, but generosity and improvidence caused him to die leaving large debts. We find many appealing scenes with him in Boswell's *Life of Samuel Johnson*, where we find Goldsmith, by nature inarticulate except with pen in hand, hopelessly trying to compete with some of the most formidable conversationalists and wits ever gathered together. That weakness is reflected in the affectionate, informal epitaph written to Goldsmith by another of the circle, the actor David Garrick:

> HERE LIES NOLLY GOLDSMITH,
>> FOR SHORTNESS CALLED NOLL,
>
> WHO WROTE LIKE AN ANGEL
>> BUT TALKED LIKE POOR POLL.

David Garrick was the foremost actor of the eighteenth century and is counted as one of the great ones of all time, in personal ability and in influence upon an era. We might ask, how is it possible to make such judgments when nothing is less permanent than the work of an actor before the age when performances could be captured on film or other recording media? What can we know of this actor dead for centuries? We know this much, that few are the actors who have left so unanimous a record of homage from an unusually broad field of admittedly discriminating judgments. It is in these estimates and testimonies that Garrick lives. His name is memorialized in one of London's most famous clubs, The Garrick, which contains an enormous collection of his own memorabilia and those of other great figures in the theatre and letters.

Garrick was born in 1717 in Lichfield, the town also distinguished as the birthplace of Dr. Johnson who, indeed, was tutor to the younger man. Garrick's father was French and his mother, English. The father had been raised in England and was a minor officer in the army. If not actually impoverished, the family was at least "low in the purse."

When Garrick came up to London, by coincidence at the same time as Samuel Johnson, he began as a wine merchant on a small scale. He and his former mentor, the "great Cham" to be, both were destined to fame. They remained friends and moved in the same brilliant conversational circles, though the ponderous and eccentric Johnson sometimes bridled at the good-natured liberties Garrick took with him.

Garrick had some literary skill, too, and his interest in the theatre was shown first in a comedy called *Lethe*. It was a success and introduced Garrick into theatrical company. Possibly from sheer sentiment he kept the little play alive in repertory at the height of his career as actor-manager.

In 1737, for political reasons, the statesman Robert Walpole imposed a licensing law for theatres which had the effect of closing all but two licensed houses, the famous Drury Lane and Covent Garden theatres. (Great theatres of that name, though not the same buildings, still stand close together at the same sites. The modern Covent Garden is an opera house.) Various dodges were worked out for evading the licensing law. In 1741 Garrick made his debut as an actor in no less a role than Shakespeare's *Richard III*, in a "concert," in a place not called a theatre, on the outskirts of London. He achieved immediate success and this pattern never changed; few actors have enjoyed such consistent triumph.

Garrick's style of acting was revolutionary in the theatre to which he came. Public approval was immediate though for a long time his methods met with hostility from other actors and some critics. The acting of the time was bombastic, declamatory. Garrick used a natural style, realistic, mirroring nature. This naturalness and studied restraint proved to have astonishing power and to lend itself to infinitely modulated effects. The elderly Colley Cibber, poet laureate, who had been a prominent figure of the high Restoration theatre both as actor and playwright, deplored Garrick's acting and wrote and spoke against it continually. Another outstanding actor summed up the matter in despair: "We are all wrong if this fellow is right."

This fellow *was* right. More and more of those who held out were forced to admit it and few were able to follow in his path quickly. Garrick was further unusual in having equal gifts for comedy and tragedy, although he was primarily what the modern theatre would call a "character actor" rather than a player of

David Garrick as Richard III. *The Bettmann Archive*

"straight parts." He was at better advantage as King Lear, or Macbeth, than as Romeo. Yet he played a tremendous range of roles in good and bad plays of his own period, as well as the Elizabethan. He became associated early with the Drury Lane Theatre. In time he became its owner and manager, making it a flourishing and profitable enterprise.

Though we have said he was restrained, in the desirable sense of the word, Garrick was nonetheless an actor of phenomenal intensity from all the impressions recorded of him. Such intensity is a primary element in great acting. In Garrick's case it was no doubt part of the sense of heady mastery which a skilled actor feels when he commands the stage. The actor's was a transient art, as we have remarked, until modern recording media made it possible to preserve it. When he walks onto a stage the audience is a limp, passive factor. It is within his power to seize it, galvanize it, control the ebb and flow of its feelings, and to walk from the stage leaving it wrung dry and emotionally exhausted. The exalting sense of magnetism and power which this gives to the actor, only an actor who has known such moments of triumph can realize.

As for Garrick's power, the story is told that in a performance of *Macbeth* his intensity was such that when he said to the hired murderer, "There's blood upon thy face!" the other player was startled quite out of his role, thrust his hand to his face, and cried, "Is there, by God?"

Garrick was often called "Roscius," the name of the greatest actor of ancient Rome. He was one of the most popular men of his time in England. Also, he had many distinguished friends and admirers in France, including that country's theatrical arbiter, Voltaire. As Voltaire had done in France, Garrick also banished intruding spectators from the English stage during performances.

We suspect that Garrick was an actor whom Shakespeare would have understood well. In spite of the fact that he, too, made adaptations, as many actors in many ages have done and will continue to do, the evidence is that Garrick restored the major Shakespearean roles to their essential integrity. A fascinating story in itself is the history of the great Shakespeare Jubilee which Garrick sponsored and managed at Stratford-on-Avon in September of 1769. It was the first step in the honoring and preserving of the Shakespeare sites and toward the Memorial Theatre and company that perform there now.

Garrick retired in 1776 and sold the Drury Lane Theatre to

Richard Brinsley Sheridan and some associates. Three years later, at the age of sixty-two, he died. He had written or adapted several plays, usually in collaboration with other writers. One of his comedies, *The Clandestine Marriage*, remains a stageworthy play.

As owner and manager of the Drury Lane, Garrick gathered to himself, encouraged, trained, or developed other fine acting talents. One of the chief of these was Charles Macklin, an older actor who had anticipated some of Garrick's reforms in the art and had begun to introduce them himself. Macklin and Garrick were intimate friends and close professional associates for several years, though they finally parted over disagreements.

One of the elements needing reform in the theatre, to which Macklin addressed himself, was costume. Since Restoration days costumes had been lavish but often were absurdly inappropriate to the character wearing them. Nothing but a sense of display seemed to determine the design of costumes.

Macklin played Shylock, in *The Merchant of Venice*, in the sombre dress appropriate to the part. His splendid performance and the striking effect of his costume created a great stir and were said to have kept King George II awake all night by their dramatic force. The performance called forth from Alexander Pope the admiring couplet:

> *This is the Jew*
> *That Shakespeare drew.*

Macklin was a man of high temper and powerful frame, qualities which made him popular with the groundlings. He was tried for murder, but acquitted, when he accidentally thrust the point of a cane into the eye of a fellow actor, when he had merely intended a threatening gesture.

A favorite stage technique of Macklin's was the skillful use of pauses for effect. He had three of these, precisely timed, which he called his short pause, his long pause, and his grand pause. One night when he was using the latter to its best effect, a stupid

Charles Macklin as Macbeth. *New York Public Library Theatre Collection*

prompter repeatedly threw the line to him. Macklin, bursting with exasperation, stepped into the wings and kicked the prompter out; then, turning to the audience, he explained blandly, "The fellow interrupted me in my grand pause."

Vigorous Macklin acted into his nineties and after his retirement, with a gleeful malice, attended the theatre faithfully, in the pit, and heckled his former colleagues.

The most prominent actress of Garrick's time, successor to the glamorous Nell Gwyn, was Peg Woffington. Like her predecessor, she sprang from the humblest origins and was carried high by her art. She was a seasoned player by the age of eleven. She, too, was ahead of the age and shared with Garrick, Macklin, and a slowly growing band of others, the belief that acting should represent real behavior. She entered into a love affair with Garrick that was the talk of London.

"Woff" was willing to play any part, and to play it in appropriate costume and make-up. She did not hesitate to play those roles which other stars did not consider fit for their fame—supporting roles. She did not hesitate to wrinkle her face and gray her hair to simulate age; nor was she unwilling to wear shabby clothes when a part called for them. She was struck by paralysis during a performance and forced to retire from the stage. She died a few years afterward.

Henry Fielding was among the eighteenth century playwrights, writing a great deal for the stage in his early years, mainly extravagant farces and burlesques, to support himself in his study of law. His work as a playwright is wholly eclipsed by his novels, particularly the celebrated *Tom Jones*.

John Gay wrote several plays but is remembered for one single work that was the greatest hit of its era on the London stage: *The Beggar's Opera*, that interspersed songs with straight dramatic action and dialogue. Jonathan Swift is said to have suggested to Gay that he write a "Newgate pastoral," an allusion to Newgate prison. The play deals altogether with criminals and is a satire on the morals of the age. Its novelty and verve made it a smash hit. A man named Rich was the manager of Drury Lane (before Garrick's time) when *The Beggar's Opera* was produced and the wits said the production had "made Gay rich, and Rich gay."

The modern German playwright Bertolt Brecht and the composer Kurt Weill made an even more sharply satirical adaptation of Gay's work, calling it *The Threepenny Opera*, which has enjoyed great popularity on the English-speaking stage as well as in Europe.

The last of the master playwrights of the eighteenth century theatre in England was Richard Brinsley Sheridan. The stage was a natural heritage to him. Thomas Sheridan, his father, was a successful actor-manager and his mother, Frances, an actress and playwright. One of Sheridan's most celebrated characters, Mrs. Malaprop, who plays havoc with language, is elaborated from a character in one of his mother's plays.

Sheridan, like Goldsmith, was an Irishman. He was born in Dublin in 1751 but was brought early to England and educated there. He studied law, as had Fielding, but devoted himself much more intensively to the theatre.

His marriage was something of a theatrical production in its own right. He fell in love with Elizabeth Linley, who was being courted persistently, to her annoyance, by a Captain Matthews. Sheridan eloped with Elizabeth to Calais and was there married to her, although they regarded this largely as a betrothal and planned a more formal marriage in England at a later date. When he came back to England, Sheridan was harassed into fighting two duels over the matter with the persistent Captain Matthews, and was severely wounded in the second of these. It is likely that the quarrelsome Lucius O'Trigger, in the play *The Rivals*, written shortly afterwards, is a caricature of the Captain.

The Rivals was produced by Garrick in 1775, the year before his retirement. The opening performance was a failure. A few adjustments were made hurriedly and eleven days later the play was repeated with instant and sensational success. It has been regarded ever since as a jewel in the theatre of manners.

In the fashion of its kind, the names of the characters define their broad types. Sir Lucius O'Trigger is addicted to duelling. Sir Anthony Absolute is a tyrannical father. Lydia Languish dotes on romance. Bob Acres is a simple man who owns a lot of land. Most famous of all is Mrs. Malaprop, from *mal apropos*, "Mrs. Inappropriate." She has passed into the language in "malapropism," meaning the use of the wrong word. She is serenely unaware of her failing and desires, in her niece's education, "that she might reprehend the true meaning of what she is saying."

On the strength of the success of *The Rivals*, Sheridan bought the Drury Lane Theatre from the retiring Garrick, in partnership with his father-in-law and a third man.

The climax of Sheridan's career was his other masterpiece, in 1777, *The School for Scandal*. A century later one of England's leading actors—the first to be honored with knighthood—Sir Henry Irving said, "Sheridan brought the comedy of manners to the highest perfection, and *The School for Scandal* remains to this day the most popular comedy in the English language." Its revivals are frequent, and its roles attract the distinguished actors of each age.

In theme the play is ageless, even though the traits it satirizes may have been particularly prevalent among a certain set at a certain time. It directs its wit against scandalmongers, revealing the havoc they wreak with their malice and lies. Its plot is so brilliantly intricate that synopsis is scarcely fair to it; it must be seen or read. Characteristic of its sharp dialogue is this exchange:

LADY SNEERWELL

> [*To Snake*]

> A villain! Treacherous to me at last! Speak, fellow, have you too conspired against me?

SNAKE

> I beg your ladyship ten thousand pardons: you paid me extremely liberally for the lie in question; but I unfortunately have been offered double to speak the truth.

Sheridan was elected to the celebrated Literary Club, which had among its members Dr. Johnson, Garrick, James Boswell, Edmund Burke (statesman, orator, and friend of the American colonies), two other liberal statesmen, Charles James Fox and William Pitt, Sir Joshua Reynolds, the portrait painter, and Edward Gibbon, author of *The Decline and Fall of the Roman Empire*.

Sheridan was elected to Parliament in 1780 and began another phase of his career. He, too, was a friend of the American colonies and a defender of the freedom of the press. His most famous speech in Parliament was his speech of accusation in the impeachment proceedings against Warren Hastings, who was charged with corruption in the administration of India. The speech was five hours and forty minutes long and was considered an oratorical masterpiece. His reputation for speaking was such that as much as fifty pounds was paid for a seat in the Parliamentary chambers that day. When the speech was over, the exhausted Sheridan collapsed into the arms of Edmund Burke. For the record, in spite of all oratory, Hastings was acquitted of the charges.

All this happened while Sheridan was still manager and chief owner of Drury Lane Theatre. John Kemble and Mrs. Sarah Siddons, subject of a famous portrait as the Tragic Muse by Joshua Reynolds, were its principal stars. A series of disasters overtook Sheridan. In 1791 the theatre was condemned as unsafe and had to be rebuilt. His wife died, and he married again, not altogether happily. In 1809 the New Drury Lane burnt to the ground to his utter ruin. He was arrested for debt and was still deeply burdened by it when he died—a melancholy close to a career of public service and lasting contribution to the theatre and the great art of comedy. Notwithstanding his misfortunes, he was buried with public honors in Westminster Abbey.

The clearly defined eras of the Restoration and the Augustan Age had closed. A series of gifted actors continued to grace the English stage. Probably the most brilliant of Garrick's long line of successors was the nineteenth century actor, Edmund Kean, of whom the poet Coleridge said that watching Kean play was "like reading Shakespeare by flashes of lightning."

The romantic poets Byron and Shelley wrote plays that were far more poetical works than stage pieces. It is late in the nineteenth century that the next wave of vigor comes to the English-speaking stage.

Chapter 12

*Theatre Comes
to America*

Playbill of the Old American Company, 1785.
Museum of the City of New York

SOME PLEASANT excitement must have been felt among the upper classes of the Virginia colony in the year 1750 with the arrival of the first professional theatrical company to be seen in America. Life was not so easy even in that southerly and most cavalier of the colonies and a novel entertainment would be welcome. Virginians had shown their interest in dramatic activities by the occasional performance of amateur theatricals, mostly farces, some of which had stirred up moral anxieties among the less sophisticated settlers and had even aroused controversies requiring settlement in the courts.

It was natural that the Virginia colony should play host to the

223

theatrical visitors. We could hardly have expected the theatre of eighteenth century England to be transplanted either to the rock-ribbed Puritans of New England or the devout Quakers of Pennsylvania. Even neutral New York, sandwiched between these two mutually suspicious pious groups, was not an ideal place for a beginning.

The Virginia venture came about because an English actor-manager, William Hallam, had undergone some severe financial setbacks. Determined to recoup his fortunes by some means or other, he hit upon the bold idea of organizing a company to send to the rapidly growing colonies where, so far, there would be no competition.

There is no record that William Hallam ever came to America himself. He gathered together a troupe, probably consisting largely of actors who had not been prospering in England. Thus, though they were professional, we can assume that the first lot were not of the best. Hallam called his venture the American Company and dispatched it to Virginia under the management of his brother, Lewis. A fairly extensive repertory of plays was rehearsed, partly in England before their departure, and partly on shipboard during the long voyage. The odds are that there were some seasick actors playing slightly nauseated comedy.

Virginia's Governor Dinwiddie turned out with all the best people to give the players a cordial reception at Yorktown, later the scene of the surrender of the British General Cornwallis, in the final stages of the Revolution. The company remained in Yorktown for some time and it was said that a certain young Major Washington was often to be seen at the play.

From Yorktown the company proceeded to the colonial capital at Williamsburg. From there they made occasional side trips to Annapolis, where one of the earliest theatres in the colonies had been built.

The business organization of the American Company was typical of its time. The actual profits of ownership were divided evenly by Lewis and William Hallam. Each one of the company held a number of shares, in proportion to which he received a portion of the receipts. This is perhaps the origin of the long-used term "stock company" for touring theatrical troupes.

Lewis Hallam received some shares in his managerial capacity, some for wear and tear on the capital investment of the company, such as costumes, stage properties, and scenery; and some shares as an actor.

The number of shares received by any actor depended on the relative importance of the roles he played. As the manager did the casting, or assigning of roles, the possibilities for favoritism are obvious, held within reasonable bounds by the fact that the company's success depended on good acting. The manager's wife usually played the leading female roles, receiving shares accordingly. The other large shareholders were the other principal actors. Lesser actors and bit players came off poorly.

A kind of bonus added to an actor's earnings came from the benefit system. A benefit in those days was not for public charity but for the personal benefit of a particular actor who received all the box office receipts for that performance. Each member of the company was entitled to a benefit every so often, at the manager's discretion, including the manager himself.

Since these theatrical beginnings in America coincided with eighteenth century drama in England it is the familiar names of plays and authors of the Restoration and Augustan ages that crop up on our own shores, along with the Elizabethan dramas in their Restoration adaptations.

The original repertory which the American Company brought to Virginia included *The Merchant of Venice, Richard III, Hamlet, Othello* (Shakespeare); *Tamburlaine* (Marlowe); *The Beaux' Stratagem, The Recruiting Officer* (Farquhar); *The Careless Husband* (Colley Cibber); *The Conscious Lovers* (Sir Richard Steele); and *The Mock Doctor* (possibly an adaptation from Molière).

In the course of time the American Company left Virginia for more heavily settled and cosmopolitan New York, where they opened a theatre on Nassau Street in what is now the modern financial district. There were hostility and opposition to this move from neighboring New England which felt the devil's minions were encroaching on its borders. Denunciations of "profane plays," echoes of Jeremy Collier, and reminiscences of the evils of cavalier influences in England were circulated. But New York was not a Puritan town and the theatre remained. The first play performed professionally in the city was *The Conscious Lovers*, a sentimental comedy by Sir Richard Steele.

Pleased with the success of the northward move, the American Company next began to prepare for an invasion of Philadelphia, the Quaker territory. Promised certain fat roles if he succeeded, a member of the company named Malone undertook to serve as ambassador to the Philadelphia authorities, seeking permission to play there. Governor Hamilton issued a temporary permit for a few performances over vigorous local protests. Many restrictions and a vigilant censorship of scripts were imposed upon the company as conditions and it was required to post a large bond against violations.

The next adventure was a tour to Bermuda. There Lewis Hallam died. He was succeeded as manager and leading player by David Douglass, who also married Hallam's widow—a thorough job of succession.

Douglass brought the company back to New York. A second attempt upon Philadelphia brought interesting results. The Quakers tried to procure an injunction to prohibit the performance. Colonial Judge Allen denied their petition. Judge Allen's wife attended the opening performance and three days later she died. The Quakers publicized this as a demonstration of swift punishment visited upon sin. It reminds us of Tertullian's example, in the later days of Rome, of the woman who went to the theatre and "at the end of five days was no longer in the world." In spite of sin and death, however, the American Company was granted a permanent license to play in Philadelphia when they chose.

In historic Fanueil Hall in Boston, scene of much agitation in preparation for the American Revolution, a theatrical performance is taking place. It is not only a seeming frivolity in a most serious time but is appearing in the Puritan stronghold of Boston, which had always barred relentlessly such worldly diversions. The explanation is that the colonies are at war for their independence and Boston is occupied at the moment by the British army.

The performance is a gala event among Tory society and the red-coated British officers. Jewel-bedecked ladies are present in most un-Puritan finery. The play is immediately topical, called *The Blockade of Boston,* and is attributed to no less interesting an author than the British General John Burgoyne, popularly known as Gentlemanly Johnny. A person whose grace and charm should not be overlooked in American patriotic zeal, Burgoyne was a survivor of the Restoration period's tradition of courtly amateur playwrights and wrote a great deal for the stage. He would have disdained the idea of being a professional in anything but soldiering.

Now, in the midst of the play's action, a soldier rushes onto the stage in high excitement and shouts, "The rebels have attacked the lines on the neck!" A ripple of applause runs through the audience at the realistic fervor of this bit player's performance. But the soldier seems bent on stealing the scene, milking his brief moment of glory for all it is worth; he repeats his line again and again. Abruptly the audience wakes up to the fact that this is not a situation in the drama but a genuine piece of military intelligence. Panic spreads, the performance is halted, and the hall is emptied as quickly as possible. Gaily attired officers abandon their jeweled ladies to rush to their posts on the lines of defense. War and enemy occupation had brought public plays to Boston, but not without attendant hazards.

The revolutionary ferment had led to some minor forms of colonial political drama before actual war began. Some of the zealots for independence wrote what were called satirical closet plays. Obviously out of the question for public performance because of their political content, they were chiefly intended for private circulation and reading; at the most for rare amateur performance behind closed doors—hence "closet" plays.

Two such incendiary plays were written by Mrs. Mercy Warren Otis of Massachusetts, wife of James Otis, a prominent rebel leader. She and her husband were friends of John and Abigail Adams. Though her little plays were not sprightly in tone they were sharp in political criticism. Both Adamses were much impressed by *The Adulateur* and *The Group*, and discuss them in their correspondence. The identity of the author was known only in their intimate circle.

Normal public play production everywhere in the colonies was halted in 1774, when the Continental Congress, girding the fledgling nation for the coming struggle, placed a ban upon the theatre along with all other frivolous, distracting diversions. "We will, in our several stations, encourage frugality, economy, and industry, and promote agriculture, arts, and the manufactures of this country, especially that of wool; and will discountenance and discourage every species of extravagance and dissipation especially all horse racing, and all kinds of gaming, cockfighting, exhibitions of shews, plays and other diversions and entertainments." It was the puritanism of purpose.

This period in our country is reflected in one the earliest, most delightful, and popular of the comedies of George Bernard Shaw, *The Devil's Disciple*, written by the Irish playwright a good century later and first performed in the United States by Richard Mansfield, of whom we shall speak later. The comedy is one of what Shaw called "Three Plays for Puritans," and one of its high points of comic genius presents Gentlemanly Johnny Burgoyne in a scene involving the trial of the hero, Dick Dudgeon, shortly before the General's military disaster at Saratoga.

The American Company discreetly retired to Bermuda for the duration of the war. After the Revolution it returned to New York and underwent reorganization. The share system was discarded. The manager took over all shares and the actors were employed on a week-to-week basis.

A new dramatic spirit now appeared in the new nation. We see the growth of an American theatre in pace with the growth of an American people. Native American playwrights appear and strongly nationalistic sentiments crop up in their plays. The first to come forward, Royall Tyler, wrote one of the two best American plays of the post-Revolutionary era: *The Contrast*.

Tyler was a versatile man, functioning successfully as soldier, jurist, politician, poet, novelist, and playwright. He served in the Revolution and later, in the rank of major, took part in the suppression of Shay's Rebellion, in Massachusetts, one of several postwar flare-ups of rural unrest. When his duties brought him to New York he was brought into contact with the American Company. Later he became Chief Justice of the Supreme Court of Vermont and a professor at the University of Vermont.

The Contrast is influenced in manner by Sheridan's *The School for Scandal*. It is a vigorous proclamation of American strength and ruggedness in contrast to what was popularly considered to be British upper class decadence and foppishness.

Dimple and Maria have been betrothed. Dimple goes to England where he is educated in those super-refined social graces in which Lord Chesterfield tutored his son in a series of famous letters. Among the Earl's precepts are: "In my mind, there is nothing so illiberal and so illbred as audible laughter" and "Courts and camps are the only places to learn the world in."

Dimple returns filled with affectations, the perfect English fop, effeminate and superficial. Maria no longer wishes to marry him, having only contempt for such artificial mannerisms. Dimple, in turn, wishes his freedom so that he may marry Letitia, a girl of wealth. Onto the scene comes Colonel Manly, the first typical, true-blue, red-blooded American on the stage. He and Maria immediately fall in love. The situation at last is resolved neatly and both couples are united in the unions which they want and deserve.

The most significant character in the play is the comic Yankee, Jonathan, the first in a long line of stage Yankees. Jonathan is played off against Jessamy, Dimple's manservant, who has been imported from England and is as full of affectations as his master.

JESSAMY

It is no shame, my dear Blueskin, for a man to amuse himself with a little gallantry.

JONATHAN

Girl huntry! I don't altogether understand. I never played at that game. I know how to play hunt the squirrel, but I can't play anything with the girls; I am as good as married.

JESSAMY

As good as married!—

JONATHAN

Why, yes; there's Tabitha Wymen, the deacon's daughter, at home. She and I have been courting a great while, and folks say as how we are to be married; and so I broke a piece of money with her when we parted, and she promised not to spark it with Solomon Dyer while I am gone. You wouldn't have me false to my true love, would you?

JESSAMY

. . . possibly the young lady has a fortune?

JONATHAN

Why, as to fortune, I must needs say her father is pretty dumb rich; he went representative for our town last year. He will give her—let me see—four times seven is—seven times four—nought and carry one;—he will give her twenty acres of land—somewhat rocky though—a Bible, and a cow.

Jonathan all unwittingly goes to see a play. He paid his money expecting to see juggling tricks and was astonished when all that happened was, "they lifted up a great green cloth, and let us look right into the next neighbour's house." As a result of this, says Jonathan, after having witnessed a great deal of other people's business:

> Why, I vow I began to smell a rat. When I came away I went to the man for my money again: you want your money, says he; yes, says I; for what, says he; why, says I, no man shall jocky me out of my money; I paid my money to see the sights, and the dogs a bit of a sight have I see, unless you call listening to people's private business a sight. Why, says he, it is the School for Scandalization.—The School for Scandalization!—Oh, ho! no wonder you New York folks are so cute at it, when you go to school to learn it: and so I jogged off.

Much emphasis was placed on the new democratic ideal. In a prologue, "Written by a Young Gentleman of New-York and Spoken by Mr. Wignell" (who played Jonathan) we find the opening lines:

> EXULT each patriot heart!—this night is shewn
> A piece, which we may fairly call our own;
> Where the proud titles of "My Lord! Your Grace!"
> To humble Mr. and plain Sir give place. . . .

The Contrast penetrated even to rock-bound Boston, where theatrical activities were beginning to stir in spite of the fierce opposition. Strictures of the law were evaded by cloaking all plays, of whatever topic, under the name of "lectures," as they had been called "concerts" in England at the beginning of David Garrick's career. Thus, we find an advertisement from *The Boston Independent Chronicle* of October 18th, 1792: "New Exhibition Room. Board Alley. Tomorrow evening will be presented A Moral Lecture in Five Parts called The Contrast, delivered by Messrs. Harper, Morris, Mrs. Murry and Mrs. Morris."

Tyler proclaimed himself an amateur and said that he had

written *The Contrast* in three weeks. He wrote several other plays, chiefly farces. *The Contrast* was actually the second play by a native American to be performed professionally. The first, a few years earlier, had been *The Prince of Parthia* by Thomas Godfrey, but it is not a work of lasting merit.

As we noted, Jonathan was the forerunner of the stock comic type of the stage Yankee (he has his low-comedy match everywhere —the stage Irishman, Dutchman and many others according to time and place). Among Jonathan's descendants, many of them inferior to him, some of them the principal stars of their plays, were such inventions as "Deuteronomy Dutiful," "Nathan Yank," "Jonathan Ploughboy," "Lot Sap Sago," "Solomon Swap," "Solon Shingle," and "Jedediah Homebred." These are not only Yankee types but sometimes represent also the shrewd rural character pitted against the city slicker and capable of outdoing him. The supreme example of the latter type, much later, is in one of the most persistent and popular plays for amateur performance, *Aaron Slick of Punkin' Crick.*

A prominent figure came to the foreground in the American theatre a few years after the Revolution. This was William Dunlap, a man of unusual talents. He began his career as a painter in London, studying under the noted American painter, Benjamin West. He was discouraged in this pursuit by the loss of one eye. Returning home he came into contact with the American Company and developed a lively interest in the drama. He wrote a play, *The Modest Soldier,* which was accepted but not produced because it lacked a part suitable for the manager's wife. Dunlap took his cue from this experience and afterward was careful to adapt his plays to the personnel of the company.

In the course of time Dunlap became manager of the American Company. He continued to operate it until 1805. At that time it failed, after a fifty-five year continuity of operation, partly because of quarrels among the members and partly because a series of yellow fever epidemics closed the theatres of New York for long periods of time. The old company had many competitors in its final years. A futile effort was made to revive it. Among the actors in that last attempt were a young couple from England, down on their luck, a Mr. and Mrs. David Poe, who have passed from the memory of man as all but the parents of Edgar Allan Poe.

Dunlap wrote a number of plays and adapted a good many from the European stage. His best work is in his original play, *André*, the story of the trial and execution of the gallant, widely admired British spy of the Revolution, Major André, who had been the British contact in the treacherous defection of Benedict Arnold.

Bland, a young American officer, is horrified to find that Major André, sentenced to die as a spy, is the man who once had saved his life by nursing him through sickness on a sea voyage. He attempts in every honorable way to save André, appealing to all authorities, even Washington himself. The situation is complicated further when Bland's father is held as a life-for-life hostage by the British. In spite of all efforts, including the entreaties of his betrothed, André goes to his death.

The simple theme of *André* is patriotism, depicted as greater than any personal or sentimental consideration. The play's importance in American theatre history is due to its emphasis of awakening national awareness.

Dunlap wrote a *History of the American Theatre*, from its beginnings until 1832. In addition to his *History* and plays, Dunlap left extensive and valuable diaries, a book entitled *The Arts of Design*, and many other writings. He was an energetic, gifted man and a staunch encourager of young, developing talents. He deserves to be remembered as the father of the American theatre; his memory and some of his works have been nurtured by the Dunlap Society.

American plays followed in rapid succession in the early nineteenth century. James Nelson Barker, soldier and politician, based his plays on native themes. In *Tears and Smiles* he contributed Nathan Yank to the growing roster of Yankee characters. *Superstition*, his best play, is the first American drama on the subject of witchcraft in New England. Its theme is summed up in the words of one of its characters: "Nothing is too ridiculous for those whom bigotry has brutalized." It is essentially the theme of a modern play by Arthur Miller, *The Crucible. Superstition* draws on a persistent legend of our early colonial years, the appearance of one of the fugitive puritan regicides mysteriously appearing from the forest to save threatened villagers from the Indians. James Fenimore Cooper later used that same story element in his novel *The Wept of Wish-ton-Wish*, and Hawthorne still later in *The Gray Champion*. Barker's play was first produced at the Chestnut Street Theatre in Philadelphia. It achieved success but one chronicler of the period says that Wood, the manager, "did not put the play on oftener because Mrs. Duff in the character of 'Mary' outshone Mrs. Wood in 'Isabella.' "

John Howard Payne was writer, composer, actor. In all he wrote or adapted some sixty plays. He composed the once massively popular sentimental song "Home, Sweet Home," which occurs in his light opera, *Clari, or, The Maid of Milan*. Payne was American consul in Tunis, Algeria, at the time of his death. One of his better plays is *Charles the Second; or, the Merry Monarch*, a comedy written with the silent collaboration of one of America's earliest important men of letters, Washington Irving.

The play which vies with Tyler's *The Contrast* for the most honors in our early drama is *Fashion*, by Anna Cora Mowatt, our first notable woman playwright, and indeed one of the earliest anywhere. *Fashion* is a satire on vanity and pretentious social ambition. It was produced in New York in 1845 and became popular at once. It has been revived often both on the professional and amateur stage. Mrs. Mowatt was a talented actress as well and was honored not only at home but also against the stiff competition of the London stage.

Interior of a New York theatre, 1822. *Courtesy of The New-York Historical Society, New York City*

The redskin has done little in America drama except bite the dust, although Indian characterizations sometimes take on a dimension beyond mere Tonto-style stock types in superior modern Westerns. The Indian appeared frequently enough in early American dramas but always in a rather elementary, or else heroic-romantic, convention.

The first Indian play was *Ponteach* (Pontiac); *or, the Savages of America,* by Major Robert Rogers. There is no record of its performance. George Washington Parke Custis, son of the stepson of the first president, wrote *Pocahontas; or, the Settlers of Virginia,* the best of many treatments of the Captain John Smith legend. *The Indian Princess,* by James Nelson Barker, and *Metamora; or, The Last of the Wampanoags,* by J. A. Stone, are other typical Indian plays.

Most of them are flowery, romantic works in the "noble Red Man" tradition that Cooper had established with his *Leather-stocking Tales.* The plays were generally cast in a most inappropriate blank verse. Arthur Hobson Quinn, admirable historian of the American theatre, says, "Very few of the forty Indian plays of which record has been made have come down to us. They were popular between 1830 and 1850, but they were usually artificial and their picture of the Indian was not a true one."

The fighting "Injun" cropped up later in the frontier drama and became and remains the stock in trade of Westerns from the nickelodeon movies to television.

Oliver La Farge's *Laughing Boy,* adapted from his Pulitzer prize-winning novel, and a compelling but highly experimental play, *The Cherokee Night,* by the Oklahoma playwright Lynn Riggs, are examples of the best modern plays about Indians. Riggs is best known for his play *Green Grow the Lilacs* which was successful on the stage. Adapted by Rodgers and Hammerstein as the musical *Oklahoma!* it enjoyed one of the longest runs on Broadway.

The Civil War made surprisingly little impact on our stage. The

new life that was to come into our theatre in the latter part of
the nineteenth century came, instead, from the far-reaching social
and economic conditions of the years after the war, together with
influences reaching us from Europe.

The Civil War plays were romantic melodramas in which the
war was little more than a military background localized and made
topical by familiar names and places. The stories themselves could
just as well have taken place in Graustark or any other imaginary
kingdom.

William Gillette's melodrama, *Secret Service*, is the well-known
formula, tricked out with excellent stage devices, of the United
States Secret Service operative who falls in love with a loyal
Southern girl during his daring duty in the Confederacy. Such
romances across the lines were the stock in trade of the Civil War
plays. Gillette was one of the most versatile showmen. Actor and
playwright, he was associated particularly in his late years with his
famous dramatization and stage performance of *Sherlock Holmes*.
His own hawklike face became the model for some illustrators' conceptions of the detective.

Other Civil War plays were *Shenandoah* by Bronson Howard
and *The Copperhead* by Harold Frederic. The early film classic of
D. W. Griffith's, *The Birth of a Nation*, and the modern film,
Gone With the Wind, based on Margaret Mitchell's novel, are
better studies of the Civil War than any of the old plays.

Dion Boucicault, an Irish actor-playwright who made America
his adopted home, wrote an interesting play, just before the war,
called *The Octoroon*, in which delicate issues of the slavery question and the mixing of the races were raised. It is essentially a
melodrama, however, and its deeper implications are lost in an
elaborate murder plot.

Uncle Tom's Cabin was dramatized by George L. Aiken from
Harriet Beecher Stowe's famous antislavery propaganda novel.
Unfortunately, when compressed on the stage, the more solid sub-
stance of the already overheated novel melted away and left a rank

melodrama which is only amusing to modern eyes. After it ceased
to be taken seriously it was played sometimes as burlesque. In its
day it was astonishingly popular. The country teemed with travel-
ling companies, called "Tom shows." Eliza crossing the ice pursued by bloodhounds, and Simon Legree cracking his whip became ultimate symbols of "mellerdramer."

A fine, though specialized, item of Civil War drama in recent
years was a concert reading adaptation of Stephen Vincent Benét's
American epic poem, *John Brown's Body*.

Frontier drama was another development. Pushing out from the
crowded centers of eastern settlement were bold men and women
who made it their business to expand the nation and find economic
freedom to match their political liberty. The frontier is an epic, a
life drama in itself; a saga of covered wagons, Indian fighters, pony
express riders, bad men, straight shooters, precious metals, rich
soil, deep forests, and turbulent, long, wide rivers. Dan'l Boone and
Buffalo Bill, Davy Crockett and General Custer, Sam Houston,
Sitting Bull, Geronimo, are all names associated with the long era
of the frontier. From this source sprang a crude, rough-and-thump-
ing brand of melodrama, peopled by the bad men, straight-shooting
heroes, sheriffs and marshals, and pure women of frontier legend.
As dramatic literature it was worthless. As entertainment for
simple, hardy, unlettered people it was great stuff.

Davy Crockett, by Frank Murdock, is a representative piece. A
typical scene is the interior of Crockett's hut. The heroine, Eleanore, has been brought there for refuge, together with her fiancé,
Neil, who lies wounded and unconscious through most of the scene.

ELEANORE

What is it?

DAVY

Keep still and listen.

[*A howl is heard*]

Poster for *Uncle Tom's Cabin*. *New York Public Library Theatre Collection*

ELEANORE

 I hear a long, low cry as of some animal in distress.

DAVY

 Ah, you hear it then? I was right, wasn't I? Thar it is again.

ELEANORE

 What is it?

DAVY

 That's wolves!

ELEANORE

 Wolves!

 [*Screams*]

DAVY

Don't be scared.

ELEANORE

But . . . is there no danger?

DAVY

Ain't I here?

ELEANORE

Yes, but they are so dreadfully near.

DAVY

Yes, they tracked you in the snow and smell blood.

ELEANORE

Blood!

DAVY

Take it easy, girl. This door is built of oak, I built it . . . and . . . blazes! The bar's gone!

ELEANORE

Gone?

[*Wolves howl all around the cabin.*]

DAVY

Yes, I split it up to warm you and your friend. Rouse him up. The pesky devils is all around the house.

ELEANORE

[*Goes to Neil*]

Neil . . . help! Help!

[*The wolves throw themselves against the door and bark.*]

DAVY

Quick there, I can't hold the door agin 'em.

NEIL

I tell you, uncle, if the girl says no, there's an end of it. . . .

ELEANORE

My God . . . he is delirious!

DAVY

What!

ELEANORE

'Tis true . . . nothing can save us.

DAVY

Yes, it can.

ELEANORE

What?

DAVY

The strong arm of a back-woodsman!

[*Davy bars the door with his arm. The wolves attack the house. Their heads are seen through the opening in the hut and under the door.*]

[*Curtain*]

Which can only be called a bang-up finish to an act. No one left the theatre before that show was over, but you couldn't get them in, today. Observe the monosyllabic, repetitive dialogue and the naive emotion.

This tradition strewed the stage with grandiose lines such as "Rags are royal raiment when worn for virtue's sake." Also, another, citified brand of ten-twent'-thirt' melodrama flourished (so called because of the scale of prices): *Bertha, the Sewing Machine Girl; Nellie, the Beautiful Cloak Model,* and others of that variety of which *East Lynne* was the most famous. Struggles for the old homestead, mortgage foreclosures, and evictions were popular subjects.

On a much higher level with the same essential appeal is *Salvation Nell,* written by Edward Sheldon, and played by the famous Mrs. Minnie Maddern Fiske. Late in the century America was thrilled, shocked, outraged, all at once, by the musical melodrama, *The Black Crook*, which audaciously presented a chorus dressed in black tights.

The latter part of the nineteenth century in America presents a theatrical panorama getting hopelessly beyond our ability to keep up with its details. New playwrights began to bring our drama step by step closer to the present-day standard in which American drama is the peer of any in the world. The best writers included Steele MacKaye and his son Percy; James A. Herne, actor-playwright, whose *Margaret Fleming* is one of the best plays of the late years of the century; William Vaughn Moody, poet and experimenter, in some ways the spiritual father of Eugene O'Neill; William Dean Howells, more famous as a novelist and critic; and the prolific student of American middle-class manners, Clyde Fitch.

It was a rich period in American acting, with Edwin Forrest, Joe Jefferson, famous for his acting in *Rip Van Winkle*, Robert B. Mantell, E. H. Sothern, and Julia Marlowe. Junius Brutus Booth pleased American and British audiences. He was followed by his still greater son, Edwin Booth, king of the American stage in his day, a tragic figure whose career was shadowed and whose life was haunted by the crime of his talented but unstable brother, the actor John Wilkes Booth, assassin of Abraham Lincoln.

Margaret Anglin and Minnie Maddern Fiske were leading actresses. Richard Mansfield, a performer and producer of superior intellectual power, carried his art to some of its heights in American theatre. His name is the more important for his farseeing selection of plays. At a time when still no writing of first-class rank had yet been done by American playwrights, Mansfield brought to the American stage several of the plays of Bernard Shaw, the difficult and beautiful *Peer Gynt* of Henrik Ibsen, and Rostand's *Cyrano de Bergerac*.

John Drew established a theatrical family line in which followed the Barrymore brothers and sister, John, Lionel, and Ethel, all of whom were exciting stage presences.

Across the late nineteenth century and on until his death in 1931 moved the bizarre figure of David Belasco, who wished to be the high priest of the American drama to such a degree that he affected a clerical collar. He was actor (but soon gave that up), director, producer, and playwright. Some of his plays were collaborations with writers whose scripts he accepted upon the condition of adjusting them himself before production—rather reminiscent of that less theatrically talented man, Cardinal Richelieu.

Belasco developed a number of stars, notably David Warfield, and his producing offices became a kind of theatrical temple. In staging techniques he was a literal realist. Unfortunately his idea of what was real did not extend to the action of the plays but simply to the details of staging. In one of his plays he put an exact duplication of a Childs' Restaurant on the stage. In another instance he purchased an old theatrical boarding house and had its interior reconstructed on his stage. In *The Auctioneer* he set up a genuine shop, down to the last detail, and boasted that there were ten thousand real "properties" on the stage.

Madame Butterfly, which Belasco wrote with John Luther Long, and his own *The Girl of the Golden West*, were among the most successful of his plays. Both were made into operas by the composer Giacomo Puccini.

Economic problems threatened the American theatre just before the turn of the century. A small clique of real estate operators and producers formed "the syndicate," and tried to corner the market in American drama through a monopoly that would give them complete control of the entertainment business. It applied to the arts a high-powered manipulative technique more associated with "robber barons" in railroads, oil, or wheat. The effort was almost successful.

In those days "the road"—the circuit of traveling theatrical companies that carried Broadway plays throughout the country—was the chief source of revenue of any production. The syndicate bought up all the good theatres all over the country. Independent managers such as Belasco, Mansfield, and the intrepid Mrs. Fiske, who would not bow to the financial dictation of the syndicate, found themselves unable to obtain theatres in which to present their productions.

The syndicate stopped at nothing to frustrate attempts to defy it. Sabotage was practiced ruthlessly in houses obtained by independents. When Belasco brought out *The Darling of the Gods*, the syndicate threw together a trashy imitation called *The Japanese Nightingale* and booked it around the country about a week ahead of Belasco's play, killing most of his business for audiences would not patronize two Japanese plays in such rapid succession.

A climax in the struggle against the syndicate was the Iroquois fire. The Iroquois Theatre in Chicago was a syndicate house. One night during a crowded performance it burned to the ground. All the exits were locked, in characteristic syndicate contempt for the safety regulations. The loss of life was appalling and created a national scandal. The theatre doors also opened inward, so that they were blocked by the pressure of panicked crowds. That tragedy resulted in the requirement of so-called panic doors that open outward from pressure on a bar.

The syndicate never was really overthrown. Natural changes altered it. By the time of the First World War it had given way to a looser form of production in which many managers had begun to follow the worst practices of the syndicate. Out of the abuses against actors which this condition created arose the movement for a union of actors. The powerful Actors' Equity Association was the result. In 1919, the young organization staged a celebrated strike. It was bitterly resisted and desperately pressed, but the actors won and Equity has been a powerful and generally constructive factor in the American theatre ever since. The story of this dramatic off-stage struggle of the players is well told in *The Revolt of the Actors*, by Alfred Harding.

Thus far, though we have seen some creditable plays and some fine actors in the American theatre, it must be conceded that there have yet been seen no great plays or writers to command attention in the world theatre. We will consider the full maturity of the American theatre in a summation of the modern stage after we have examined the large events in the nineteenth-century theatre of England and Europe.

Henrik Ibsen. *Norwegian Information Service*

Chapter 13

Romanticism to Realism

THE NINETEENTH-CENTURY THEATRE in Europe and England experienced a host of movements or trends, following each other in succession, coexisting, overlapping, sometimes in the work of a single man. Many labels were applied here and there—not always with wide agreement as to what they meant: romanticism, realism, naturalism, expressionism. Taking them loosely as rough guides, and not getting caught in a doctrinaire commitment to any of them, romanticism and realism will serve the purposes of our quick look at some major figures.

246

The French theatre struck a vein of romanticism that led to a remarkably large number of its successful plays being transmuted into some of the most popular tragic grand operas.

The two Alexandre Dumases, father and son, known to the French respectively as Dumas *père* and Dumas *fils*, both were popular novelists and playwrights. The father's sheer bulk of output was amazing and he is remembered best in English for the series of romantic novels beginning with *The Three Musketeers*. His plays, which included *Henry III*, *Charles VII*, and *Antony*, followed close behind the first romantic dramas of Victor Hugo and helped to break the confines of French neoclassicism. A mulatto, and the illegitimate son of a marquis, Dumas *père* cut a colorful swath through French society himself, making large sums of money which still could not keep pace with his extravagances. In his older years, he joined the cause of Garibaldi, working for the liberation and unification of Italy, showing himself to be a political romantic as well as a theatrical one.

An adaptation of his novel *The Count of Monte Cristo* was a long-time staple of English and American melodrama. James O'Neill, the father of the playwright Eugene, made a career for many years as its hero.

Dumas *fils*, who had to sustain his spendthrift father in his last years, was also a man of talent but less prolific and versatile than the elder. His most enduring work is the novel, *La Dame aux Camélias* (*The Lady of the Camellias*), which is generally known in English as *Camille*. Dumas' own dramatization of this was a favorite on the stage and remains so in its form as the opera, *La Traviata*, by Verdi.

It is the story of the courtesan, Marguerite Gautier, who renounces her love for young Armand Duval so that she will not ruin his career. Having pretended fickleness to conceal her sacrifice, Marguerite dies of a combination of tuberculosis and broken heart. Even those beyond the pale of respectable society, it tells us, are not without their deeds of virtue and greatness; though perhaps it tells us this with a slight excess of tears.

Young Dumas had based this story in part on a real person. He had regarded it as a potboiler and yet it proved to be his major work. Also, even within its romantic story, there were the seeds of his growing interest in social problems and a belief that drama should contribute to the needs of society which made Dumas *fils* one of the earliest influences toward the development of a realistic, or as he called it a "useful," drama.

Eugène Scribe wrote so many plays of various kinds that he operated a virtual play factory. He worked with numerous regular collaborators, in his employ, many of whom he regarded as specialists—one man for dialogue, one for plots, one for jokes—an organization almost as elaborate as the staff of writers for a television comedian. He was an adept craftsman, whose plays appealed mostly to the new French middle class. The more romantic vein was expressed in the numerous opera librettos he wrote, for several composers, which include *The Huguenots* and *L'Africaine* of Meyerbeer, and *La Juive* (*The Jewess*), by Halévy, the latter of which provided one of the greatest roles of the tenor Enrico Caruso, in our century.

The early life of Victorien Sardou sounds like a scene from *La Vie Bohème*. Impoverished after the ruin of his family's fortune, he reached a low point when he was literally dying in a garret, of typhoid fever, in a mound of rejected play manuscripts. He was nursed back to life by a woman who then aided his career, and whom he later married.

When the hard-attained success finally came it was immense and he was prolific and varied in production—a seeming characteristic of French writers of the nineteenth century. He wrote plays of the romantic school, many with historical backgrounds, and also several which would be called realistic, satirizing aspects of French middle-class life, customs, laws, and attitudes.

He custom-tailored many plays for specific players, including the great French actress, Sarah Bernhardt, and the English actor, Sir Henry Irving, for whom he wrote *Robespierre* and *Dante*. Irving also played in other of his works, including *Madame Sans-Gêne*, a story of Napoleon, and *A Scrap of Paper*. His play, *La Tosca*, a romantic melodrama, became the basis of the vastly popular opera by Puccini.

Sardou, and to some extent Scribe, became identified with the phrase "the well-made play," used disparagingly to suggest a slick, glib craftsmanship used to produce superficial, contrived work, such as the fashioning of fat roles commissioned by actors. Bernard Shaw, who was one of the men who would bring a new depth to playwriting, in his days as a critic assailed the well-made play and invented the word "Sardoodledum" as a derisive label for it.

Victor Hugo was the dominant literary figure of the age. It was he, followed soon by the elder Dumas, who established the sharp romantic break with the former classicists. His play *Hernani*, a Spanish romance, produced at the Théâtre Français in 1830, became the symbol of the revolt against the old style. The controversial furor it aroused was so intense that duels were fought and literary feuds pursued at great length over it. The forty-five performances given it at the Théâtre Français were called "the battles of *Hernani*."

Hugo is best known in English for three great novels, *Notre Dame de Paris*, also called *The Hunchback of Notre Dame*, *Toilers of the Sea*, and *Les Misérables*. They illustrate the curious borderline between romanticism and realism. All three are realistic in many minute details of French life at varying historical periods, and in their passionate plea for justice for the oppressed whose plight is starkly portrayed. Yet all three are also touched with romanticism in their idealism and enlargement of characters beyond life size, as in the case of Jean Valjean, the hero of *Les Misérables*.

We will cap this view of French romantic playwrights with one we have met in passing already, Edmond Rostand. His *La Princesse Lointaine* (*The Distant Princess*) provided a role for Sarah Bernhardt. *L'Aiglon* (*The Eaglet*) was about the imprisoned son and heir of Napoleon. *Chantecler,* a satirical animal fantasy, and *The Last Night of Don Juan* are among his plays. His masterpiece is the much loved *Cyrano de Bergerac* which has attracted both audiences and actors since its first appearance in 1897.

When it was played in New York by Richard Mansfield the anticipation was so great that high speculative prices were paid for seats at the opening. It is scarcely just to summarize the gay, bravura story of Cyrano, he of the enormous nose and the genius for improvised poetry, who sacrifices himself to the happiness of his beloved Roxane, adroitly wooing and winning her for another man. His own long-suffering love is acknowledged and recognized only at the point of death. It is the perfect romance of tears and laughter. Cyrano, formidable fighter, braggart with some justification, poet, and unselfish lover, is a swashbuckling hero of the highest order and provides an actor's field day. The best of several English translations is that by Brian Hooker which was used by the actor Walter Hampden, and most who have played it since on the English-speaking stage.

Before we consider the countercurrent to romanticism in nineteenth-century playwriting we can make brief acquaintance with certain of the actors of the era, household names in their own times and often far beyond the borders of their own countries.

Rostand's dedication to *Cyrano de Bergerac* reads:

> *It was to the soul of Cyrano that I intended to dedicate this poem. But since that soul has been reborn in you, Coquelin, it is to you that I dedicate it.*

The tribute was deserved. Some of the enormous and swift success the play achieved was due to the superb performance given by the foremost French actor of the day.

Benoît Constant Coquelin's triumphant career brought him into the roster of the principal organization of the French theatre, the Comédie Française. He did not stay with this company because its schedules imposed too many limitations on the freedom of his energetic personality. He organized a company of his own with which he made many successful tours outside of France. In 1900 he toured America with the famous Sarah Bernhardt. Coquelin, though particularly celebrated for the brilliance and dash of his comedy, was a thoughtful actor and a master of tragedy, too. He wrote some important critical works and studies of the drama and the art of acting.

Sarah Bernhardt, his contemporary, is still a legend of the stage. It is possible that her powerful and magnetic personality, her sheer presence, caused her to be overrated as an actress.

Bernhardt was born in Paris, of Jewish parentage, in 1845. At an early age she began training for the stage at the Paris Conservatory. While struggling to make a place for herself in the French theatre she appeared in musical burlesques.

Her real success came almost simultaneously with the disastrous Franco-Prussian War of 1870. Bernhardt worked energetically as a nurse in the ambulance service during the unsuccessful defense of Paris.

The French public was enthralled by her performances in the *Phèdre* of Racine, and in *Hernani* and *Ruy Blas*, the two Spanish romances of Victor Hugo. She had become a great name rapidly, not only in France and the rest of Europe, but in America, where she made her first triumphal tour in 1880.

"The Divine Sarah," as her admirers called her, was a talented sculptress and also the author of a play, *The Confession*, written as a vehicle for herself. Perhaps her most notable roles were in Sardou's *La Tosca* and Dumas *fils' Camille*. She created a sensation by the tour de force of playing Hamlet, and at the age of fifty-five still was playing the roles of young men.

From all accounts of Bernhardt's style of acting, modern tastes would find it heavy, a little given to tearing a passion to tatters. She carried this off where a lesser actress could not by the magnificence of her temperament and stage presence. A little of her acting is preserved, without benefit of voice, in a film, *Queen Elizabeth,* which she made in 1912.

The First World War called forth her patriotic zeal again. Although she underwent the amputation of a leg in 1915, she continued her career, a rather grim picture of an aging romantic actress with a wooden leg. She devoted her enormous energy to performing at the battle front for the entertainment of the troops.

The veteran actress, seemingly inexhaustible in her vigor, continued to play actively and was about to turn to the medium of films again when she died, in 1923, at the age of seventy-eight.

In England, the son of a shopkeeper brought a new social dignity to the acting profession, after having started his adult life as a clerk. This was John Henry Brodribb, known to the world by his professional name of Sir Henry Irving, the first English actor to be honored with a knighthood.

The critical prestige and persuasiveness of George Bernard Shaw has led many to speak slightingly of Henry Irving in spite of his professional success and prominence. He was accused of not using his talents with a sense of vision or perception of great drama. Shaw claimed that Irving simply could not, or would not, rise to what might have been expected of him.

He worked his way to the top of his profession by the slow and tedious road of stock companies and he remained something of a stock actor even in his splendor. His first big success was in the melodrama, *The Bells.* His popular tour de force in the role of Mathias, a character haunted and driven mad by the guilt of an undiscovered murder, was more congenial to him than genuinely great roles he might have played.

As actor-manager he operated a flourishing company at the Lyceum Theatre, in London, for twenty-three years. Sardou meant as much to him as Shakespeare. Though he played a large Shakespeare repertory he was accused of carrying mutilation of Shakespeare to extremes, paring down the plays to emphasize and exaggerate his own roles, and often to diminish and reduce in importance the roles of his supporting company. Shaw charged him with stifling the talents of the fine actress, Ellen Terry, who was long associated with him. Irving set too much value on easy theatrical effects—what Shaw called a series of tricks to simulate acting—carried off with a flourish that seemed to dignify them. The most damning fact is that he was blindly hostile to the plays of the greatest dramatists of his time, Ibsen and Shaw, and never supported any progressive or advanced influence in the theatre. In all this he is in marked contrast to Richard Mansfield in America, part of whose glory was the perception of the great plays and playwrights of his age.

A hero-worshipping biography of Irving was written by his company manager and long associate, Bram Stoker, whose literary efforts are more generally remembered for the blood-curdling vampire classic, *Dracula*, a thriller of quality. Irving died the traditional trouper's death, collapsing after a performance while on tour in 1905.

Ellen Terry was one of the two best actresses on the English stage at a time when the general level was high. The child of actors, she was on the stage from the age of eight. Three sisters and a brother also were actors.

Though she played a wide range of roles she enjoyed particular fame as a Shakespearean actress, especially in the light, joyous touch she brought to his comedy roles. For more than twenty years she was the leading actress in Irving's Lyceum Theatre.

One of the most interesting theatrical documents is the published correspondence between George Bernard Shaw and Ellen Terry. Shaw professed a kind of Platonic or remote courtly love for her. Their letters contain brilliant discussions of the art of acting and other elements of the theatre and include Shaw's chief criticisms of Irving. Shaw wanted her to play several roles in his plays but her commitments to Irving blocked it and Irving would have nothing to do with Shaw's plays. In 1906, the year after Irving's death, Ellen Terry played Lady Cicely Waynflete in *Captain Brassbound's Conversion*, which Shaw had written specially for her. The triumph bore out all Shaw had claimed about their potentially fruitful relationship as author and actress, but it was too late in her career for more to come of it.

Ellen Terry was made a Dame of the British Empire, an honor equivalent to Irving's knighthood, and was the first actress to be so honored. Her son, Gordon Craig, became a distinguished stage designer and influenced some developments in the modern theatre.

Beatrice Stella Tanner, better known as Mrs. Patrick Campbell, shared stardom on the English stage with Ellen Terry and also shared an epistolary courtship—perhaps a little less Platonic—by Bernard Shaw. Their letters, too, have been published. She played in works of both Ibsen and Shaw, creating the role of Eliza Doolittle in *Pygmalion*.

Harley Granville-Barker, actor-manager-dramatist-critic, was a strong and constructive force on the English stage. In production partnership with J. E. Vedrenne, he produced most of Shaw's plays, playing many leading roles, and also several of Ibsen's plays. Apart from his own plays, adaptations, and translations, he wrote other works on theatre and drama, one of the most valuable being his *Prefaces to Shakespeare*, which are perceptive studies of the plays.

Most people concede to Eleonora Duse the rank as greatest actress of her time, a claim always disputed by partisans of her contemporary and rival, Sarah Bernhardt. As Garrick had been in his day, and as Mansfield and Granville-Barker were, she was a reformer and creator of a modern acting style. She was a restrained, balanced artist, a genuine servant of the theatre, who chose to reflect its most profound possibilities in the art of acting rather than to use that art simply as a springboard for personal display.

Duse was the third generation of an Italian family of actors. Her childhood background was like that of a *commedia dell' arte* troupe of strolling players. Her early life was filled more with hardship and suffering than with glamor. She was born in a third-class railway carriage and dragged about by her actor parents during all her childhood. Her first recorded performance on stage was at the age of four, when she appeared as the child, Cosette, in a dramatization of part of Hugo's *Les Misérables*. She played Shakespeare's Juliet at fourteen, about the age of the character herself, though for modern sensibilities it is played usually by much more mature women.

To discriminating tastes, Duse's restraint had more power than the florid style of Bernhardt. Hers were living interpretations, adapted as readily to the realistic as to the romantic type of theatre. She played the great feminine roles of Ibsen, helping to advance the new drama.

In 1895 a famous contest of actresses occurred in London when both Duse and Bernhardt undertook to play the role of *Magda*, by the German playwright Sudermann (it might be called a romantic melodrama with a touch of realism). The event caused much excitement. In the opinion of Bernard Shaw and other best judgments of the day it was Duse who triumphed with her more profound and perceptive interpretation.

Duse, whose health was failing, retired just before the First World War. She returned in 1923 and made special appearances in London, then undertook a limited tour of America, starting in New York with a triumphant series of performances at the Metropolitan Opera House. The tour was not finished. Weakened by the strain she died, in 1924, in Pittsburgh, Pennsylvania. Mussolini had offered her a pension, which she had refused. Upon her death, when she could embarrass him no longer by declining Fascist favors, he caused her to be brought back to Italy and buried in state.

For the first of the nineteenth century's master playwrights and the pioneer of a new realism in drama we turn to a country unmentioned until now in our chronicle: Norway. Henrik Ibsen, in his youth, was apprenticed to a druggist in the small Norwegian town of his birth. He broke away from this uninspiring occupation and attended the University of Christiania, which is the old name of Oslo, the nation's capital. There he became interested in the theatre and entered the profession as a manager and director.

Soon he began to write plays. His earliest ones were relatively conventional in the prevailing romantic spirit, but then within two years, 1866–67, came *Brand* and *Peer Gynt*. These at once disclosed a poet, a romanticist still, but with an element much more profound than anything since, perhaps, Goethe's *Faust*.

Peer Gynt is a fanciful, philosophical, poetic drama. Many who will never see or read it have heard in concert halls the lovely suite of incidental music composed for it by Ibsen's countryman, Edvard Grieg. Various of its movements—Aase's Death, The Hall of the Mountain King, Anitra's Dance, and Solveig's Song—superbly match the play's gamut of brooding tones, grotesque supernaturalism, exoticism, and yearning.

It is a study in self-centeredness. Peer is a charming, irresponsible, self-indulgent, resourcefully imaginative scalawag. An incorrigible liar, he makes the most fatal of errors—he lies to himself, also.

Peer hastens the death of his mother, Aase, leaves his sweetheart, Solveig, travels the world as a swindler and opportunist, making and losing fortunes, and at the end seeks to evade even the reckoning with death and judgment.

The image of Peer's world is that of the Trolls, the mountain goblins of Scandinavian lore. In their world and Peer's private one alike, nothing is real, all is false, is illusion. When he is led into the Troll King's hall by the King's daughter, a clue to the play lies in part of Peer's dialogue with the ugly monarch.

THE TROLL KING

What is the difference between Trolls and Men?

PEER GYNT

There isn't any, as far as I can gather;
Big trolls would roast and little ones would claw you—
Just as with us if only we dared do it.

THE TROLL KING

True; we're alike in that and other things too.
Still, just as morning's different from evening,
So there's a real difference between us,
And I will tell you what it is. Out yonder
Under the skies, men have a common saying:
"Man, to thyself be true!" But here, 'mongst Trolls,
"Troll, to thyself be—enough!" it runs.

A little later the King adds:

You're cut out for a Troll. Why, look, already
You bear yourself quite in a Troll-like fashion!

Peer has a frightening encounter with the Great Boyg, an invisible Troll who, when asked who he is, replies, "Myself. Can you say as much?"

Peer dedicates his whole life to the pursuit of what he calls

The Gyntian Self!—An army, that,
Of wishes, appetites, desires!

His only prayer is, "Do look after me, Lord! . . . . Leave other folk's matters alone!"

At the end, Peer meets the Button Moulder, who is going to melt him down in his ladle. To Peer this is unendurable,

. . . losing all
The attributes that make a Gynt—

The Button Moulder says that is no matter—

You never yet have been yourself.

His orders, he shows Peer, say,

> "You will fetch Peer Gynt.
> He has defied his destiny.
> He is a failure, and must go
> Straight into the Casting-ladle."

On that turns the cryptic ending. He is given a chance to escape the ladle if he can prove that he has a real self under the falseness of his life. On the morning of Pentecost, in despair, he meets the long-abandoned Solveig again. In answer to his query,

> Tell me, then—where was my real self,
> Complete and true—the Peer who bore
> The stamp of God upon his brow?

Solveig replies:

> In my faith, in my hope and in my love.

By this he wins a reprieve. Is it final? The Button Moulder says,

> At the last crossroads I shall meet you, Peer;
> Then we'll see—whether—! I say no more.

This remarkable play has attracted and often defeated actors. Richard Mansfield was the first to attempt it in America, in 1906. He played the taxing role gallantly and well, though he was then dying of cancer, continuing in it until his strength and his career were ended. In 1964 the Old Vic, in London, staged a production that was received with acclaim.

From this philosophical fantasia Ibsen switched abruptly to an altogether new vein. Taking the neatly carpentered frame of the well-made play, à la Sardou, he took it to a new dimension, not of form but of content. Abandoning poetry he began to address himself in prose to contemporary social problems.

Pillars of Society is about a hypocritical and corrupt merchant who nearly loses his son by his scheming. In *An Enemy of the People*, townsfolk turn on the doctor who shows that their mineral

Scene from Ibsen's *Peer Gynt. Norwegian Information Service*

baths are polluted, because it will make them lose money. *Ghosts* is about the then utterly taboo subject of venereal disease. *A Doll's House* is about a woman's determination to become a person in her own right, not an appendage to her husband.

From the sociological he shifted again toward the psychological. *Hedda Gabler*, in his own words, is about a woman who has nothing to do. *The Wild Duck* presents a fanatical, destructive obsession with telling the truth. *The Master Builder* is about youth and age, and a builder's dread of a new generation coming to displace him. These psychological plays shade into another aspect, a mysticism which is partly a return to the vein of *Brand*. In such plays as *Rosmersholm*, *The Lady from the Sea*, and *When We Dead Awaken*, there is sometimes a rhapsodic eloquence that suggests the poetry he had left behind.

Ibsen died in 1906; in the preceding years he had suffered two paralytic strokes, the last of which began to undermine his mental faculties. He died partly the victor and partly the vanquished. Sometimes he had been depressed by a conviction that his battle was futile, that the world would not change, that he could not win the reforms for society which his plays showed as so necessary. That was both true and false. His plays had raised a storm of protest and resistance, and though our fundamentally cussed human nature does not change, so many changes in some attitudes and practices have taken place that no one today is outraged by the problems and ideas which Ibsen stated so boldly at the end of the nineteenth century. Some of the plays have suffered the penalty of the successful reformer and have become dated.

Yet he was the victor in that, more than any other man, he had shaken the European theatre and infused it with new life. He had taken the stilted form of the well-made play and shaped it into mature realistic drama. Ibsen the poet never was submerged wholly by Ibsen the prophet. As master craftsman, his influence upon modern dramaturgy was immense.

He ran into the fact of the transience of topicality by contrast with the permanence of universality. What remains of his socially shocking plays is their historical interest and their psychological validity. *Peer Gynt* is ageless and will have a message as long as there is anyone to hear it.

In England, two critics united to praise and encourage performances of Ibsen. William Archer also ably translated some of the plays. Bernard Shaw wrote a small book called *The Quintessence of Ibsenism*, as he had written *The Perfect Wagnerite* to advance the Wagnerian cause.

There are two other important Scandinavian playwrights. Another

Norwegian, Björnstjerne Björnson, is best known outside his country for his two-part play, *Beyond Our Power*. August Strindberg, a Swede of great brilliance but tragically unstable temperament, varies from stark psychological realism in *The Father* and *Miss Julie* to Gothic fantasy in *The Ghost Sonata*.

In the wake of Ibsen other realistic playwrights appeared in Europe. In France Émile Zola wrote realistic novels and dramas. He probed into pockets of suffering, oppression, and brutality in such novels as *Thérèse Raquin*, *L'Assommoir* (*The Bludgeon*), and *Le Débâcle*, and several plays. Some of the novels were adapted to the stage by other hands. In 1894 France was thrown into violent controversy over accusations of espionage made against a certain Captain Alfred Dreyfus, a Jew, who was convicted and sent to the terrible penal colony, Devil's Island, off the coast of French Guiana in South America. Zola believed Dreyfus was innocent and partly the victim of anti-Semitic malice. He wrote a strong pamphlet called *J'Accuse*, attacking Dreyfus' persecutors. It led to temporary exile for Zola but was influential in forcing a new trial in which Dreyfus' innocence was established. Zola died at work one night, overcome by fumes from the defective flue of the stove in his room.

Also in France, Eugène Brieux wrote extensively in the realistic mode. His *Damaged Goods*, like Ibsen's earlier *Ghosts*, dealt with venereal disease and shocked audiences, particularly in the United States. Brieux, like all literal realists and topical propagandists, has faded with social change and acceptance of his subject matter. Topicality and shock in themselves never are more than nine-days' wonders.

In Germany, Gerhart Hauptmann wrote many social plays. The most famous, *The Weavers*, was a new type—a mass drama, in the sense that a group was the protagonist instead of an individual. The subject was the machine-wrecking movements that occurred in England and Europe as the earliest reactions to the industrial developments that have now reached the stage that we call automation. In Hauptmann's play, handweavers feel that their wages and their jobs are threatened by the power looms.

In England we escape the heaviest hand of realism.

Oscar Wilde, born in Dublin, esthete, poseur, poet, novelist, and wit, wrote the sprightliest comedies of manners since Sheridan, in such still popular plays as *The Importance of Being Earnest, Lady Windermere's Fan, An Ideal Husband,* and *A Woman of No Importance.* His one poetic tragedy, *Salomé,* so shocked Victorians that it was banned from the English stage. It was about the murder of John the Baptist to gratify the whim of Herod's vicious stepdaughter. Sarah Bernhardt played it in France (Wilde wrote it in French) and it was made into one of the most powerful of modern operas by the German composer Richard Strauss. Like Wagner's operas, it has an all but overpowering orchestral score; a popular story was that in conducting rehearsals for it, Strauss shouted to the orchestra: "Louder! louder! I can still hear the singers."

Though there were many other able English playwrights in various modes, the towering figure, not just for the British but for the world stage, was George Bernard Shaw, who came to be known widely simply as G.B.S. His career was so versatile and so long that he is *a* principal figure, if not *the* one, in the theatre of both the nineteenth and twentieth centuries. Different though he is in all respects from his precursor, it is hard to deny him the rank of greatest playwright to appear since Shakespeare.

Born in Dublin, that fertile source of dramatic talent, in 1856, Shaw came to London as a young man, interested from the start in socialist politics of the mild sort known in England as Fabian Socialism, so called from Quintus Fabius, a Roman general whose tactic was to move slowly, delaying and harassing the enemy. The Fabians urged evolution, not revolution—an idea pursued years later in Shaw's ambitious theatrical experiment, *Back to Methuselah.*

In his youth he wrote four novels, all unsuccessful, and numerous political pamphlets. In three art fields he was a critic, capable on painting, brilliant on music and drama. We know already of his writings in support of Wagner and Ibsen. His collected musical criticisms have been published and also his drama reviews. The latter volumes, *Dramatic Opinions and Essays,* are the most important body of their kind after Lessing's *Hamburg Dramaturgy,* full of wisdom on acting, writing, and other aspects of theatre.

Not until his forties did he begin in earnest to write plays. The first three, though interesting, were confined chiefly to social preaching. Then the natural theatrical-comic genius bloomed and an astonishing outpouring followed of plays, good, excellent, nearly great, and several very great indeed. There was a natural falling off in plays written between the ages of seventy-five and ninety-four. His masterpiece, *Saint Joan,* was written at sixty-seven in 1923.

Shaw brashly declared himself a didactic playwright, one using the stage to teach, lecture, preach, and reform the world. That has been enough to blight many playwrights, but Shaw's theatrical sense was so unerring, his comic spirit so boundlessly irrepressible, that we swallow his lectures, or dismiss them as we are inclined, for his laughter, showmanship, and penetration of character win us all. He can rock audiences with laughter and at the same time tease or shock them into fresh ideas.

The undoubted great plays are *Caesar and Cleopatra, Man and Superman* (whose "Don Juan in Hell" dream sequence often is performed separately, sometimes as a dramatic reading), *Major Barbara, Pygmalion, Heartbreak House,* and *Saint Joan. Back to Methuselah,* which he called "A Metabiological Pentateuch," is an extraordinary theatrical experiment, not wholly successful, ranging from the Garden of Eden to "As Far as Thought Can Reach."

Heartbreak House is one of the most impressive. In its loose conversational flow, seeming (deceptively) unorganized, it imitates and even subtly parodies the manner of Chekhov, whom we shall discuss soon. Shaw gave it the descriptive subtitle, "A Fantasia in the Russian Manner on English Themes."

George Bernard Shaw. *Consulate General of Ireland*

It assembles a host of characters ranging from the upper to the lower classes and representing many walks of life in the country house of the aged, eccentric Captain Shotover, one of the most remarkable characters set upon any stage.

Among these, with the mingled threads of their loves, fears, ambitions, and hatreds, Shaw generates a brilliant conversation piece reflecting the confusion, drift, and decay of values among English people in the period just preceding the First World War. The frustrations, distortions, and bewilderment of each are laid bare. The "Heartbreak House," Shaw proves, is England itself. Sardonically he did not end the play by any turn of plot, but brought it to a stop in the tumult of a droning, thundering air raid, unforeseen at any time in the play. Yet some of the characters welcome it as the only thing which can galvanize them into awareness, shake them out of lethargy.

Captain Shotover, a retired sea captain, often resorts to the metaphor of a ship. One of the characters invokes Providence:

CAPTAIN SHOTOVER

> Every drunken skipper trusts to Providence. But one of the ways of Providence with drunken skippers is to run them on the rocks.

The danger is not in drink but in drift. He adds:

> Let a man drink ten barrels of rum a day, he is not a drunken skipper until he is a drifting skipper. . . . It is the man who lies drinking in his bunk and trusts to Providence that I call the drunken skipper, though he drank nothing but the waters of the River Jordan.
>
>   . . . . .

HECTOR

> And this ship that we are all in? This soul's prison we call England?

CAPTAIN SHOTOVER

> The captain is in his bunk, drinking bottled ditch-water; and the crew is gambling in the forecastle. She will strike and sink

and split. Do you think the laws of God will be suspended in favor of England because you were born in it?

HECTOR

. . . What am I to do?

CAPTAIN SHOTOVER

Do? Nothing simpler. Learn your business as an Englishman.

HECTOR

And what may my business as an Englishman be, pray?

CAPTAIN SHOTOVER

Navigation. Learn it and live; or leave it and be damned.

The role of Shotover was created by Sir Cedric Hardwicke, who played it in the appropriate—and since then traditional—make-up of a Shavian white beard. The play came about in a remarkable cycle, proving prophetic in a little more than twenty years, by which time "Heartbreak House" was not just England but the world. The air raiders came again and more terribly. England's "drunken skipper" was displaced and she found a navigator in Sir Winston Churchill. Through it all, aged Bernard Shaw sat in beleaguered England while the last act of *Heartbreak House* played itself out around and above him. He saw the end of it, a prototype of his bearded, prophetic Captain Shotover. In fact, with a grand contempt for the hazards of war, he supervised and completed the filming of his *Major Barbara* in London in spite of the continual dangers and interruptions of air raids.

In *Saint Joan* the play of his wit is unabated but a new depth of feeling is present. When someone was quoted as saying that Shaw's plays had no emotion, the playwright is supposed to have said, "Let him read *Saint Joan*." The laughter is there, but *Saint Joan* transcends the comic spirit. It is in a border realm not far from tragedy. Its tender, touching portrait of Joan—the best in literature—is accompanied by some of his most probing comments on history and human nature in the trial scenes.

Many writers have been fascinated by this peasant girl, guided by supernatural voices, who led French armies to victory and was burned for heresy by a Church that soon reversed itself and canonized her as a saint. Some of the writers fell into the pitfalls of stuffy piety or sentimentality. Shaw is touched by the mystery of Joan but the detachment of his ironic view of life protects the play from excessive sentiment and gives it the balance that makes an exciting clash of ideas.

Shaw refuses to portray any of Joan's persecutors as villains. Instead, each is convinced that he is acting rightly and for the good of his particular cause. Shaw presents a Joan crushed by the clash of opposing ideas, one of which, nationalism, she herself has let loose. This brilliant drama, being an imaginative, even argumentative, work, is not history. But it helps us to be aware of the vast enigma of history and to be skeptical of simplified accounts of it. Above all, it is superb theatre.

Shaw wrote so-called "Prefaces" to all the plays. Actually they are addenda, additional reflections on the ideas that had been the conception of the play, but not to read them is to miss an important facet of his work.

Shaw was almost ninety-five years old when he died in 1950. He was a legend in his time, a world figure, a symbol of caustic wit from the days when he was a red-bearded, faintly Mephistophelian image, to his late years as a white-bearded, sharp-tongued sage and jester who might have been Shotover or one of the ancients in *Back to Methuselah*. For years he was a personality of London, gadding about its streets on foot with unflagging energy, observing every level of its life, often conspicuous in odd, faddish woolen garb. He was gifted with genius, was garrulous, often an irritating gadfly, at rare moments gentle, and in sum, great.

Chapter 14
The Theatre
Today

Anton Chekhov. *New York Public Library Theatre Collection*

As WE COME fully into this century and draw close to our own time the spread and diversity of theatre is more than we can encompass. The broad story which was our purpose is told, of how man arrived at this prolific and varied theatre we know today up a long road from primitive campfires and grassy Greek dancing circles. Within this book's scope there remain only some threads to be picked up, some test samplings of the modern theatre's current spirit—which is always changing—and some words of summary.

We must look back a bit to speak of the Russian people's undoubted genius for the theatre arts. Contemporary with Shaw's early period was the Russian physician and man of letters, Anton Chekhov. He was born in 1860 in southern Russia. His grandfather and father were serfs, or slave peasants, who managed to lift themselves into better circumstances and buy their freedom.

268

The father was a grocer during Chekhov's youth. Much of the boy's time was spent either assisting his father in the grocery, or visiting with his grandfather who had, by then, become supervisor of a country estate. He studied, and practiced, medicine before his attraction to literature.

He is a master of the short story, but his first fame is as a playwright. Of more than a dozen plays, the finest are *The Sea Gull, Uncle Vanya, The Three Sisters,* and *The Cherry Orchard.*

They are in a manner uniquely his own though profoundly Russian in pervading spirit. *The Sea Gull* is a tragedy, a study of frustrations and unfulfilled ambitions and desires. The successful novelist, Trigorin, bored with his life and empty triumphs, is tormented by the knowledge that he has fallen short of real and lasting fame: ". . . when I die, my friends, passing by my grave, will say: 'Here lies Trigorin. He was a charming writer, but not so good as Turgenev.'" Irina, a middle-aged actress already beginning to lose popularity, is vaguely troubled by the knowledge that her public success is vanishing and that she has spent no time making a success of her human relationships. Constantin, her son, writes obscure plays and novels which are not understood by his mother and are somewhat scorned by Trigorin. The boy loses Nina, whom he loves, to the more sophisticated Trigorin. Nina, filled with ambition for the theatre, is abandoned by Trigorin and left to pursue what she knows already will be a hollow life on the stage. Constantin caps the picture of defeat and frustration by killing himself.

The last and greatest of Chekhov's plays is *The Cherry Orchard.* A common but gross error is to call it a tragedy. In the first place, its melancholy overtones are essentially pathetic rather than tragic. Chekhov passionately protested that it was misread and misplayed by people who "see in my play something absolutely different from what I have written." He stipulated firmly that it is a comedy, and though proper productions are rare, such a one as done in 1962 by the Royal Shakespeare Company in London bears him out. The mistake was easy to make, especially for Russians and Westerners with a preconception about Russians. We might say, if you have a Russian comedy you don't need a tragedy.

The story of how the charming but distraught and ineffectual Madame Ranevsky loses her family estate, with its beautiful cherry orchard that she and her brother, Gaieff, have loved since childhood, is viewed with comic, critical, bittersweet detachment.

Madame Ranevsky is a spendthrift, a woman of tempestuous affairs and impulsive behavior. Gaieff is an impractical, aging dandy, absentmindedly gesturing and calling imaginary billiard shots: "Off the white on the right, into the corner pocket."

The means are at hand to save something from their bankruptcy, if they will compromise, consent to some inevitable changes. But they are lost in dreams, cannot make decisions or act effectively, so they lose all under the auctioneer's hammer. At the end, while their trunks are being carried out of the house, the axes can be heard at work felling the beloved orchard to make way for a real-estate development.

The true protagonist is the bumbling, newly rich merchant, Lopakhin, who buys the estate, marveling:

> The cherry orchard is mine now, mine! (*Roars with laughter*) My God, my God, the cherry orchard's mine! Tell me I'm drunk or crazy or dreaming . . . (*Stamps his feet*). . . . I've bought the estate where my grandfather and my father were slaves, where they weren't even allowed to enter the kitchen. I'm asleep; it's only a dream, an illusion. . . .

Observe the resemblance to Chekhov's origins. His ironic laughter encompasses both those who are declining in the world and those who appear to be rising.

Chekhov was intimately associated with Russia's foremost producing company, the Moscow Art Theatre. They did most of his plays, and did them best, except that even they, in the year of his death, 1904, played *The Cherry Orchard* in the erroneous tragic spirit that so upset him. After their production of *The Sea Gull* the Moscow Art Theatre adopted the wings of a gull as its emblem. Chekhov married one of the company's leading actresses, Olga Knipper-Chekhova. He was only forty-four when he died, victim of tuberculosis that had shadowed his life for years.

We have noted the relationship between Shaw's *Heartbreak House* and Chekhov's plays.

Maxim Gorky rose from peasant poverty to be a major literary figure, claimed as their own by Soviet Russia for his social dramas. He lived until 1936 and wrote much, yet his best play was written in 1903, a year before Chekhov's death, and performed by the Moscow Art Theatre. This was *The Lower Depths* (sometimes called *A Night's Lodging* or *At the Bottom*). It is an almost actionless play, though it does contain a murder. It interests by its varied gallery of sharply individualized characters and its splendid dialogue. It involves the events of one night in a tramps' lodging house—American slang would call it a "flophouse." Its chief message is uttered by Luka, a wandering pilgrim, who urges the derelicts to reassert their dignity as men.

Gorky remained in Russia after the revolution, as its principal literary ornament. Yet he was reported to have chafed under the repressions of the regime and at his death it was rumored—but not proved—that he had been murdered to prevent his open expression of disillusionment.

One of Gorky's interesting books is a small memoir of his younger days, called *Reminiscences of Tolstoy, Chekhov, and Andreyev*, which is absorbing as an insight into the personalities of the men and the artistic-intellectual climate of the turn of the century in Russia.

The Moscow Art Theatre was dominated by its leading director and actor, Constantin Stanislavsky. He was the supreme exponent of internally motivated realistic acting. His book, *An Actor Prepares*, and his autobiography, *My Life in Art*, became the bibles of the Stanislavsky Method, the root of all modern "method" acting as taught and practiced currently by the Actor's Studio group of

New York. It is fine for some kinds of roles, chiefly the ultra-realistic. It is not well adapted to more frankly formal playing and is especially poor training, if it is the only training the actor receives, for the Shakespearean tradition or the comedy of manners. It has led to a current lowering of the standards of American stage diction through a cult of naturalness coupled with a vogue for plays about inarticulate characters of low class.

The other principal producer and director in Moscow before the revolution was V. E. Meyerhold, who began his career under Stanislavsky but left him because he wished to experiment. Instead of trying to be "real," Meyerhold started the modern movement back toward frankly make-believe theatre. He carried his style to the point of using nearly bare stages, with ladders, steps, platforms, and machinelike structures to suggest the industrial age. His sympathies were with the revolution and after it he organized the official theatre department of the Soviet Government. Yet in the 1930's, in his sixties, he became convinced that the narrow communist control of thought and subject matter had stifled the Russian theatre. He had the bravery to say so bluntly in a speech at an important public banquet. Immediately afterward, Meyerhold disappeared and neither his whereabouts nor the nature of his fate have yet been learned in the West.

There are magnificent Russian traditions in the novel, drama, ballet, music including opera, acting, stagecraft, and the art of film. These talents did not disappear from communist Russia—indeed the film art has been entirely under that regime—but all have suffered in their relative ways the inevitable muzzling of art under totalitarian regimes with their censorship and thought control. Techniques that are nonpolitical, such as music and ballet, are practiced with skill; those that involve free expression of ideas and choice of subject are muted. Even composers have been judged politically at times. Since the death of Stalin there has been some easing of controls, known as the "thaw." It is an improvement, though compared to the freedom of the West, the freeze still is on. When the creative talents of Russia become free, she will certainly contribute again to world theatre. A Soviet playwright, Aleksei Arbuzov, visiting the United States in 1964, remarked, "The Soviet theatre is an audience's theatre; the audience is better than the theatre and deserves better than it gets."

Even in the West, before World War II, left-oriented artists were developing a political theatre. In Berlin the communist playwright Bertolt Brecht, author of *The Threepenny Opera* mentioned earlier, and the director Erwin Piscator developed a didactic style of writing and staging which they called epic theatre. Piscator later conducted a fine Drama Workshop under the auspices of the New School for Social Research in New York. Brecht's didactic dramaturgical theories and some of his plays, *Mother Courage*, *The Caucasian Chalk Circle*, and *Galileo*, have enjoyed great vogue in some theatre circles since the Second World War. Piscator's "epic-drama" adaptation of Tolstoy's *War and Peace* has been produced both in Europe and the United States.

This century has seen a number of fine Irish playwrights who remained Irish nationalists in the emotional as well as political sense, not becoming expatriates as Wilde and Shaw did. Those who stayed in Dublin wrote for the exciting acting company of the Abbey Theatre in that city. From that Irish wellspring have come wonderful plays, some comic, some tragic, some a mixture: *Riders to the Sea* and *The Playboy of the Western World*, by J. M. Synge (the latter caused riots when first performed, as some thought its robust, crude vitality an insult to the Irish); *The Whiteheaded Boy*, by Lennox Robinson, and *Juno and the Paycock* and *The Plough and the Stars*, by Sean O'Casey.

The best Irish drama combines tragedy with bursts of laughter and rich comic characterizations. This rare blend is found in O'Casey's *Juno and the Paycock*. In it we see a lower-class Dublin family caught in the net of the bitter, underground civil war for Irish independence.

In the family of the strutting "paycock," Captain Jack Boyle,

Scene from an Abbey Theatre performance of *The Playboy of the Western World* by Synge. *Irish Tourist Board (Bord Fáilte Photo)*

we see a daughter abandoned by her lover, the execution of a son for betraying a young fighter for independence, and the collapse of the ill-founded hope of an inheritance. In the midst of disaster the worthless Boyle and his drinking companion Joxer waste their time in empty boastings and denunciations of fate. Boyle's drunken protest, which closes the play, is the garbled phrase: "th' whole worl's . . . in a terr . . . ible state o' . . . . chassis!"

The tragedy is in the cry of women who have lost sons through political murders—a cry like a modern echo of *The Trojan Women*—calling on God to "take away our hearts o' stone, and give us hearts o' flesh! Take away this murdherin' hate an' give us Thine own eternal love."

The dominant figure is Juno, the wife of the shiftless Boyle. In her enduring strength she casts off the useless men around her. When her daughter bewails "My poor little child that'll have no father!" Juno says, "It'll have what's far betther—it'll have two mothers."

In England at the present there are many skilful playwrights involved in the theatre-as-entertainment, including the prolific Terence Rattigan and the versatile actor-comedian-director-playwright, Peter Ustinov. Representing the avant-garde are writers of the younger generation, such as John Osborne and Harold Pinter, experimenting with both content and techniques.

After Shaw, the elder statesman of British drama, American by birth but long a British subject by choice, was the distinguished poet, critic, and playwright, T. S. Eliot, who died in 1965. He turned to the theatre relatively late in an impressive career. His *Murder in the Cathedral* is about the death of St. Thomas à Becket and studies the subtle temptations that can lurk even in martyrdom. *The Cocktail Party* is a curious and theatrically effective blend of witty drawing-room comedy with mystical religious experience—the natural and the supernatural. His other plays are *Family Reunion* and *The Confidential Clerk*.

Christopher Fry should be mentioned for his revival of poetic drama, most notably in his comedy, *The Lady's Not for Burning*, and his religious play, *A Sleep of Prisoners*, written to be performed in church in the medieval spirit, though its treatment of the agony of man's search for God in wartime is wholly modern.

France has several prominent contemporary playwrights. Jean Giraudoux, whose *Amphitryon 38* was mentioned in the Roman chapter, wrote *Tiger at the Gates*, in which the Trojan War is seen from the Trojan side, *The Madwoman of Chaillot*, a sharp-edged satirical fantasy, and the gently comic fairy tale, *Ondine*.

Jean-Paul Sartre, one of the most eminent of French men of letters and leader of the French wing of the so-called Existentialist philosophy, has used the theatre as a social and ideological medium in such plays as *No Exit*, *The Flies*, and *The Condemned of Altona*.

The most prolific and versatile, in sheer theatrical terms, is Jean Anouilh, who ranges from historical dramas such as *Becket* (a great contrast to T. S. Eliot's approach) and *The Lark* (a treatment of Joan of Arc, indebted to Shaw, yet original) to a bittersweet romance in modern setting on a mythical theme in *Eurydice*, a striking adaptation of *Antigone* which is politically penetrating and makes Creon, rather than the girl, its central figure, and a play of manners in an eighteenth-century mode, *The Rehearsal*, and numerous other works.

American drama came to maturity after World War I with the emergence of our first playwright to have his greatness recognized around the world. Eugene O'Neill was the son of James O'Neill who, as we noted, made a career out of *The Count of Monte Cristo*. He was born in the old Cadillac Hotel, in the heart of the Broadway theatre district.

O'Neill began with some fine one-act plays written for the Wharf Theatre in Provincetown, Massachusetts. For a while he continued to develop his skills with this venturesome group at the small Provincetown Playhouse in Greenwich Village. Soon his work moved uptown to Broadway, most of it produced by the Theatre Guild, a great producing organization that made immense contributions to the American theatre in the 1920's and early 1930's.

Psychological probing was O'Neill's gift, and he experimented with forms also. In *Strange Interlude*, which shocked and fascinated its audiences and was banned in Boston, he created a play in nine acts that ran for over four hours and used long "asides" in which characters spoke their real thoughts interspersed with what they said directly to the other persons of the play. *Ah, Wilderness!*

Eugene O'Neill. *Ewing Galloway*

was his only comedy and is an engaging picture of American youth around the turn of the century. Its title cloaks an amusing aspect of theatrical promotion. In its source—it is a quotation from the *Rubáiyát* of Omar Khayyám—it is "Oh, Wilderness," but presumably on the producer's recommendation it was changed to "Ah" to place it high in the always alphabetical listing of current plays in the newspapers.

Several of his plays are exceptionally long. *Mourning Becomes Electra* is his modernization, in a New England setting, of the Oresteia trilogy of Aeschylus. *The Iceman Cometh* uses the riffraff of a Bowery bar for a tragedy of disillusionment and death. Several important posthumous works have been played since he died in 1953: the autobiographical plays, *Long Day's Journey into Night* and *A Touch of the Poet, A Moon for the Misbegotten,* and most recently, *Hughie,* which is a variation on the theme of *The Iceman Cometh.*

One of his early and most interesting plays, *The Emperor Jones,* was made into an opera by the composer Louis Gruenberg, and had its premiere at the Metropolitan Opera in 1932 with the American baritone Lawrence Tibbett in the title role.

Leaping over many fine craftsmen in the American theatre since O'Neill, three eminent names among American playwrights are Tennessee Williams, Arthur Miller, and Edward Albee. But when we speak of contemporary times, how soon those now prominent will fade, and how soon new claimants will appear, can be seen only in the perspective of time.

The modern theatre long since broke out of the confines of the picture-frame stage and realistic scenery, though plays use them if they are appropriate. Among those who most helped to free our stage of literal representation is Thornton Wilder, a distinguished novelist as well as playwright. We have mentioned his borrowings from the Oriental theatre. Quoting a phrase from Molière, he has

Scene from Thornton Wilder's *Our Town*. *Vandamm Collection of the New York Public Library Theatre Collection*

stressed that the essentials of drama are simply "a platform and a passion or two."

In his much loved *Our Town*, played on a bare stage with make-shift props, at one point the Stage Manager-Chorus indicates two plain garden trellises that are shoved out from the sides and re-marks: "There's some scenery for those who think they have to have scenery." In *Our Town* the mechanics of the dramatic process are exhibited candidly and add a certain interest of their own, like seeing the works in a glass-cased clock.

The arena stage and theatre-in-the-round are ultimate steps in carrying theatre into the midst of the audience. Remembering the ancient link between worship and drama, it is interesting that many modern churches have placed the altar in the center and celebrate the Eucharist in the midst of the worshipers. In the theatre such free forms have their own limitations and rigidities, too, and should be used with discretion in the selection of plays most suitable for them. Production technique should not be an end in itself, but the servant of the play in communicating with the audience.

The most radical aspect of contemporary theatre is philosophical. There is a cult of the so-called—indeed well-called—"theatre of the absurd" in which nothing makes coherent sense, dialogue and action both are random and obscure, or else the scenes of life and action are carried to ridiculous grotesqueries.

The absurd, in the sense of the bizarre, the fantastic, or startlingly novel, is not new. We have it in the plays of the Italian experimenter of the 1920's, Luigi Pirandello, whose *Six Characters in Search of an Author* has enjoyed recent revivals. There are absurdities in Thornton Wilder's *The Skin of Our Teeth* and Giraudoux's *The Madwoman of Chaillot*. But these are madness with a method. They use absurdities to startle us into new ways of seeing.

The "theatre of the absurd," exemplified in the plays of Samuel Beckett and many imitators, rests on the assertion that existence is absurd, that life and human action are meaningless. Ironically this view is wholly antidramatic, as also is any philosophy that denies the concepts of good and evil. If life is absurd, if there is neither good nor evil, if the existence of man is without meaning and everything that happens to him is random, then drama as the human race has understood it since the Greeks becomes impossible. There can be no clash of forces, no conflict of interests, no moral decisions worth our attention. The "theatre of the absurd" is the expression of a small, but for a time fashionable and influential, wing of the theatre. It is not for a broad and diversified audience.

We are not suggesting that writers must not write such plays, or attempting to invoke rules, like the French classicists, to show why they cannot "succeed." The law of the theatre is simple—it asks only what will work within the mood of a given time. You can do anything, from the manner of Aeschylus, to Shakespeare, to a "Tom show," to the "theatre of the absurd," so long as you can get people to pay to see and stay to watch. That is the practical side: other critical values are matters of individual taste and standards.

People are even speaking of a "theatre of brutality" as a label for the ugly strains of violence and hate on the modern stage. No one can say how long these elements will last. In time their vogue will pass, as do all vogues.

The Broadway theatre is commercial—the term is not used as a slur but to note the fact that it is a business enterprise that must earn a profit or fail, whether productions are artistically good or bad, profound or trivial. Success there is measured by earnings. As production costs have risen staggeringly, the alternatives have become extreme—a play must be a smash hit or fail. There is no room for a modest success playing to houses less than full.

One of the principal burdens of cost—though not the only one— is the demands of the theatrical unions, not only in salary levels but also in arbitrary requirements and specialization of labor which make necessary the hiring of superfluous people.

Rising costs also mean rising prices for tickets. The Broadway theatre has become so expensive that many theatre lovers cannot afford to patronize it. This has led to the practice of block-booking, the selling of whole houses, or sections of them, for benefits for charitable causes, or to theatre clubs. The result often is a semi-captive audience of tired businessmen dragged reluctantly to the theatre because their wives have supported a charity. Actors dislike playing to block-booked houses. They are not like audiences of theatre lovers who have come through choice and enthusiasm. Yet some productions cannot open unless they can offer a writer of reputation, and star players, on the strength of whom they can build up a substantial advance sale of block-bookings. In some cases this has led to the irony of a play or musical that few people liked, running a while on the advance bookings alone.

The Broadway economic squeeze led to the rise of the "Off-

Broadway" theatres, located in various sorts of auditoriums from
hotel ballrooms to remodeled churches. By being outside the
Broadway area, under existing production codes, great savings are
possible in everything from rent to union salary scales. Plays could
run for a year or more, earning a modest profit at comparatively
low ticket prices, without having to have a packed house every
night. Thus many new plays and revivals can be produced, experiments can be tried, actors and directors can gain the essential range
of experience for their growth.

Since the first honeymoon days, Off-Broadway costs have risen
too—the ironic penalty of success. Now there are even Off-Off-
Broadway theatres. What is important is that many plays of all
kinds are being performed.

England and most European nations have some government subsidized theatre companies, believing them to be an asset and a
source of national cultural pride. That has not been the tradition
in the United States, for better or worse—certainly some price is
always paid in controls, however indirect. As part of the W.P.A.
(Works Progress Administration) emergency employment program
in the 1930's, during the great depression, the Federal Theatre
Project was subsidized. It lasted a few years, ending like the rest
of the programs when the economic emergency was over. The Federal Theatre was valuable. At a time when commercial theatre was
languishing, it staged some fine productions of old and new plays,
throughout the country as well as in New York, conducted some
interesting experiments as in the documentary "Living Newspapers," and most important of all, nurtured through a lean time
some of the best talents in all phases of theatre who have since
become prominent on our stage.

There are some limited forms of government aid, federal or
local, to community art centers such as the Lincoln Center in New
York. With or without subsidies to augment private funds, the
most heartening development in recent years in the American
theatre is the springing up of vigorous community repertory companies in widely scattered cities of the United States.

The theatre, especially that of Broadway but by extension all of it, often has been called "the fabulous invalid," because pessimists periodically announce its imminent death from economic woes, dearth of talent, or other causes. Yet the fabulous invalid remains alive—like the rest of us, in better health at some times than at others. Unlike the rest of us, it is not likely to die.

Keep up with the plays and players of your own period, for they are still, in some measure, in Shakespeare's words, "the abstracts and brief chronicles of the time."

A SELECTED BIBLIOGRAPHY

GENERAL

Cheney, Sheldon. *The Theatre: Three Thousand Years of Drama, Acting, and Stagecraft.* New York: Longmans, Green & Co., 1959 (revised edition).

Clark, Barrett H. *European Theories of the Drama: With a Supplement on the American Drama.* New York: Crown Publishers, Inc., 1947.

Cole, Toby, and Chinoy, Helen Crich, eds. *Actors on Acting.* New York: Crown Publishers, Inc., 1949 (comprehensive and historical).

Freedley, George, and Reeves, John. *A History of the Theatre.* New York: Crown Publishers, Inc., 1940.

Gassner, John W. *Masters of the Drama.* New York: Random House, Inc., 1940 (comprehensive).

Gassner, John W. *Theatre at the Crossroads.* New York: Holt, Rinehart & Winston, 1960 (modern).

Hartnoll, Phyllis, ed. *The Oxford Companion to the Theatre.* New York: Oxford University Press, 1957 (2nd edition).

Simonson, Lee. *The Stage Is Set.* New York: Theatre Arts Books, 1962 (paper).

SOME OTHER BOOKS

Brown, Ivor. *How Shakespeare Spent the Day.* New York: Hill & Wang, 1963.

Grene, David, and Lattimore, Richmond, eds. *Complete Greek Tragedies.* Chicago: University of Chicago (4-vol. set boxed, or 9 vols. paper).

Hamilton, Edith. *The Greek Way.* New York: W. W. Norton & Co., Inc., 1930.

Hamilton, Edith. *The Roman Way.* New York: W. W. Norton & Co., Inc., 1932.

Kitto, H. D. F. *Greek Tragedy.* New York: Doubleday & Co., Inc., 1954 (paper).

Rowse, A. L. *William Shakespeare*. New York: Harper & Row, Publishers, Inc., 1963.

Taubman, Howard. *The Making of the American Theatre*. New York: Coward-McCann, 1965.

This brief bibliography is intended only to start the reader along the road in any direction he might wish to pursue his reading about the theatre. The general works are comprehensive and offer detailed, classified bibliographical guidance. The other items are listed simply because of the special pleasures they afford. Except for the University of Chicago edition of the Greek drama, which contains the best translations, no plays are listed. Plays old and new are abundantly available in libraries in numerous anthologies or in separate editions. They may also be found in both hardbound and paperback form, in any good bookstore.

Index

Index

ABOUT THE AUTHOR

EDMUND FULLER is an author, editor, critic, and teacher. He has written three novels: *A Star Pointed North, Brothers Divided,* and *The Corridor.* His diversified nonfiction includes *Man in Modern Fiction* and *Books with Men Behind Them.* His reviews and articles have appeared in the *New York Times,* the *Wall Street Journal,* the *New York Herald Tribune,* the Chicago *Tribune,* the *American Scholar, Saturday Review,* and *Horizon.* He has taught at Columbia University and Kent School and now is on the faculty of St. Stephen's School, Rome. In the field of textbooks he is co-author of *Adventures in American Literature* and General Editor of the series, *Adventures in Good Books.*